Community Housing Choices for Older Americans

M. Powell Lawton, Ph.D., has been Director of Behavioral Research at the Philadelphia Geriatric Center since 1963. In addition to his pioneering work in the environmental psychology of later life, he has contributed heavily to the development of methods for assessing the competence of older people, and to the theoretical understanding of the psychological wellbeing of older people. He graduated from Haverford College and received his Ph.D. in clinical psychology from Columbia University in 1952. He currently serves as Adjunct Professor of human development at Pennsylvania State University and as medical research scientist at Norristown State Hospital. He has served as Secretary and as Vice President of the Gerontological Society, and as President of the Division on Adult Development and Aging of the American Psychological Association. He is author of *Planning and Managing Housing for the Aged* and *Environment and Aging*, as well as editor or coeditor of a number of other books and several hundred articles and presentations.

Sally L. Hoover, M.A., is a demographer, who, after receiving her master's degree from the University of Southern California, served as a project director of several research projects at the Philadelphia Geriatric Center dealing with the housing of the elderly. She was an author of the first U.S. Department of Housing and Urban Development report on housing the elderly from the Annual Housing Survey. Since 1980, she has worked in the research division of the Bureau of the Census on topics dealing with the victimization of the elderly. She has delivered a number of papers at professional meetings on demographic aspects of aging, and has consulted with a variety of community organizations.

Community Housing Choices for Older Americans

M. POWELL LAWTON, Ph.D.
SALLY L. HOOVER, M.A.
Editors

Foreword by Bernard Liebowitz

SPRINGER PUBLISHING COMPANY
NEW YORK

Springer Publishing Company, Inc.
200 Park Avenue South
New York, New York 10003

81 82 83 84 85 86 / 10 9 8 7 6 5 4 3 2 1

Printed in the United States of America

Library of Congress Cataloging in Publication Data

Main entry under title:

Community housing choices for older Americans.

    Based on a conference, held in Philadelphia in Apr. 1978.
    Includes bibliographies and index.
    1. Aged—United States—Dwellings—Congresses.
I. Lawton, M. Powell (Mortimer Powell).
II. Hoover, Sally L.
HD7287.92.U54C65   363.5'9   81-9071
ISBN 0-8261-3640-0   AACR2
ISBN 0-8261 3641-9 (pbk.)

CONTENTS

FOREWORD

This book is the first to be devoted exclusively to the housing situation of that great bulk of older Americans that lives in self-chosen homes in the cities, towns, and rural areas of all states. It is hoped that the material will provide impetus for others to continue the search for the housing alternative that best meets a particular older individual's needs. Diversity is one of the major goals of any such effort simply because people themselves are so diverse.

The Philadelphia Geriatric Center has been a leader in the past in its early actualization of congregate housing ideas, in the community housing described in Chapter 16 in this volume, and in the neighborhood in-home services plan also depicted in this volume. We hope that this book will itself constitute another such effort-motivating stimulus.

The conference, "Community Housing Choices for Older Americans" held in Philadelphia in April 1978, that produced most of the papers appearing as chapters in this book was one of the tasks accomplished under a grant from the Administration on Aging to the Philadelphia Geriatric Center more broadly directed toward analyzing the housing problems of community-resident elderly. The conference was planned by a broad group of people representing organizations with shared concerns in this area:

Action Alliance of Senior Citizens, Philadelphia—David Kuhn, Terrence O'Conlon, Marie Taylor, Michael Tyson

Bryn Mawr College—Merle Broberg

Bucks County Adult Services—Elizabeth Claugh

Chester County Services for Senior Citizens—Donna Baker

Delaware Division on Aging—Bonny Anderson

Federation of Jewish Agencies of Greater Philadelphia—Susan N. Gordon

Gray Panthers—Ernestine Allred, Martha I. Thomas

Homeowner's Association of Philadelphia—Harry Zaslow

Housing Association of Delaware Valley—James Berry

Jewish Family Services, Philadelphia—Ruth G. Cohen

Mayor's Commission on Services to the Aging—Arthur J. Ocinski

Montgomery County Office of County Commissioners—Richard Stoddard

New Jersey Department of Community Affairs—Vivian Carlin, Martha Senseman

Pennsylvania Association of Older Persons—Claire Patterson

Pennsylvania Office for the Aging—Paul D. McLaughlin

Pennsylvania Regional Training Institute for Aging Programs—Joanne Muir Behm

Penn State University—Arthur H. Patterson

Philadelphia Chapter of American Institute of Architects—Peter Arfaa

Philadelphia City Planning Commission—Sandra Garz, Barbara Kaplan

Philadelphia Corporation for Aging—Joseph Walsh

Philadelphia Geriatric Center—Maurice Greenbaum, Rose Locker, Avalie Saperstein

Philadelphia Housing Authority—Marlene Sheppard

Stephen Smith Geriatric Center—Hobart Jackson

U.S. Bureau of the Census, Philadelphia—David Lewis

U.S. Department of Housing and Urban Development, Philadelphia—Richard Krakow

University of Pennsylvania—William Grigsby

University of Southern California—Judith Hamburger

The conference was attended by almost 400 people and was followed two months later by a dissemination report summarizing program and policy suggestions made at the workshops and discussion groups.

The Philadelphia Geriatric Center also wishes to acknowledge the major contributions to the conference and to the ultimate form of this book made by Commissioner Robert Benedict and Dr. Martin Sicker of the Administration on Aging; and William Oriol, then Staff Director, Senate Special Committee on Aging, and presently Associate Director, International Center of Social Gerontology.

Bernard Liebowitz, M.S.W.
Executive Vice President
Philadelphia Geriatric Center

CONTRIBUTORS

ARLENE ADLER
Department of Psychology
New York University
New York, New York

JAMES BONAR
Executive Director
Los Angeles Community Design
  Center
Los Angeles, California

HERMAN BROTMAN
Consulting Gerontologist
3108 Holmes Run Road
Falls Church, Virginia

ELAINE M. BRODY
Director, Department of Human
  Services
Philadelphia Geriatric Center
Philadelphia, Pennsylvania

VIVIAN F. CARLIN
Division on Aging
New Jersey Department of Community
  Affairs
Trenton, New Jersey

TERRENCE L. CONNELL
Office of Policy Development and
  Research
U.S. Department of Housing and
  Urban Development
Washington, D.C.

DEBORAH DEVINE
Social Science Research Analyst
U.S. Department of Housing and
  Urban Development
Washington, D.C.

BARBARA J. FELTON
Department of Psychology
New York University
New York, New York

RICHARD FOX
Executive Director
Plainfield (N.J.) Housing Authority
Plainfield, New Jersey

LEONARD E. GOTTESMAN
Director, Education and Consultation
Philadelphia Geriatric Center
Philadelphia, Pennsylvania

DEBORAH GREENSTEIN
Program Analyst
U.S. Department of Housing and
  Urban Development
Washington, D.C.

MICHAEL GUTOWSKI
The Urban Institute
Washington, D.C.

STANLEY LEHMANN
Department of Psychology
New York University
New York, New York

BERNARD LIEBOWITZ
Executive Vice-President
Philadelphia Geriatric Center
Philadelphia, Pennsylvania

PAUL F. NOLL
Visiting Professor, Department of
  Urban and Regional Planning
Florida State University
Tallahassee, Florida

VICTOR REGNIER
Department of Architecture
University of California, San
Francisco
San Francisco, California

JULIO L. RUFFINI
Medical Anthropology Program
University of California, San
Francisco
San Francisco, California

AVALIE SAPERSTEIN
Director, In-Home Services
Philadelphia Geriatric Center
Philadelphia, Pennsylvania

BETH J. SOLDO
Center for Population Research
Georgetown University
Washington, D.C.

EDWARD STEINFELD
Department of Architecture
State University of New York at
Buffalo
Buffalo, New York

HARRY F. TODD, JR.
Medical Anthropology Program
University of California, San
Francisco
San Francisco, California

RAYMOND J. STRUYK
The Urban Institute
Washington, D.C.

EDWARD C. WALLACE
Assistant Executive Director
The National Center on Black Aged
Washington, D.C.

THOMAS J. WALSH
U.S. General Accounting Office
Washington, D.C.

I
Overview of the Aged and Housing Programs

1
Introduction

M. POWELL LAWTON
SALLY L. HOOVER

This book deals with a strangely neglected topic. Among all those related to the problems of older people, housing as a generalized area of concern is not neglected. The Housing Act of 1937 specified "safe and decent housing" as a right for every American, and the Older Americans Act of 1965 reiterated this right with respect to the elderly population. Both the gerontology literature and the popular press are replete with discussions of housing for the elderly. Almost invariably, however, these articles turn out to deal with planned, clustered housing, exemplified by high-rise "senior-citizen housing," retirement communities, and so on. This type of housing has been extremely successful, and its success has become well known.

Attention in the gerontological literature has been lopsidedly given to planned, rather than unplanned, housing. The same is true of the national effort in housing assistance, where federal dollars have gone overwhelmingly into new construction of planned housing for the elderly, rather than to elderly homeowners and renters living in homes scattered throughout ordinary communities.

The purpose of this book is to begin to redress the difference in emphasis between planned and unplanned housing. It is hoped that the material presented here will motivate the professional and research community of gerontologists to look much more broadly and deeply into current conditions and potential programs than has been done heretofore. What is presented here is clearly just a beginning. Despite the fact that all the chapters in this volume were commissioned explicitly for a conference dealing with this subject and for ultimate use in this book, many areas are omitted or inadequately treated; such soft spots require later treatment by others.

We hope that this volume will provide one impetus for the mutual courtship between the housing and the social service sectors. While a major achievement would be a true functional alliance of the U.S. Departments of Housing and Urban Development (HUD) and Health and Human Services (HHS) on all housing problems of the elderly, working toward less imposing goals constitutes a necessary first step. The first such goal is this collection of a variety of reports from people who have been working in community-oriented housing. In this effort we have searched for authors who speak to policy, service delivery, and research issues. We have sought representation of points of view that cover specific subgroups of elderly housing consumers. Finally, we sought authors who could represent both the private and public sectors of housing-related services.

The book begins with the editors' most general overview of the housing occupied by the older people of the United States and a recapitulation of the housing programs of the federal government. The achievements of planned housing programs are seen to be impressive. Those for smaller scale assistance to existing housing are also reviewed and found lacking.

Chapter 3 of Part I, written by Raymond Struyk, brings the federal view of the relationship between research and public programming. In his role as Deputy Assistant Secretary for Research at HUD, Struyk was a consistent advocate for the development of programs for the elderly, and specifically, for research to guide us toward the most efficacious new programs. The dispassionate critic of federal performance over the years must in all honesty feel that HUD has invested very little in research related to its largest user constituent, the aged. The research directions projected by Struyk suggest that this imbalance is in the process of correction.

Part I concludes with the overview of the aged as a group offered by Beth Soldo and Herman Brotman. As demographers they remind us of the essential facts that we must know in order to work at our problem. The elderly are growing in number, especially the older (and potentially less independent) segment. Income and health are frequently problems of direct relevance to their housing needs. Their households differ radically from those of the population at large.

If an older person lives in a household shared with other family members, the social and physical support available often minimizes both the need for outside services and the probability of institutionalized placement. For older persons living alone, self-care and housing-maintenance problems can be serious challenges to the continuation of independent living.

Because of differential mortality rates and additional social factors, the single-woman household is the second most frequent, after the husband-wife households. Additionally, the proportion of widowed women increases with age; thus, older women are less likely to have someone to help them cope with housing-related problems at the time when physical declines are most likely to occur.

Part II considers in greater depth some subgroups of the elderly. As part of the general background, Edward Wallace reminds us where our planned housing programs have been, insofar as their attempts to meet the needs of black aged are concerned. While this book emphasizes unplanned housing, we must understand the factors associated with the participation (or nonparticipation) of the black aged and other minorities in existing programs. Substantial structural barriers to participation exist. At the same time, as Wallace reminds us, individuals from one subgroup or another may choose not to participate, or demand to participate in a manner consistent with their preferred lifestyles. If we translate some of these considerations into the assistance programs for unplanned housing, they may sometimes lead us to bolster indigenous, neighborhood-based groups in preference to either the existing housing or aging establishment in getting services to minorities.

Sally Hoover offers more detail in examining the housing situations of black and Spanish elderly (Chapter 6). The Annual Housing Survey is especially notable in affording long-sought data on the housing of Americans of Hispanic background. While the first run-through of basic housing information is primarily descriptive, a variety of provocative questions are raised by the descriptive data.

Is the consistently lower housing quality of older blacks in part a function of lifetime income level, differences in living arrangement patterns, and average age of the dwelling? Why do more older whites choose mobile homes as a low-cost means to homeownership? What are the differences in housing quality for the six subcategories of older persons of Hispanic heritage?

Paul Noll presents an overview in Chapter 7 of the federal performance in dealing with housing needs in rural areas. Particularly where the elderly are concerned, the Farmers Home Administration (FmHA) programs have not been notably good performers. However, a new commitment to the aging appears to have been made, as evidenced in both the stepped-up Section 504 grant program and the experimental congregate-housing developments in the Section 515 construction program initiated in 1979. It is clear that considerably greater study is required to understand the needs of the rural elderly, their receptiveness to federal assistance, the willingness of rural communities to devote resources to housing programs for the elderly, and the place of local-level FmHA personnel in the total effort.

The last special group to be considered is the suburban elderly. In

Chapter 8, Michael Gutowski lays out current information regarding the suburban elderly and then considers some general issues of housing and neighborhood-based services as they may apply to the suburban elderly.

This group is "a group to watch." For the first time, in the mid-1970s more older whites lived in suburban areas than in central cities. One indicator of this aging-of-the-suburbs phenomenon is the median age of suburban dwellers, which rose from 27.4 in 1970 to 28.1 in 1974, and to 29.1 in 1977 (U.S. Bureau of the Census, 1978). Additionally, between 1970 and 1975, the growth rate of the suburban elderly population (27%) was about 3½ times that of the older population in central cities (8%). In the suburbs themselves, the older population increased at about 3 times the rate of the total suburban population. This pattern of residential distribution reflects the residential inertia of middle-aged and older populations (Golant, 1979).

While housing quality is generally better in the suburbs, local services are often worse than in central cities or small towns. Thus, the aging of the suburbs may bring increasing problems to those who age within the suburbs. In addition, the housing stock of the older suburbs may deteriorate or become the object of urban renewal efforts, either of which may selectively disturb the living patterns of the elderly.

Part III is minimally concerned with housing in its limited sense. Basic to our view of transactions between the older person and the environment is a package of services—human, organizational, and physical services. People most frequently compose an essential element of the link between the older person and the physical environment. Physical services are delivered by people; physical resources are allocated by individuals and organizations; linkages such as transportation require human intermediaries; and people are enabled to use and enjoy their homes, neighborhoods, and communities by the efforts of family, friends, and formal services. Each of the chapters in Part III is meant to illustrate some aspect of this person-environment service system.

Thomas Walsh presents the results of one of the most influential studies of the service networks of older people that has yet been conducted, the General Accounting Office Cleveland study. In mapping the relationship between individual competence and the types and costs of services delivered, Walsh reminds us that an immense portion of our health and welfare effort is, in fact, devoted to the maintenance of an independent living style within one's own domicile. Thus, the highest quality dwelling or neighborhood may not be usable if the individual cannot obtain basic life-supporting services. This study demonstrates in quantitative terms how the great proportion of the costs of such supportive services is borne by older individuals and their families, and it is worth underlining that housing costs were included in the totals and that public housing tenants are given separate attention in Walsh's chapter.

The next four chapters move to specific locales for looks at how total neighborhood-wide service structures operate. First, the service organization in the Sunset District of San Francisco is described by Julio Ruffini and Harry Todd. The neighborhood services are in a relatively early stage of development as described here, and will no doubt progress to cover a variety of other service sectors in the future. Then, in Chapter 11, Todd and Ruffini speak as legal anthropologists in painting pictures of real people working out relationships to their neighbors in the Sunset District of San Francisco. The particular area chosen for study may have more than its share of problems. But the ethnography of Todd and Ruffini is focused on *negotiation of conflicts*, rather than making any attempt to portray the entire spectrum of life for the elderly in the Sunset District. It is too easy to romanticize the "informal network" and the help-giving structure of a neighborhood; this chapter portrays older people at work in coping with the realities of everyday life and neighbors.

Similarly, Leonard Gottesman and Avalie Saperstein focus on the technical aspects of service organization in a Philadelphia neighborhood. Each of these programs has unique aspects, some because they are tailored to the needs of a unique group, and others because they are pacesetting ideas. While no claim is made for absolute uniqueness, each of these programs contains elements that are eminently capable of being adapted in other locales. It is important to note that wherever explicit housing services of the type considered in this book are delivered, they do or will fit into a larger context of integrated and coordinated services. The quality and efficiency of housing-related services would be enhanced greatly if they were always worked into a total context that coordinated formal and informal supports, information, and community-centered, in-home, and institutional services.

Finally, Victor Regnier presents a different type of look at a neighborhood in terms of its naturally occurring services. It is important to remind ourselves periodically of the fact that most older people obtain most of their resources on their own, rather than through formally organized services. Regnier underlines how the presence of a structure in the mind that aids in satisfying resource needs is necessary to coping with these needs. Further, his hard research data illustrate how relatively dependent many people are on very local services, but they also show the great variation in use and locale of use that exists among the elderly. The work reported here should be particularly useful to planners of services and those concerned with matching urban change to individual needs.

Part IV turns back to explicit housing services, under the general rubric of "housing alternatives." There is an amazing diversity of ways for people to live. Had we looked further we could no doubt have found material that deals with older people living in boats, in rooming houses, or even in caves. Certainly it would have been no trouble to commission chapters on condominiums, boarding homes, or mobile-home living. Rather than attempting the impossible task of comprehensive treatment, some representative settings and services are discussed by the authors of the chapters in Part IV.

Edward Steinfeld provides a discussion of the concrete aspects of home maintenance and repair services that will be a basic reference for any organization considering such a program. Planning, funding, and delivery problems are discussed. Steinfeld's emphasis is on variety and the different ways that a program package can be put together. This approach is ideal in encouraging local effort to construct a program that suits its own situation. While central funding and standards for services seem to be an inevitable need for the future, the wide autonomy encouraged by the Block Grant program and some other programs seem essential to maintain the investment of a community in contributing to its own maintenance and improvement through attention to the housing of its older people.

Raymond Struyk and Deborah Devine report on a specific instance of a home maintenance program. Their research reminds us that the most sophisticated methodological approaches may be used to shed light on extremely cogent issues. The substance of their findings, however, has major implications for future policy regarding small home-repair programs. Thus, control over their use may be necessary to insure that any added income is turned into maintenance effort and that assistance goes to those in need. The single-person household is marked as being an instance of particular need.

The chapters by Elaine Brody and Bernard Liebowitz and by Vivian Carlin and Richard Fox address a topic that has caught the fancy of many gerontologists: the use of existing housing stock by older people in some form of shared-space arrangements. Brody and Liebowitz describe the model and survey the most recent research on the well-known community housing of the Philadelphia Geriatric Center. This housing very carefully plans private facilities with a modicum of shared social space. Brody and Liebowitz contrast this model with a variety of other shared, communal, and congregate living arrangements, indicating that while the variety represented by this array is highly desirable, there are probably limits to the appeal or feasibility of some of these housing arrangements.

Carlin and Fox give a very specific case history of a home-sharing plan where the separate identities of homeowner and tenant are maintained, to the mutual advantage of both. While it is shown to be not an easy program to implement, an innovative proposal for long-range financing and production is offered.

Another style of living either chosen by or fallen into by a small slice of the elderly population is the urban hotel, discussed in Chapter 18 by Barbara Felton, Stanley Lehmann, and Arlene Adler primarily with reference to its single-room occupancy (SRO) version. Some segment of the elderly also live in relatively high-cost hotels with many services. These authors carefully review the research and the issues concerning the SRO as a viable locus for living. They rightly emphasize that we must separate in our minds (and in our research) the characteristics of the users of the SRO from the effects of living in such environments. We remain uncertain of the latter. The fact that the SRO may represent the best ecological niche for some older people is hard for many of us to accept. Yet Felton's team and other researchers have demonstrated clearly that the SRO has a social milieu consistent with the personal needs of some older people; when it also provides at least minimum-quality physical shelter, the case is made for its support, despite the efforts of many forces to ease its demise.

Still another approach, so new that it has yet to be implemented, is contributed in Chapter 19 by Victor Regnier and James Bonar. They present the consensus of a team of service planners and designers grappling with the tripartite issues of providing housing for the elderly, using still-sturdy building stock, and upgrading an off-central-city core area in Los Angeles. Their suggestions regarding the recycling of industrial buildings are an example of the many possibilities inherent in the recycling concept. Similar possibilities have been suggested, and some implemented, in relation to college dormitories, elementary schools, run-down hotels, and insolvent motels. It is important to underline that the elderly seem very frequently to become the gratuitous beneficiaries of cast-off buildings of all kinds. This propensity is likely to continue. Our task is neither to gullibly grasp all such opportunities nor to reject them automatically as second rate. Regnier and Bonar's discussion provides a model by which the positive and negative features of any proposed conversion may be estimated. The final decision will hopefully weight heavily the potential effects of the site and structure on the quality of life for the older person.

Part IV ends with a summary report by Terrence Connell of the high points of the way older people have responded to one of the largest social experiments ever formally evaluated, the Experimental Housing Allowance Program, conducted over a period of years by the U.S. Department of Housing and Urban Development. Now nearing its end, the housing allowance experiment has provided an immense variety of data and information on how individuals, housing markets, and whole communities respond to the opportunity to pay a lesser proportion of one's income on housing. We shall be hearing about these results for many years, and the effects of the results on national programming are likely to be major. Connell's chapter provides an overview of the characteristics of elderly users, and their housing-service delivery comes from the results.

The reluctance of older people to move is demonstrated once more. The conclusion is reached that success is most likely when the subsidy is applied to the residence where the older person presently lives, rather than forcing the person to move. However, the last words are not yet in on the success of the program in meeting its basic goal of elevating the quality of the housing.

This generalization in a sense provides the guideline for the whole volume. We must find ways to improve what is, and give up placing all our hopes in solutions that both cost (as of 1979 in some urban areas) $80,000 per unit for new construction and require the older person to relocate. It is hoped that each of the chapters to follow will contribute to the ability of local housing and social agencies to meet the needs of the 90% of elderly with whom we are concerned.

REFERENCES

Golant, S. M. Central city, suburban, and nonmetropolitan area migration patterns of the elderly. In S. M. Golant (Ed.), *The location and environment of elderly population*. New York: V.H. Winston, 1979.

U.S. Bureau of the Census. Social and economic characteristics of the metropolitan and nonmetropolitan population: 1977 and 1970. *Current population reports*, (Series P-23, No. 75), Washington, D.C.: U.S. Government Printing Office, 1978.

2
Housing for 22 Million Older Americans

M. POWELL LAWTON
SALLY L. HOOVER

This chapter will sketch briefly the new construction programs in federally assisted housing and then proceed to an overview of the housing occupied by the great majority of older Americans who do not live in planned housing. This section will be followed by a definition and brief discussion of housing-related services and a description of existing public programs serving these needs.

FEDERALLY ASSISTED PLANNED HOUSING PROGRAMS

Public Housing

While what we know as public housing began in the Housing Act of 1937, the first such units designated explicitly for the elderly were mandated in the 1956 Housing Act. The housing is under the auspices of local housing authorities with financing and operating expenses assisted by federal funds. Tenancy is limited to those who fulfill local income eligibility standards; rent may not exceed 25% of the individual's income (Brooke Amendment of the 1969 Housing Act). While relatively little new public housing is under planning today, this program has provided the largest number of units for the elderly of any new construction program. A recent audit of the number of units produced under the various federal programs is shown in Table 2.1.

There have, to be sure, been problems with public housing. Sites for such housing have often been located in undesirable spots, and the proximity of some to family housing or to high-crime neighborhoods has been very stressful to older tenants. On the whole, however, research has shown clearly favorable effects of such new housing on life

TABLE 2.1
Elderly Occupancy in HUD-Assisted Programs, June 1976

	Total Units	Occupied By Elderly[a]	Percent Elderly
Public housing	1,035,861	455,779[b]	44
Section 236	550,000	192,000	35
Section 202	45,275	45,275	100
Section 231	54,606	54,606	100
Section 8[c]			
New construction	25,636	22,548	88
Substantial rehabilitation	4,341	3,233	75
Existing	232,505	110,621	48
Loan management	95,292	44,015	46

[a]"Elderly" includes ages 62+ and younger handicapped people.

[b]Includes elderly in both elderly-designated units and non-designated units.

[c]Figures as of December 31, 1977.

Source: Welfeld, I., and Struyk, R. J. Housing options for the elderly. Washington, D. C.: Occasional Papers in Housing and Community Development, No. 3. U. S. Department of Housing and Urban Development, Office of Policy Development and Research, 1978.

satisfaction, housing satisfaction, social interaction, and participation in activities (Carp, 1966; Lawton & Cohen, 1974; Sherwood, Greer, Morris, & Sherwood, 1973).

Section 202 Housing

Section 202 of the 1959 Housing Act authorized 50-year direct loans at 3% interest to nonprofit sponsors for building housing limited to the handicapped or to people aged 62 and over. This program has been extremely successful, both in providing a wide range of enriching environments for lower middle-income older people and in its extremely low rate of financial failures. About 45,000 units were produced in this original 202 program. The program was replaced by the Section 236 program (see next section), but revived recently with interest rates just under market levels. However, by coupling the 202 program with Section 8 subsidies (to be described), rentals may be kept within the limits of the Brooke Amendment and range upward on a sliding scale, again according to income eligibility limits. While about 18,000 new units were approved in fiscal year (FY) 1978, the demand in completed applications was more than 4 times that number, and many problems in the processing of applications have occurred since these functions were dispersed into HUD area offices where little expertise in housing for the elderly exists.

Section 236 Program

Created under the 1968 Housing Act, this program required mortgages at market rates, but federal interest reimbursement was made to the sponsor (either nonprofit or commercial entity) on a sliding scale proportional to the number of low-income tenants housed, down to a rate as low as 1%. The long-range cost of this program was very high, and it was abolished when Section 8 was established in 1974. As Table 2.1 indicates, about 192,000 units for the elderly were produced.

Section 231 Program

The 1959 Housing Act also authorized federal mortgage insurance on market-rate loans to profit and nonprofit organizations for housing serving people in higher income ranges than did the public housing and 202 programs. More than 50,000 units were produced. However, this program experienced a high failure rate and although not abolished, it has been relatively inactive for a number of years.

Section 8 Program

The major form of federal housing subsidy is now the Section 8 program, authorized in the 1974 Housing Act. This program guarantees the owner of a rental property a per-unit subsidy consisting of the difference between 25% of a low-income tenant's income and the market rate. The developer may be either a profit-making entity or a nonprofit sponsor (in which case the development is often done under the 202 program). Section 8 subsidies may be applied to new construction, substantially rehabilitated housing, or existing housing.

The existing housing program will be described in more detail later in this chapter. Table 2.1 indicates that the elderly have been the major beneficiaries of new construction units (88%) and substantial rehabilitation units (75%), and still disproportionately large beneficiaries of Section 8 existing units (48%). It is noteworthy, however, that as of 1979, less than one third of Section 8 new construction units for which funds were authorized have been able to get to the construction contract stage.

"Congregate housing" is not a federal program but refers to a service package superimposed on a variety of housing funding types. Congregate services must include group meals served in a common dining room and may include a variety of other supportive services, such as personal care, housekeeping, counseling, and so on. Almost all congregate services now in existence must either be paid for by the user or subsidized by the sponsor. However, the 1978 Housing Act provided for the first time a small amount of funding within the HUD budget to finance congregate services in both public and 202 housing. A substantial development of such congregate services seems likely to occur as an alternative for marginally independent people who might otherwise require care in a more restrictive setting.

Farmers Home Administration

No Farmers Home Administration (FmHA) programs are earmarked exclusively for the elderly. The FmHA Section 515 program has been used widely for the elderly and had provided 29,000 units as of the end of 1976; overall, these represented about one third of all Section 515 units. In 1979, the Administration on Aging and the FmHA entered into an agreement to jointly sponsor ten congregate housing sites for the elderly, with financing under the Section 515 program and a service package planned and coordinated for a 3-year demonstration period by HEW with the participation of the local area agency on aging. If the demonstration is successful, this could be a most significant development on the rural housing scene.

While public housing and 202 housing have been the prime targets for research evaluation, most of the programs reviewed above have been relatively successful in providing favorable physical and psychosocial environments for older people. There have been some problems in the development and administration of the housing, and not everybody thrives in these kinds of environments. The much greater problem has been the limitation in the number of units produced in comparison to the need. In 1971, in a survey of public and 202 housing, for example, for every occupied unit in these kinds of housing there were 1.5 people on the waiting list. The 1971 White House Conference on Aging called for the production of 120,000 new units of planned housing per year for the elderly. The total production figures over almost 20 years shown in Table 2.1 give the picture of how dismally the effort to reach this goal has failed. The point for emphasis in this volume is that no matter how the country may try, national resources are insufficient to meet more than a fraction of the housing needs of the elderly through new construction. The efforts of the past have not kept up with the need. The efforts of the future will be even more difficult, with the tremendous restrictions on public expenditures facing the decade of the 1980s.

NONPROGRAMMATIC HOUSING

With these considerations in mind, it behooves us to devote considerably greater energy to determining how we can improve the housing conditions of older people living in ordinary housing in "normal" communities. There are several arguments in favor of this effort. First, the nation has been profligate in allowing its housing stock to deteriorate or be replaced before it has lived out its useful life; limitations in our resources require better use of what we have. Second, the cost of new construction would be patently prohibitive if we thought of this option as our only one for improving the living environments of the elderly. Third, the evidence is strong from many sources that large numbers of older people, probably the great majority of them, would prefer to remain in their own homes no matter how much new housing was built. Finally, the good of society at large is served, in addition to that of older people, if we can maintain the quality of the housing occupied by the elderly up through the time it becomes turned over to younger occupants. This step, if accomplished, would do more for neighborhood preservation than any renewal or rehabilitation program could.

WHERE THE OLDER POPULATION LIVES

Despite the public visibility of older migrants to the Sunbelt and the desertion of rural areas by younger people, geographic variations in the proportion of people aged 65 and over are, on the whole, rather mild. For example, as compared to the 1979 national proportion of just under 11%, the most age-dense state is Florida (16%) and the most age-sparse states, aside from Alaska, are Nevada, Utah, and New Mexico, each with less than 8% elderly. Across all regions, the elderly are underrepresented in suburban areas (i.e., outside the central city of Standard Metropolitan Statistical Areas [SMSA]) and slightly overrepresented in small towns. Among the elderly group only, as one might imagine, elderly blacks are concentrated in central cities (55%, as compared to only 29% of all white elderly), and grossly underrepresented in suburban areas (11%, as compared to 34% of white elderly).

In 1977 the median income for all elderly-headed families was $9,110 or about half the median income of $18,264 for the total population that year. However, the median figures for the older population ranged from $5,120 for households headed by an older black woman to $15,599 for older male-headed households where the wife is employed full time. The median income levels were substantially lower for unrelated individuals aged 65 or older. The median for all older unrelated individuals was $3,829 in 1977. Half of the older black females had an annual income of $2,621 or less; unrelated white males had a median income of $4,441 (U.S. Department of Commerce, 1979a).

In 1977 the proportion of older persons with an income level below the poverty level varied by household type and race. The proportion of all older persons in families with incomes below the poverty level was 8% as compared to 27% of the older unrelated individuals. Older whites living in family settings had the lowest proportion living in poverty, about 6%; between 4 and 5 times as many older blacks living in family settings had a poverty-level income. All unrelated individuals were more likely to have an annual income below the poverty level: 20% of the white males, 26% of the white females, 39% of the black males, and 61% of the black females existed on poverty incomes or less (U.S. Department of Commerce, 1979b).

X   HOUSING TENURE X

Essential to the understanding of all topics covered in this book is the fact that more than 70% of all housing units headed by the elderly are owner-occupied, and of these, 86% are unencumbered by a mortgage. For many, the owned home is the only major asset. While it cannot normally be turned into cash income, the owned home is the source of a major saving in one's monthly budget. For example, half of all elderly renters spend 30% or more of their incomes for housing; an equitable housing-cost percentage benchmark of 25% has been established for low-income families under federally assisted housing (Struyk, 1977b). By contrast, only 38% of elderly homeowners with current mortgages and 14% of owners with paid-up mortgages spend 30% or more of their incomes for housing. Looked at from a different vantage point, the older homeowner often cannot afford to live anywhere else. Since the owned home is likely to be old and in an older section of the community, its market value is low, far lower than the cost of most replacement housing. In addition, moving to rental housing risks doubling housing costs.

The homeowner also has many reasons for being emotionally attached to the dwelling. It is a symbol of a lifetime's hard work and a last bastion of emotional security. Associations with the time of early marriage or raising of children may enhance its perceived value. Finally, one comes to know one's home intimately, learns how to adapt to and accept its deficiencies, and understandably becomes reluctant to make a change, even if objectively it might be for the better.

While only 30% are renters, as we shall see, the elderly renter is apt to have even more housing problems than the homeowner, beginning with the previously mentioned problem of rent as an excessive proportion of income. Many renters are nonetheless attached to their dwellings or neighborhoods in the same way as owners, and will almost always face an increase in housing costs if they move. The subsidized planned housing programs have overwhelmingly served former open-market renters, as well as displaced people. Relatively few people elect to sell homes to move into assisted housing, though in another, higher income bracket, one sees a frequent use of proceeds from the sale of a home to purchase a home or care in a retirement community.

The 1976 Annual Housing Survey (AHS) shows that 9.7% of owner-occupied homes of the under-65 population are valued at less than $15,000, as compared to 22.5% among over-65 owner-occupied homes. At the other end of the scale, 47.5% of under-65 units as compared to only 29% of over-65 units were valued at $35,000 or more. Among renter-occupied homes, 12.6% of younger heads paid under $100 per month, while 33.7% of over-65 heads paid this little. Almost twice as many younger heads (33.7%) paid $200 per month as did older heads (17.3%).

Not surprisingly, older homeowners have lived in their present homes longer than renters. In 1976 35% of homeowners had lived there since 1950 or earlier, as compared to 9% of renters. Owned homes tend to be single-family homes (84%), while almost half of all older renters live in multiple-unit (five units or more) housing. The median number of rooms in owner-occupied housing is five, as compared to three in rental housing.

It is of interest to note that the 1976 AHS sample estimates that 0.6% (in the neighborhood of 130,000 people) of elderly heads of families lived in hotels and 4.9% in mobile homes; this latter figure has increased precipitously in recent years and may be a continuing trend for the future.

QUALITY OF HOUSING OCCUPIED BY THE ELDERLY

One rough guide to housing quality is the age of the housing. The median age of both owner-occupied and rental housing of the elderly was over 35 years (i.e., built before 1940) in 1976; only 35% of the housing occupied by heads under 65 was this old.

More specific indicators of the quality of housing may be found in the various structural and utility systems of the dwelling unit. The Annual Housing Survey asks informants about a variety of deficits. Table 2.2 shows the frequency of 19 deficits separately for the under- and over-65 populations by tenure in 1976.

Overall, the prevalence of most deficits is quite low. In general, however, the housing of the aged is slightly poorer than that of the under-65 segment, and rental housing slightly poorer than owned housing. The most frequent deficits are in the heating system and the presence of rodents. Comparison of these results with similar figures from only 3 years previously shows a highly regular improvement in quality over this short time.

Struyk (1977a) demonstrated the great disparity between the quality of elderly-occupied housing in rural and urban areas in the 1973 data. While the full distribution by place sizes is not available on later surveys, the variation between those living inside and outside SMSAs is in the same direction. Deprived statuses combine to result in very high incidence of deficits among blacks, those living outside metropolitan areas, and those living in the South. For example, the deficit rate for blacks living outside SMSAs in the South for wall sockets is 38%, incomplete kitchen 26%, incomplete plumbing 37%, leaking roof 23%, presence of rodents 42%. The extreme contrast group is whites living in Western SMSAs, where these same deficit rates range from 1% to 4%.

Housing quality also varies by type of household. If the structural aspects of the housing unit are compared for older couples, older single males, older single females, and multigenerational households where the head was under age 65 (but at least one household member was

TABLE 2.2
Percentages of Units with Housing Deficiencies by Age
and Tenure, 1976

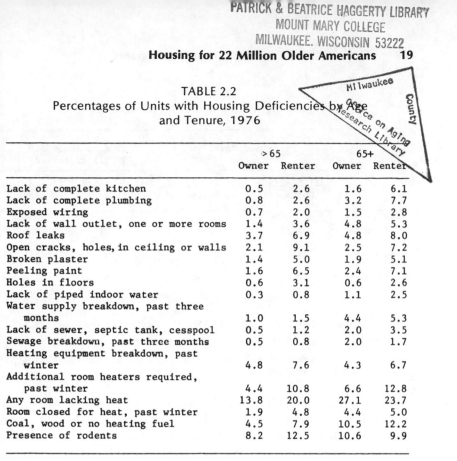

	> 65		65+	
	Owner	Renter	Owner	Renter
Lack of complete kitchen	0.5	2.6	1.6	6.1
Lack of complete plumbing	0.8	2.6	3.2	7.7
Exposed wiring	0.7	2.0	1.5	2.8
Lack of wall outlet, one or more rooms	1.4	3.6	4.8	5.3
Roof leaks	3.7	6.9	4.8	8.0
Open cracks, holes, in ceiling or walls	2.1	9.1	2.5	7.2
Broken plaster	1.4	5.0	1.9	5.1
Peeling paint	1.6	6.5	2.4	7.1
Holes in floors	0.6	3.1	0.6	2.6
Lack of piped indoor water	0.3	0.8	1.1	2.5
Water supply breakdown, past three months	1.0	1.5	4.4	5.3
Lack of sewer, septic tank, cesspool	0.5	1.2	2.0	3.5
Sewage breakdown, past three months	0.5	0.8	2.0	1.7
Heating equipment breakdown, past winter	4.8	7.6	4.3	6.7
Additional room heaters required, past winter	4.4	10.8	6.6	12.8
Any room lacking heat	13.8	20.0	27.1	23.7
Room closed for heat, past winter	1.9	4.8	4.4	5.0
Coal, wood or no heating fuel	4.5	7.9	10.5	12.2
Presence of rodents	8.2	12.5	10.6	9.9

Source: Annual Housing Survey, 1976; public-use tape.

aged 65 or older), a larger proportion of both older single males and females had to cope with housing deficits such as incomplete plumbing facilities, peeling paint, lack of working electrical wall outlets, and an inferior type of heating equipment than did other households. Preliminary findings from the 1976 Annual Housing Survey data indicate that on the average, older Americans currently living with younger families not only enjoy housing of better structural quality, but also have a higher standard of living. Only older marital pairs appear to have a comparably good home environment (Hoover, 1978).

The 1975 survey data showed only 12% of all units without any of 25 deficits. About 24% had 4 or more deficits (Lawton, 1978).

One would expect that, with older and somewhat poorer quality housing, older owner occupants would face the necessity for more frequent repairs. Table 2.3 shows the percentages of all owners and those over age 65 who reported having done different types of jobs on their homes during the past year. The elderly in fact, reported most of

86- 917

TABLE 2.3
Housing Maintenance and Remodeling

| | Performed Past 12 Months | | Cost More Than $100 (Of All Performed) | |
	All Dwelling Units	65 and Over Heads	All Dwelling Units	65 and Over Heads
Additions	5.8%	2.9%	93.0%	89.0%
Alterations	22.2	10.1	74.5	73.4
Replacements	20.8	18.1	76.5	77.6
Repairs	46.7	30.9	50.1	54.7
Expectations	41.2	27.1	76.5	78.8

Source: U. S. Bureau of the Census, Annual Housing Survey, 1974.
Public-use tape.

these jobs much less often than did people in general. Yet, when these jobs were done, the elderly paid about what everyone else did. It thus seems probable that many owners are deferring needed maintenance, knowing that the cost they will pay will represent a disproportionate percentage of their income.

Perceived Neighborhood Quality

The AHS also asked people to evaluate their local areas on a variety of attributes and services. Table 2.4 shows the percentages of older people indicating that a variety of undesirable conditions were present, the percentage indicating that the existing condition was bothersome, and the percentage indicating that the condition was bad enough to make them want to move. For almost all attributes older people expressed greater satisfaction than did those under age 65. Many fewer are seen as bothersome than are experienced as negative conditions, and only tiny fractions indicate that any poor conditions dispose them to wish to move. A similar analysis of the 1974 data showed that 12% wished to move because of one or more bothersome neighborhood conditions. Comparatively low satisfaction was expressed with public transportation, shopping, and medical resources, followed by street noise and crime.

Table 2.4
Percentages of People Aged 65 and Over Indicating Presence
and Evaluations of Neighborhood Conditions, 1976

	% Condition Exists	% Bothered	% Wish to Move		% Inadequate	% Wish to Move
Street noise	34.6	11.2	2.7	Public transportation	32.8	1.4
Street traffic	37.2	8.8	2.4	Schools	2.4	0.1
Streets need repair	14.3	6.5	1.0	Shopping	15.8	1.1
Streets impassable (snow, mud)	7.9	3.4	0.6	Police protection	8.4	0.9
Inadequate street lighting	18.5	4.6	0.6	Fire protection	4.5	0.3
Neighborhood crime	15.5	9.8	2.6	Medical resources	12.1	0.6
Trash, litter	14.2	8.5	1.8			
Abandoned structures	5.6	1.8	0.5			
Rundown houses	7.4	3.0	1.0			
Industrial activities	20.1	1.9	1.3			
Odors, smoke	7.9	4.6	1.3			
Airplane noise	19.5	6.0	0.8			

Source: U. S. Bureau of the Census, Annual Housing Survey, 1976. Public use tape, unpublished data.

Before concluding that older people are, on the whole, very satisfied with their neighborhoods, a brief warning is required. Considerable evidence exists to suggest that older people are selectively more likely to express satisfaction with the status quo than are younger people (Campbell, Converse, & Rodgers, 1976). A variety of reasons may contribute to this tendency to look on the bright side: the lack of any other genuine alternative, the scaling down of aspirations with age, ego defensiveness, or the reduction of cognitive dissonance. When the question of moving is introduced ("so bothersome that you'd like to move"), the defensive denial becomes extreme. In any case, older people's degree of satisfaction is unquestionably inflated by this type of consumer survey format.

This section on the type of housing occupied by older people living in ordinary communities has shown, rather consistently, that the elderly occupy older housing of slightly lower quality than that occupied by younger people. The economic security represented by an owned home or relatively low rental payment is accompanied by a general state of cash unavailability for housing-related expenses, such as ordinary maintenance. Being relatively immobile because of economic and other types of constraints, older people typically make the best of remaining where they are. They feel positively about "standing pat" for both positive reasons of attachment and negative reasons of the several types discussed above. While realities of statistical generalizations force us to talk about the "average" older person, target groups of distinctly deprived older people emerge upon a closer look: the resident of rural areas, the black, the renter, and the female unrelated individual.

HOUSING-RELATED SERVICES

The discussion above has implied the need for a variety of services related to housing. In many ways, the need for income support cuts across all housing problems. Research done in the Experimental Housing Allowance Program conducted over the past 6 years by HUD calls into question, however, whether an increase in income necessarily becomes converted into needed home maintenance (Office of Policy Development and Research, 1978). It is probable that a variety of programs is required to identify explicit housing needs and provide for their satisfaction.

Steinfeld discusses a variety of housing-related services in Chapter 14 of this volume. An abbreviated and slightly revised outline of housing-related service types is shown in Table 2.5.

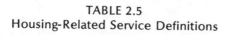
TABLE 2.5
Housing-Related Service Definitions

Housing-Related Services Provided to Community-Resident Elderly[a]

I. *Substantial rehabilitation skilled maintenance, major repairs:*
Extensive repair and reconstruction that usually requires skilled tradesman to complete.
Examples include:
1. Extensive electrical wiring
2. Major structural repairs such as roof reconstruction or housing conversion
3. Replacement of sidewalks and driveways
4. Plumbing

II. *Repairs:*
A. Emergency repairs: Repairs which, unless attended to promptly, may result in either sickness or accidents to the occupants, or abandonment or major damage to the building.
Examples include:
1. Damage caused by a break-in
2. Utility breakdowns
3. Removal of heavy snow which prevents access to or egress from dwelling
B. Minor repairs: Unskilled or semiskilled home maintenance tasks that improve the livability of homes, and that can be made at moderate cost and without specific technical knowledge.
Examples include:
1. Plastering repairs
2. Laying new floor surfaces
3. Plumbing repairs
4. Repair or replacement of major appliances (washer, dryer, refrigerator, stove)

III. *Accessibility modifications:*
Structural adaptations that meet the special needs of elderly disabled.
Examples include:
1. Installing a stair lift or ramp
2. Modifying appliance and electrical controls for easier manipulation
3. Widening doorways

IV. *Chore services:*
Home maintenance tasks that an individual can no longer perform himself and that help to maintain the individual's health and safety in the home. These tasks do not include any housing construction or homemaker activities.

(Continued)

TABLE 2.5
(Continued)

Examples include:
1. Replacing window panes, fuses, electric plugs
2. Heavy indoor cleaning and outdoor cleaning
3. Snow shoveling and grass cutting
4. Nonexpert insect and rodent control

V. *Weatherization:*
Repairs, modifications, or supplies that protect a dwelling or its occupants from the effects of weather, conserve energy, or provide alternative energy sources to heat or cool a dwelling.
Examples include:
1. Providing and installing storm windows, insulation
2. Servicing a heating system

VI. *Security modifications:*
Measures that prevent accidents, fires, or intrusion into a dwelling.
Examples include:
1. Installing secure door and window locks
2. Addition of exterior flood lights or lights along access walks
3. Installing smoke detectors, fire escape or alarm systems

VII. *Housing counseling:*
A. Advice or printed material provided to elderly homeowners to assist them in improving or financing their own homes
B. Assistance in finding new and better housing or in selling their own homes
C. Assistance with financial matters related to housing
D. Assistance in dealing with landlords, utilities, movers

[a]Adapted from Steinfeld, E., Holmes, M.B., & Holmes, D. *Planning handbook: Residential repair and renovation services guide for state and area agencies on aging.* New York: Community Research Applications, 1978.

It is possible to view any community-based services, especially those delivered in the home, as housing-related in the sense that they may help the person remain in the community rather than enter a more dependent living situation. However, each of those services shown in Table 2.5 has some more explicit relationship to housing needs, as compared, for instance, to home health, meals on wheels, or legal services.

Most of the services shown in Table 2.5 are relatively familiar. It may be a surprise to many to learn that none of them is available on a statutory basis to every class of needy older Americans. A brief sketch of programs that do provide some of these forms of assistance will suffice, since there are so few available.

The HUD Section 312 Rehabilitation Loan Program has been in operation for a number of years and a fairly steady 12% of its users have been people aged 65 and older. Considering that almost 25% of owner-occupied households are headed by older people, this figure clearly shows that older people are underrepresented. HUD officials are very explicit regarding the reasons for this underrepresentation: The financial stability of the 312 program depends on the payback capabilities of its users, and the elderly are thought to constitute poorer risks. The interest rate is low. However, the program is available only in specified areas such as urban renewal, code enforcement, or block grant areas. Furthermore, there are major administrative problems and delays in getting HUD approval and in paying contractors. The 312 program has been one of the most difficult to use. In 1977 only about 5,200 loans were granted, 855 of them to people aged 65 and over. The average size of each loan was $7,591 for the elderly; major rehabilitation work is thus performed under this program.

The Community Development Block Grant Program (CDBG) subsidizes a number of the types of housing services listed above. However, because the CDBG operates only in selected (usually urban) areas and there is a high degree of local determination, it is difficult to summarize activity in this program. First, substantial amounts of major rehabilitation occur under this program. Often the process is somewhat easier than in the case of the 312 program. However, the extent of use by the elderly is not known. Most CDBG agencies operate a loan and grant program that serves small repair, emergency repair, major repair, and accessibility or security modifications. These funds are relatively accessible to older people in the designated areas, but ease of use varies radically among cities. The elderly are high users, but the uniform complaint is made by agencies that their funding is inadequate.

The Title III Program of the Older Americans Act comes the closest to being a national source of assistance for home maintenance. Housing services and chore and homemaker services are two of the in-home services that may be designated in fulfilling the mandatory services requirements for local and state plans. While all states included housing renovation and repair services in their plans for fiscal year 1978, a national total of $3.3 million was expended, clearly a minuscule amount. Chore services are in somewhat better supply, but it is impossible to estimate their volume separately from homemaker services, which account for the majority of the total in that category. In any case, many local areas have no Title III funded housing-maintenance programs at all, and where they do exist they are grossly underfunded.

The Section 504 Home Repair Program of the Farmers Home Administration, after many years as a low-use program concentrating on loans with full payback requirements, has recently been used as a grant or combination loan and grant program. Although not targeted explicitly to the elderly, most grant users are low-income elderly. Funding has improved recently, though it is still at a low absolute level. Persistent problems occur with lack of outreach or active encouragement to use at some local levels.

There have been several varieties of assistance in weatherization through the Community Services Administration, the federal Department of Energy, and other channels. Funds are in relatively good supply, but the marketing of the weatherproofing, heating system, and fuel cost aspects of the programs has been variable in its effectiveness among local areas.

The Section 8 program of HUD should be mentioned in this connection as a vehicle for improving the quality of renter-occupied housing. Such subsidies have been used by the owners of rental housing in return for making improvements for tenants already occupying their housing (if occupied housing already meets Section 8 quality standards, the subsidy may be used purely as an income support). There is some possibility that the Section 8 program might be extended to older homeowners in the future.

Other programs have been used for various purposes. The Title XX Social Services Program may be used for chore and other housing-related services, but these uses are at local option. Most often the service is not age restricted and a means test is applied.

A variety of housing counseling activities occur in relation to federal loan and neighborhood renewal programs. Most often they are directed toward younger people with the specific aim of protecting against default and deterioration of the stock. Few efforts to deal with the far broader problems of the elderly have been located. There are a number of locally sponsored home repair or chore services not funded by any of the federal programs.

In any case, the summary above allows us to conclude, first, that there is no assurance that every area will have available a program to serve the housing needs of low-income elderly. Second, without exception, programs where they exist are grossly underfunded. Third, there are no rules to guide the ideal organization of such services where they do exist; some are delivered by free-standing agencies, some by neighborhood organizations, some by housing-oriented agencies, and some by welfare-oriented agencies. Finally, the lack of coordination between the housing and the welfare sector works against the development of a technical expertise in delivering hard housing services within a social service framework that recognizes the special needs of the elderly.

In conclusion, we consider the case firmly established that greater attention is required for the housing problems of community-resident aged owners and renters. Existing programs are too few, too capricious in coverage, lacking in technical expertise, and poorly coordinated.

REFERENCES

Campbell, A., Converse, P. E., & Rodgers, W. L. *The quality of American life: Perceptions, evaluations, and satisfactions.* New York: Russell Sage, 1976.

Carp, F. M. *A future for the aged.* Austin: University of Texas Press, 1966.

Hoover, S. L. *Housing characteristics and quality of multigenerational households.* Paper presented at the annual meeting of the Gerontological Society, Dallas, November 1978.

Lawton, M. P. The housing problems of community-resident elderly. *Occasional Papers in Housing and Community Affairs* (Volume 1). Washington, D.C.: United States Department of Housing and Urban Development, 1978.

Lawton, M. P. & Cohen, J. The generality of housing impact on older people. *Journal of Gerontology,* 1974, 29, 194–204.

Office of Policy Development and Research. *A summary report of current findings from the Experimental Housing Allowance Program.* Washington, D.C.: U.S. Department of Housing and Urban Development, 1978.

Sherwood, S., Greer, D. S., Morris, J. N., & Sherwood, C. C. *The Highland Heights experiment.* Washington, D.C.: U.S. Department of Housing and Urban Development, 1973.

Struyk, R. J. The housing situation of elderly Americans. *Gerontologist,* 1977, 13, 130–139. (a)

Struyk, R. J. The housing expense burden of households headed by the elderly. *Gerontologist,* 1977, 17, 447–452. (b)

U.S. Department of Commerce. *Money income in 1977 of families and persons in the United States.* Current Population Reports (Series P-60, Number 118). U.S. Government Printing Office, March 1979. (a)

U.S. Department of Commerce. *Characteristics of the population below the poverty level: 1977.* Current Population Reports (Series P-60, Number 119). U.S. Government Printing Office, March 1979. (b)

3
Research in Housing for the Elderly: The U.S. Department of Housing and Urban Development

RAYMOND J. STRUYK
With Deborah Greenstein

The research activities of the U.S. Department of Housing and Urban Development (HUD) with respect to the aged, as of 1978, indicate the way of the future. The results of this research will need to be in hand before strong concrete proposals regarding new initiatives can be made either to the Office of Management and Budget or to the Congress that will be found acceptable on technical grounds.

HIGH-PRIORITY AREAS FOR RESEARCH

The first point about HUD's research program on the elderly is that in 1977 Secretary Harris and her principal staff agreed that housing for the elderly should be one of six high-priority areas for our research resources. Those who have been following HUD research over the years will realize that this represents quite a change.

The adoption of this priority bodes well for several reasons. First of all, it means that there are more resources available, more contract dollars, and more HUD staff to work on these problems. But much more importantly, it means that there is an interest in these issues among the principal staff and the secretary. There is an audience, and without an audience, the best research in the world will not get translated into action.

The general thrust of the research is on housing for the "independent elderly," that is, the noninstitutionalized elderly and those who are not living in HUD-assisted projects. There is a concern for

28

supporting the wish of the elderly to remain in their own homes, particularly in light of the department's past strong focus on the renter side. The majority of HUD's attention will be devoted to elderly homeowners.

Six current research activities are described, followed by a look at what the future has for both the research program and the operating programs in HUD.

Quality of Housing

The first research task is the monitoring of what is happening to the quality of housing in which the elderly live and the fractions of their incomes that they are having to devote to that housing, using the Annual Housing Survey data collected for the department by the U.S. Bureau of the Census. HUD is concerned not only in the global sense but in looking carefully at different household types, those in different locations, those with different incomes, and so on.

These measures are, after all, part—and only part—of the bottom line of how well the department is doing. We can talk about business cycles, count housing units and production, and be aware of rent control, but the basic question is: How well are the elderly housed? We are using that definition as our metric and hope to issue reports on this situation to the Congress on a consistent basis, so that they can be used as a yardstick to measure our progress.

One important outcome of this work is an increased ability to target the department's resources on those who are in the greatest need, either in terms of physical quality of the housing unit or in terms of housing-expense burden.

Demand for Housing Programs

The second research activity is the investigation of the demand side of housing programs. The most familiar is the current Experimental Housing Allowance Program (EHAP) (described in detail in Chapter 20, this volume). A demonstration of a full-scale housing allowance demand program is now in process in two market areas, Green Bay, Wisconsin, and South Bend, Indiana; a total of about 17,000 households have been enrolled since the program began 4 years ago and 8,000 are currently receiving payments. The results of these, plus related efforts in 10 other cities, will determine the feasibility of the program on a national scale. We are, of course, monitoring what is happening there very carefully.

HUD has also finished the first wave of its evaluation of the Section 8 Housing Assistance Payment Program, which is the major current housing assistance program of the department.

We are closely examining how the elderly are faring under EHAP and Section 8. How do their participation rates compare to other households and what impediments are there to their participation? How are they expending their additional funds; how much goes for improved housing, how much goes simply to reduce rent or home-ownership cost burdens? What are effects on mobility, and finally, for homeowners, what are the effects on their dwelling-unit maintenance and repair activities?

Housing Maintenance Activities

The third area examines the determinants of housing-maintenance activities by elderly homeowners. It is my personal perception that the department is placing greater emphasis on the improvement of the physical housing environment, as opposed to relief of the housing-expense burden, and that this emphasis will continue in the future. This emphasis is consistent with the department's broad objectives of neighborhood and central-city revitalization. For this reason the whole set of determinants of the housing-maintenance decisions of the elderly take on a special interest.

How sensitive are home-maintenance activities to substantial increases in income? Is there a clear increase in repair activity? How sensitive is the completion of these activities to the occurrence of impairments in household members? How does the provision of social services, of supportive services, or repair services affect the quality of housing-unit maintenance? To what extent does repair activity vary among household types, husband and wife or single individuals? An answer to this question would reveal much about whether internal support at home, such as that between couples, is likely to result in better maintenance.

Supportive Services

A fourth research area concerns the relationships between explicit housing services and housing-related supportive services. Traditionally such supportive services have been thought of primarily as means of assisting elderly householders to remain in their own units. HUD is taking a slightly different view that is consistent with the mission of the department: Does the receipt of chore services, housekeeping services, or even personal-care services significantly affect the physical environment that is occupied by the elderly?

Theoretically it is fairly clear that this effect could occur through direct substitution, that is, tasks that the impaired elderly formerly did for themselves would be performed through formal services. Alternatively, the effect could be complementary: "Helpers" could assist the elderly person in doing things that they would not be able to do alone. Finally, a support function is possible whereby frail elderly could be provided with one kind of service (e.g., chore) which would leave them with more energy and personal resources to take on a number of other jobs. It may be that the burden of walking five blocks to shop for groceries is severe; removing that burden could allow a person the energy to do more housecleaning or the energy to call a contractor to arrange for repairs to be made.

We have been examining the effect of the provision of some of these services on the quality of housing occupied by the elderly using the Survey of the Low-Income Aged and Disabled that was done in 1973 and 1974, before and after the implementation of the Supplemental Security Income Program. The early analysis suggests that there really are some complementary effects, particularly for renters. These findings have formidable implications for the enlightened self-interests of HUD and Health and Human Services (HHS) and their joint action. The findings strongly suggest that a great deal can be achieved in conserving the resources used in providing services to the elderly. This work is still in process and more will be reported in the future.

Maintenance Services

A fifth project is HUD's participation with the Ford Foundation in a demonstration and evaluation of the provision of maintenance services to elderly-headed households in Baltimore. The idea behind this program is very similar to taking out a service contract when you buy a washer or dryer. In exchange for an annual or monthly fee, the seller will fix the appliance when it breaks.

This is a heavily subsidized program that is now in the early operating phases. My personal view is that this type of program has enormous possibilities because many of the elderly are unaware of fairly major deficiencies in their units. When asked a direct question, they often perceive no problem with a particular system, whereas a trained evaluator would say it really does need to be repaired. In an analysis of 1,600 elderly homeowners (reported at greater length in Chapter 15, this volume), about half of the systems that clearly needed repairs were unrecognized as such by the elderly.

Simply providing a marginal increase in household income will probably not increase their perceptions of the problem at all. Thus it is not surprising that an increment in income does not spontaneously induce much additional maintenance and repair activity.

Data from another study, Boston's Housing Improvement Program, which is funded through the Community Development Block Grant Program, indicate that detailed technical assistance—How do I get it done?—provided by appraisers and inspectors, is very instrumental in getting work started.

These findings together suggest a much more "hands-on" approach to improving housing quality among elderly homeowners than most of our programs now entail.

Housing Adjustments

The final research activity goes back to an essential problem: our current inability to describe with any confidence the process by which elderly households adjust to their changing housing needs. Cross-sectional data panels are available, but we do not know how individual households react to various changes in their health status, income status, or family composition.

By housing adjustments I mean two things. First are modifications to the currently occupied dwelling. The use of rooms may change, for example, a den may be converted into a bedroom because it is simply too difficult for one member to go up and down the steps anymore, or units may be allowed to depreciate as various kinds of maintenance expenditures are foregone. A second, more traditional type of adjustment is shifting between dwelling units, or residential mobility. To fill the gap in understanding the adjustment process, we are beginning a 10-year survey of housing adjustments by elderly people in two metropolitan areas, using a cohort of persons aged 55 years and over in the first year and conducting a longitudinal study.

We wish to know not only how these adjustments take place but in addition, if government is to intervene in a constructive fashion, we want to know the proper set of incentives that will maintain or upgrade dwelling-unit quality or foster timely relocation. How sensitive are the elderly to various factors? When is the right time, the appropriate moment, for the government to offer assistance? When are people on the verge of making these adjustments themselves without the heavy hand of government?

LOOKING TOWARD THE FUTURE

Turning to a more general view of the future, enormous demographic swings will occur in this country over the next several decades (discussed at length by Soldo and Brotman in Chapter 4, this volume). As we begin the 1980s the United States is building a huge number of single-family structures to satisfy the post–World War II baby-boom household-formation groups. This trend will probably continue for another decade, but within 2 or 3 decades we could have a relative surplus of single-family housing.

At present, a major policy question is whether we should foster adjustments in markets where single-family housing is in very tight supply and we are building it at a high rate. One must recognize the issue of people wanting to stay in their own homes as well as a series of other questions. But we do not really know how to foster adjustments because we do not know what factors now drive such adjustments. On the other hand, in loose housing markets, which characterize many of the Northeastern and North Central cities, the last thing needed is new housing other than, perhaps, special-purpose housing for the elderly. Given the market situation, I would strongly argue against any massive building program in such areas, for the elderly or any other group.

What does the future hold for HUD? I would like to be able to say something definitive, but I fear that such a clear forecast is impossible. In the near future my office will be developing a research agenda from which we hope to work in the next 3 years or so. In December 1977 we sought the advice of a small group of scholars, local government officials, our colleagues from the Administration on Aging, and representatives of aged organizations on what they perceived to be the strongest policy questions that we ought to consider in the research program. At the time of this meeting we also sponsored a conference at which several background papers on the independent elderly were presented and published in a new publication, *Occasional Papers in Housing and Community Development*, being edited for HUD by American University.

It is much more difficult to forecast HUD programs than HUD research. For the 1979 fiscal year (FY) budget, HUD requested a 10,000-unit Section 8 program initiative for elderly homeowners, but this was disallowed by the Office of Management and Budget. The budget process in the future will clearly involve consideration of a much broader set of program options for the elderly than has been the case in the past.

Feasibility for some programs is difficult to document now; for a number of them we may have to wait until we know more before we can make a strong case to the secretary and the Office of Management and Budget.

In conclusion, it is my view that HUD will have to be much more willing to crawl out of its traditional shell of assisted rental housing and take some innovative steps to overcome the housing problems of the elderly. I believe that with a genuine willingness by the principal staff and the secretary to do this, the next few years will be important ones for elderly Americans.

Appendix

A GUIDE TO COMPLETED HUD RESEARCH ON ELDERLY HOUSING

DEBORAH GREENSTEIN

The results of several of the research projects on the elderly supported by the Office of Policy Development and Research are available in print. A description of these projects follows, as does information on ordering the reports.

1. *Low-rise housing for older people—Behavioral criteria for design* attempts to translate available research on the needs of older people in housing into performance criteria for designers, and into possible design solutions. Housing is divided into six categories: inside the unit, unit edge, places for neighboring, community activity spaces, on the site, and links to the town. In each category the report presents performance criteria, possible design solutions in both words and pictures, several annotated plans, and a set of design review questions. The report received an award from *Progressive Architecture*, which called it "the best single-volume summary of design and program guidelines for low-rise housing for the elderly." Available from the U.S. Government Printing Office—Stock Number 023-000-00434-8.

2. *Evaluation of the effectiveness of congregate housing for the elderly* looked at 27 congregate housing sites around the country in order to see if congregate housing is a viable type of housing for the elderly, what type of elderly is best served, if it enhances independence, and what services are essential rather than frills. The findings were that congregate housing is a successsful way of extending the elderly person's ability to remain independent, but that the service-delivery package is very expensive to provide and that federal and state support for it is undependable. Available from the U.S. Government Printing Office—Stock Number 023-000-00378-3.

3. *Congregate housing for older people—an urgent need, a growing demand* presents the papers prepared for a HUD-HEW supported conference

on congregate housing. Papers included address seven areas of concern: the current situation, assessing the market, design, research utilization, management, financing housing and services, and what comes next. The papers stress the difficulty of paying for services and the need for future HUD-HEW cooperation. Available from the U.S. Government Printing Office—Stock Number 017-062-00107-3.

4. *Property tax relief program for the elderly—An evaluation; a compendium report; final report* is a three-volume examination of the property relief programs in all fifty states, covering such elements as eligibility, outreach, administration, and costs and benefits. The study showed that the effect of the property tax relief programs in reaching their objectives of reduced regressivity, keeping the elderly in their homes, slowing neighborhood decline, influencing voting, and the like were mixed. Basically a form of income transfer, the programs reached their peaks in the days of state government surpluses. Available from the U.S. Government Printing Office—Compendium Stock Number 023-000-00332-5; Evaluation Stock Number 023-000-00331-7; Final Report Stock Number 023-000-00330-9.

5. *Elderly participants in the Administrative Agency Experiment* is a report on a special study of the elderly participants in one part of the Experimental Housing Allowance Program. The study found that the percentage of eligible elderly who actually participated was lower than that of the nonelderly, but that once selected, the elderly were more successful in meeting the requirements of the program. Available from National Technical Information Service—PB 265-685.

6. *Housing for the elderly and handicapped* is the result of an in-house evaluation of the Section 202 program conducted by the Policy Development and Research Office's Division of Special Studies. The report points out that 202 has predominantly served a white, middle-class population, and that much of its success was due to the small size of the program and to the special attention given to it by HUD Central Office staff. The new decentralized Section 202 program may differ substantially because of its larger size, its higher interest rates, and its tie to Section 8 rent subsidies. Available from the U.S. Government Printing Office—HUD-PDR-301.

7. *The housing listening post: Final report* describes a statewide toll-free telephone housing information and referral service operated by elderly volunteers. The program grew in response to the need of the HUD office in Seattle and the State of Washington Office of Community Affairs for an efficient, consistent way to respond to a large volume of telephone calls seeking housing assistance. The service operated successfully for 2 years, serving over 25,000 residents of the state of Washington. It is estimated that over 29,000 hours of time was volunteered by the elderly staffers at a savings of $110,000 in personnel costs. Available from the U.S. Government Printing Office—Stock Number 023-000-00333-3.

4
Housing Whom?

BETH J. SOLDO
HERMAN B. BROTMAN

Because institutionalized adults generate an extensive demand for services they have attracted considerable attention from researchers, policy makers, and planners alike. Despite their disproportionate utilization of national health care resources, the older institutionalized population at any point in time is relatively small; in 1976 approximately 50%, of individuals 65 years of age or older, resided in some type of custodial care setting. [Prior research (Myers & Soldo, 1977) indicates that the lifetime probability of institutionalization is considerably higher than that suggested by the small proportion of elderly institutionalized at a single point in time.]

The vast majority of older persons live in the community. The community-based older population, far from being a homogeneous entity, includes persons from 65 to well over 95 years of age of varied historical, cultural, and educational experiences. Older persons living in a community setting also differ in their family-friendship networks, personal resources, and interests, as well as in their financial status. Location in the community does not even imply uniformity in the health characteristics of older persons; while a substantial number are impairment free, a small proportion of older noninstitutionalized persons are housebound and totally disabled. The basic demand for shelter is met, in turn, by a wide variety of living arrangements and housing accommodations ranging from single-person to multigenerational households, and from underserviced suburban residences to well-serviced public housing projects for senior citizens.

Living arrangements and housing assume unique social significance at the older ages as health declines and dependency needs are likely to increase. Troll's (1971) reinterpretation of disengagement theory (Cumming & Henry, 1961) suggests that the aging process can be characterized as a process of disengaging from the economic sector and reengaging into the household sphere of activities. Even for those individuals, particularly women, who were not actively involved in the labor force, the context of household living may become more salient at

the older ages as secondary contacts with the job market are severed
due to spouse's retirement or death. Other channels of social contacts
are similarly constrained by physical disabilities and/or financial
difficulties.

In households shared with other family members, primary roles
and social supports are immediately available to the older person. Even
in households occupied by an older husband and wife or a sibling pair, a
delicate balance of care and compensation often is struck that
minimizes the need for outside services or, in extreme cases, precludes
institutionalized placements. In the absence of kin within the household, the type of living arrangement limits the number and kinds of
supports available. Particularly for older persons living alone, repeated,
acute, or chronic illness episodes or housing-maintenance problems are
serious challenges to continuation of independent living in the
community. Prior research demonstrated the importance of living
arrangements not only for the support networks available to older
persons (Shanas, Townsend, Wedderburn, Friis, Milhøj, & Stehouwer,
1968; Townsend, 1965; Treas, 1977) but also for life satisfaction of the
elderly (Beyer & Woods, 1963; Murray, 1973; Wolk & Telleen, 1976),
patterns of geographic mobility (Aizenburg & Myers, 1977), and even
attitudes toward death (Swenson, 1961).

Because of the importance of living arrangements and housing for
the well-being of older persons and the organization of social resources,
this book was planned to direct attention toward community-based
older persons—an extremely large but somewhat neglected segment of
the older population. The target population of the conference was
defined in terms of the significant sociodemographic and economic
characteristics of community-based elderly. The factors that affect
living arrangements at the older ages also are identified and analyzed.
An understanding of the process that determines housing patterns of
older persons suggests the scope of housing-related problems and
potential intervention points.

CHARACTERISTICS OF COMMUNITY ELDERLY

When older persons living in the community are compared with their
institutionalized counterparts, they emerge as a distinct demographic,
social, and economic group. In general, community-based elderly tend
to be somewhat younger, in better health, with greater financial
resources and larger kin networks than those residing in some type of
long-term care facility.

Age-Race Distribution

Table 4.1 shows the age distribution of the older population by residential location and race in 1970. Whereas the majority of those institutionalized are "old old" (75 years of age or older), nearly 75% of those in a community setting are 60–74 years of age, or "young old." (This is to be expected as the risk of institutionalization increases sharply with age. In a previous study, Soldo (1977) found that after age 80, the odds that an older woman would be institutionalized were at least equal to the chance of living with her husband in their own household. By age 85, however, the probability of institutionalization was greater than that of living in an intact husband-wife arrangement.) Both the white and nonwhite community populations are younger than the comparable institutionalized groups.

The nonwhite population in the community has a younger age structure than the white population because of racial differentials in both mortality (Kitagawa & Hauser, 1973) and fertility (Kiser, Grabill, & Campbell, 1968). Proportionately more aged nonwhites than whites, however, live in the community. In 1970 nonwhites comprised 8.9% of the total elderly population, but only 6.4% of those institutionalized were nonwhite. The overrepresentation of nonwhites in the older community population is linked to their relatively low incomes (Myers & Soldo, 1977), de facto discrimination in the admission policies of some nursing homes (Kart & Beckman, 1976), and the functional strengths of the extended nonwhite family (Hill, 1972). Older nonwhites, therefore, are likely to remain in a community setting regardless of disability levels and even at the extremes of old age.

Sex Composition

There is an excess of females in the older population as a whole since the death rates for males are higher than those for females at any age, but particularly in old age (Retherford, 1975). In 1970 there were 131 females for every 100 older males. Among older persons in the community in 1970, women outnumbered men also, but only by a factor of 1.28. In 1970 there were nearly twice as many females institutionalized as males.

Marital Status

Substantial sex differentials in mortality, reinforced by the cultural norm of women marrying slightly older men, also affect male-female differences in the distribution of marital status among older persons

TABLE 4.1
Distribution of the Institutionalized and Community-Based Population Aged 60 and Over, by Age and Race: 1970
(base numbers in parentheses)

Age	Total Population			Older Persons in the Community			Older Persons in Institutions		
	Total	White	Nonwhite	Total	White	Nonwhite	Total	White	Nonwhite
60–64	29.7%	29.5%	31.6%	30.4%	30.3%	32.0%	9.5%	9.0%	17.7%
65–69	24.5	24.2	27.5	25.1	24.8	27.7	11.3	10.6	20.8
70–74	19.1	19.1	18.2	19.3	19.3	18.3	13.8	13.7	16.1
75–79	13.7	13.9	11.3	13.5	13.7	11.2	18.5	18.6	17.0
80–84	7.9	8.1	6.1	7.4	7.5	5.9	21.2	21.8	12.5
85 and over	5.2	5.2	5.7	4.4	4.4	4.9	25.6	26.3	15.9
Percent total	100.0% (278,125)	100.0% (253,420)	100.0% (24,705)	100.0% (267,714)	100.0% (243,674)	100.0% (24,040)	100.0% (10,411)	100.0% (9,746)	100.0% (665)

Source: 1970 Public Use Sample of Basic Records: 1/100 File
5% Neighborhood Characteristics File

residing in the community. Most older women living in a community environment are widows (53% in 1976), while most older men in a similar setting share a private household with their spouse (76% in 1976). In long-term care facilities the majority of older patients—male or female—are widowed.

Incomes

Very few older noninstitutionalized persons are totally lacking in financial resources. The data shown in Table 4.2 indicate, however, that a number of older persons, particularly women, exist in the community with meager financial resources. In 1970 approximately one third of the older community population lacked any cash income or reported only a very low annual income. One in five older persons living in the community, however, had incomes falling into the highest quintile group. "Young old," who are concentrated in the community, tend to have annual incomes exceeding those of persons 80 or 85 years of age.

Health

While proportionately more institutionalized than noninstitutionalized older persons are greatly or extremely impaired (Comptroller General, 1977), approximately half of those living in the community are disabled (i.e., limited in their mobility) in some way. As shown in Table 4.3, more blacks than whites and more males than females are severely limited. Despite the prevalence of physical disabilities associated with chronic conditions, only 5% of older whites and 8% of older nonwhites in 1975 were totally housebound.

Living Arrangements

Living arrangements of older persons in the community vary by age and sex as shown in Table 4.4. Because most older men are married, maintaining a husband-wife household is the most common living arrangement for males 65 years of age and over. The proportion of married men living with spouses declines with age and this trend is offset by proportional increases in those heading independent non-family households as primary individuals. Older women, however, are considerably more likely than their male counterparts to be widowed and consequently are less likely to reside with their spouse in old age. For unmarried older women, living alone is the most common alternative to intact nuclear family living. For either older males or

TABLE 4.2

Income Distribution for the Institutionalized and Community-Based
Population Aged 60 and Over, by Race: 1970

Income[a]	Total Population			Older Persons in the Community			Older Persons in Institutions		
	Total	White	Nonwhite	Total	White	Nonwhite	Total	White	Nonwhite
No income	11.3%	11.6%	13.3%	11.2%	11.1%	12.6%	25.1%	24.2%	37.7%
$1 – 1099	22.6	20.6	31.2	21.0	20.0	31.1	34.5	34.5	35.0
$1100 – 2199	22.4	22.2	27.3	22.5	22.0	27.5	25.5	25.9	18.5
$2200 – 5099	22.9	23.6	19.1	23.6	24.1	19.4	12.7	13.0	8.1
$5100 and over	20.8	22.0	9.2	21.5	22.8	9.4	2.3	2.4	.6
Percent total	100.0% (278,125)	100.0% (253,420)	100.0% (24,705)	100.0% (267,714)	100.0% (243,674)	100.0% (24,040)	100.0% (10,411)	100.0% (9,746)	100.0% (665)

[a]Refers to total personal income and was categorized to create proportionately equal-sized groups of those reporting any income in the calendar year prior to the 1970 Census enumeration.

Source: 1970 Public Use Sample of Basic Records: 1/100 File
5% Neighborhood Characteristics File

41

TABLE 4.3

Percentage Distribution of Persons 65 Years of Age and Over, by Disability Status, Sex, and Race: 1975

Sex and Race	DISABILITY STATUS				TOTAL
	Unable to carry on major activity	With limitation in amount or kind of major activity	With limitation but not in major activity	No limitation	
White males	28.6	15.3	4.8	51.3	100.0% (7,770,844)
Black males	42.7	13.1	4.6	39.7	100.0% (726,465)
White females	7.5	26.7	7.9	57.8	100.0% (11,104,384)
Black females	15.7	32.9	6.3	45.1	100.0% (1,003,120)

Source: Unpublished data from the Health Interview Survey, National Center for Health Statistics. Data are based on interviews of the civilian, <u>noninstitutional</u> population.

TABLE 4.4

Living Arrangements of Persons 65 Years of Age and Over,
by Sex: 1976 (numbers in thousands)

Living Arrangements	Male		Female	
	65 – 74	75+	65 – 74	75+
In families				
Head, spouse present	81.3	66.7	----	----
Spouse	----	----	46.4	21.3
Other head	2.8	4.5	8.7	8.9
Other Relative	1.8	7.2	7.7	19.8
Primary Individual	13.3	20.5	36.4	48.8
Secondary Individual	.8	1.1	.8	1.2
In Households	100.0%	100.0%	100.0%	100.0%
	(5944)	(2969)	(7778)	(4971)

---- Represents zero. Living arrangements as defined by
the U. S. Bureau of the Census stipulate that in a
husband-wife household, the male will be designated
the head of household. Females are never enumerated
as the head if the husband is present, and similarly,
a married male living with his wife is never classified
as a spouse.

Source: United States Bureau of the Census.
Current Population Reports, Series P-20, No. 306,
"Marital Status and Living Arrangements: March 1976."
Issued January 1977.

females, living with relatives is not a widely used option, although the
proportion of those sharing a relative's household increases with age.

DETERMINANTS OF LIVING ARRANGEMENTS

Prior research indicates that the living arrangements of the elderly are
neither isolated nor random events in the context of an individual's life
cycle. Rather, living arrangements are the outcome of a lifelong series
of interactions between decisions, experiences, and behavior. Moreover, the determinants of living arrangements at the older ages are not
confined strictly to postretirement behavior, resources, or attitudes

(Soldo & Myers, 1976). Hence, a number of demographic, social, economic, and health-related characteristics have been identified previously as affecting housing behavior and preferences at the older ages (Murray, 1971, 1973; Shanas, 1969; Shanas et al., 1968).

A life course framework for analyzing the determinants of living arrangements is shown schematically in Figure 4.1 (Note that this representation is not a formal path model. The diagram implies a temporal, or life cycle ordering, rather than a causal structure. Such a representation suggests the ways in which relevant variables are inter-related developmentally.) In reviewing the components of this model, our concern is with those factors that affect both the probability of community residence in general and the likelihood of specific types of living arrangements in the community in particular.

Figure 4.1 shows that the demographic factors of age, sex, and race are temporally prior to living arrangements and correlated with each other. Their temporal priority derives from the fact that they are ascribed, or fixed characteristics. They are shown as interrelated because the factors conducive to community living—good health and effective support networks—vary jointly with age, sex, and race.

Chronological Age

Chronological age, in and of itself, does not affect the probability of living in the community or the utilization of different types of living arrangements. Age, in general, is a "surrogate for the experiences which cause changing probabilities of behavior of various kinds" (Ryder, 1964, p. 449). Just as the probability of widowhood and subsequent changes in living arrangements vary directly with age, the likelihood for additional status changes that favor one type of arrangement over another also vary with age. Underlying at least part of the relationship between age and living arrangements at the older ages are changes in health status. The measurement of health status is extremely complex and no single measure is satisfactory for all purposes (Sullivan, 1966). The dimension of health most relevant to an analysis of living arrange-ments behavior is that which assesses the capacity of older persons to perform normal roles and activities required to maintain their own households.

The relationship between age and functional capacity has been examined in numerous national surveys (e.g., see the National Center for Health Statistics, 1973), and one directed solely at the elderly

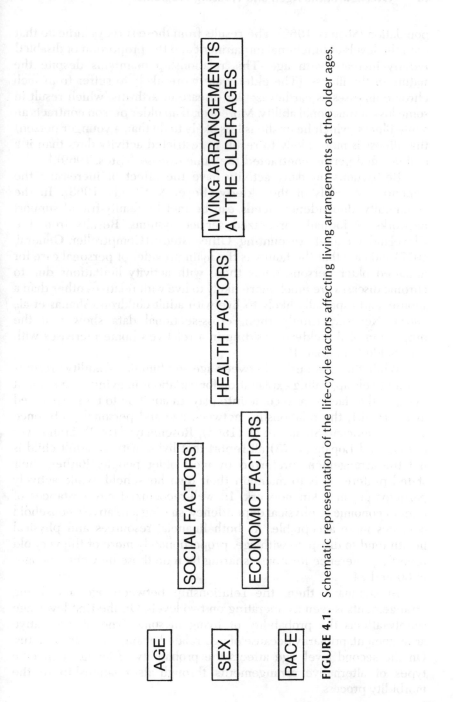

FIGURE 4.1. Schematic representation of the life-cycle factors affecting living arrangements at the older ages.

population (Shanas, 1962). The results from these surveys indicate that both the levels of functional impairment and the proportion of disabled elderly increase with age. This relationship maintains despite the nature of the illness. [The elderly are more likely to suffer from such chronic illnesses as cardiovascular disease or arthritis, which result in some loss of functional ability. Moreover, if an older person contracts an acute illness (which he or she is less likely to do than a younger person) that illness is more likely to result in restricted activity days than if a middle-aged person contracted the same disease (Estes, 1969).]

Restrictions on daily activity have the effect of increasing the dependency needs of the elderly (Beyer & Woods, 1963). In the community, dependency needs can be met by family-friend support networks or formally organized service systems. Results from the Cleveland General Accounting Office study (Comptroller General, 1977) indicate that the family is the main provider of personal care for impaired older persons. Thus those with activity limitations due to chronic diseases are much more likely to live with relatives other than a spouse, and especially likely to live with adult children (Shanas et al., 1968). Not surprisingly then, cross-sectional data show that the proportion of the elderly residing in a relative's home increases with age (Soldo & Lauriat, 1976).

While the relationship between age and functional ability presents an intuitively appealing explanation for variations in living arrangement by age, other factors also come into play. In addition to those specified in Figure 4.1, the relationship between age and personal preference also is significant. Shanas et al. (1968), Rosenmayr (1963), Stehouwer (1965), and Lopata (1973) all report that living with an adult child is not the arrangement preferred by most older people. Rather, their stated preference is to maintain their own household, while actively participating in a kin network. In well-recognized circumstances of either economic or physical dependency, sharing a relative's household becomes more acceptable. As both financial resources and physical health tend to dissipate with age, proportionately more of the very old report a preference for house sharing than do those between the ages of 60 and 74.

In summary, then, the relationship between age and living arrangements is seen as operating on two levels. On the first level, age simply affects the probability of living in some type of alternative arrangement, primarily because of age-related changes in marital status. On the second level, age affects the probability of living in specific types of alternative arrangements through its relationship to the morbidity process.

Sex and Race

The factors underlying the effects of sex and race on types of living arrangements can be specified in a similar manner. Although proportionately more men have spouses, those who do not are less likely either to live alone or with a relative, and more likely to be institutionalized than nonmarried women. These observed tendencies reflect lifelong differences in family relationships and intergenerational roles. Across the life cycle, kinship ties are more salient to women than to men (Aldous, 1967; Gans, 1962; Reiss, 1962; Shanas et al., 1968). At the older ages, widows tend to be considerably more integrated into a kin network of mutual aid and support than widowers. Although one might surmise that, lacking familiarity with household tasks, widowers would find it more difficult to maintain a home than widows, both McKain (1969) and Shanas et al. (1968) report that older widows are much more likely to move in with adult children than are older widowers. Frequently, it is the closeness of the mother-daughter tie that facilitates the sharing of a household (Adams, 1970; Newman, 1977). Often this arrangement is mutually beneficial, with the widow also providing such family services as babysitting.

Troll (1971) summarizes the effects of sex differentials in family structure by noting that "the options for widows, who are more kinship oriented, include both remarriage and turning to other kin; those for widowers, only remarriage" (p. 269). Older men lacking strong kin ties and failing to remarry are subject to a higher risk of institutionalization, for as Townsend (1965) has demonstrated with British data, most institutionalized individuals are confined because they have no one outside the family to care for them. Similarly, Brody et al. (1978) hypothesize that the absence of an effective family care unit is a crucial factor in an institutionalized episode.

Racial differences in patterns of living arrangements also are linked to life cycle differences in family structure. Nonwhites, regardless of age, are more likely to maintain a nontraditional but family-based living arrangement than are whites. In middle age, this pattern is exemplified by the significantly higher proportions of nonwhite family households headed by women. Consistent with these earlier life cycle patterns, elderly nonwhites are more likely either to head family households (without a spouse present) or live with a relative than are whites.

Prior research also indicates that when income is controlled whites and nonwhites do not differ significantly in terms of their attitudes toward familism or participation in a kin network (Sweet, 1972).

Rather, observed racial differences in family structure are closely linked to the distribution of marital status by race.

Social and Economic Characteristics

Both the social and economic characteristics of individuals are represented in Figure 4.1 as intervening between the effects of the demographic factors and the outcome variable—living arrangements. These factors occupy an intervening position for two reasons. First, the variables included in either the social or economic components are, for the most part, indicators of mid-life experiences. Unlike the effects of the demographic variables, which are givens, social and economic characteristics are contingent upon earlier life cycle patterns of behavior. Within a life cycle perspective they are temporally intermediate, preceding the establishment of a living arrangement at the older ages. Among the factors included in these components are marital status, family size and structure, educational attainment, and social class.

Second, social and economic variables are identified as intervening because they qualify or condition the effects of age, race, and sex on particular types of living arrangements at the older ages. If age, race, and sex completely determined the distribution of living arrangements, no differences would be observed by other characteristics within age, sex, and race categories. This is clearly not the case. Prior research has documented significant differences in living arrangements by the social and economic characteristics listed above (Myers & Soldo, 1977; Shanas et al., 1968; Siegel, 1975). These factors serve as constraints on the number and type of options available to an individual, given their demographic characteristics and their marital and health statuses. Theoretically, the whole range of alternatives is open to older people, but in reality their options are often restricted by decisions and behavioral patterns of mid-life. A low level of income in old age, for example, reflects occupational and educational origins, and may constrain the ability of the individual to live alone. If other shared accommodations are available, meager financial resources certainly militate against living alone.

Marital Status

Let us examine the effects of marital status within this framework. While all unmarried elderly by definition live in some type of arrangement other than the husband-wife household, the distribution of alternative living patterns varies by marital status. (Any arrangement that represents a deviation from the traditional middle-aged pattern of a husband-wife household is seen as an alternative arrangement.) The main differences are between those who have never been married and those who have, regardless of the duration of that marriage or the age at marriage. Although a small group in absolute numbers, the distribution of living arrangements among the never-married is quite distinct from those widowed, divorced, or separated in the older ages. The never-marrieds have approximately twice the chance of being institutionalized at the older ages than do unmarried older people. The never-marrieds also are less likely to head a family household. For those elderly whose marriages were terminated, the widowed are more likely to live with relatives and somewhat less likely to live alone than those whose marriages were disrupted by divorce or separation. Proportionately more widows, however, are institutionalized than their divorced or separated counterparts.

The effects of marital status on living arrangements can be misrepresented if they are examined apart from their social and economic correlates. Much of the variation in living arrangements by marital status can be attributed to variations in age, family size, and structure by marital status. Most of the elderly whose spouses are still alive, regardless of whether they are living with them or not, are younger than those who are widowed. It is not surprising, then, that the divorced and separated elderly tend to be concentrated in basically independent types of arrangements, and less so in those involving financial and physical dependency, such as institutionalization.

Marital status also tends to be correlated with family size, with widows having had, on the average, slightly more children than those who were divorced or separated some time prior to their current living arrangement. The effect of family size operates within the broad context of trends in family roles and structures. Riley and Foner (1968) estimate that only 30% of the noninstitutionalized population is kinless. Evidence gathered by researchers during the 1960s overwhelmingly indicates that geographic separation from kin does not necessarily signify family isolation (Adams, 1970; Kerckhoff, 1965; Litwak, 1960a, 1960b). While the nuclear unit within the kin system has become dominant over any other previous structural forms, kin networks exist based on generational ties of conjugal units (Adams, 1970; Shanas, 1980; Streib, 1965).

Family Networks

Survey results indicate that older people value financial and household independence. However, norms of filial and kin duties are such that elderly persons expect kin to assist them in such times of need or crisis as illness or death of spouse (Streib, 1965). Acts of filial and kin responsibility are, for the most part, performed voluntarily, without law or compulsion (Adams, 1970; Blenkner, 1965; Schorr, 1980). Most older people interviewed by Streib (1965) saw the major responsibility of their adult children as proffering ties of affection. Children of older parents surveyed by Shanas (1962, 1979) report, however, a willingness to extend their affective commitments to assuming household and/or financial responsibilities.

Family networks, then, are important resources for coping with age-related changes in living arrangements. Using the 1960 published census data, Shanas (1962) described variations in living arrangements by family size. She found that childless elderly are more likely to live alone or as nonrelatives in a household than those with children; 23% of those with children in 1960 lived alone or as a nonrelative, compared with 63% of those without children.

Using data from the 1970 census, Soldo and Myers (1976) have recently found that the effect of family size, expressed in terms of the number of children born to a woman, is constant across all age groups of elderly women who are not living with a spouse. Childless women, regardless of age, are also more likely to be institutionalized than those with children. The effect of family size on the rate of institutionalization is generally interpreted in terms of compensating care and support systems. The larger the family the more likely it is that the financial or service supports will be available, which either postpone or totally preclude the necessity of an institutionalized episode.

Financial Security

In general, financial security is extremely important, "because it largely determines the range of alternatives older people have in adjusting to aging" (Karasik, 1973, p. 4). With respect to living arrangements, income, like family size, sets realistic limits on the number and kinds of housing options available to the elderly. In a 1972 study of the living arrangements of widows, Chevan and Korson noted that "income as a social class indicator reflects the accumulation of resources and the *financial ability to maintain an independent household*" (p. 48) [italics added]. Shanas (1969) also conceptualizes income as an indicator of the autonomy of the elderly.

Data collected by the Social Security Administration in 1968 supports these views. Murray (1971), in reporting the survey results, shows that those elderly with low incomes are more likely to live with relatives than are those at higher income levels. Using unpublished census data from 1970, Soldo and Lauriat (1976) showed that regardless of age, sex, or race, higher incomes tend to be associated with independent living and lower incomes with dependent types of situations.

While a low income has the same effect on all elderly, proportionately more women than men, more nonwhites than whites, and more of the very old than the young old are concentrated in the lower income brackets. As level of income at the older ages is contingent on previous occupation, education, marital status, and demographic factors, economic status reflects a host of life cycle differences.

Health-Related Factors

The effects of health-related factors are shown in Figure 4.1 as immediately prior to living arrangements (the outcome variable of interest) and modifying the effects of all preceding components. The process determining living arrangements among older persons with health-related problems is significantly different from the process affecting persons in good health. A change in health status at the older ages, be it sudden or gradual, is likely to reorganize the determinants of living arrangements and modify the saliency of the demographic, social, and economic characteristics.

For the disabled, their living arrangement must not only meet their minimal needs for housing within the limits of their budgets, family structure, and preferences but it also must allow for their dependency needs. For the most part, the severity of limitation is positively correlated with the extent of support provided by the housing environment. Extremely impaired older persons, for example, have the greatest probability of institutionalization (Comptroller General, 1977).

A number of recent studies (Barney, 1977; Maddox, 1975; Morris, 1975) have demonstrated, however, that continued residence in the community is not predicated solely on good health. For chronically ill or disabled older persons, access to an effective family care and support unit is critical for sustained residence in the community. Townsend's (1965) British data not only show that fewer aged with relatives enter institutions but also that those living with relatives prior to institutionalized placement remain in the community to a more advanced stage of impairment. The newly released report by the Comptroller General (1977) offers additional evidence concerning the importance of family care units and provides additional impetus for direct family assistance programs.

SUMMARY

The preceding review of the literature has been presented to emphasize several points. First, living arrangements are the outcome of a life cycle process. Whether or not consciously considered, the effect of decisions regarding family size, kinship patterns, and occupational opportunities are carried through to old age. While the probabilities of widowhood or disability are externally determined, the social and economic resources available to cope with age-related adjustments are determined earlier in the life cycle. Rather than the distribution of living arrangements among the elderly being random, it manifests the effects of these factors and their distribution among relevant cohorts. Patterns of living arrangements among older persons are likely to change in the next 10 to 15 years simply because of differences in the life course of currently middle-aged persons and their predecessors.

Second, it has been emphasized that living arrangements are the outcome of a complex life cycle process. Prior research has identified a number of factors thought to be important determinants of living arrangements among the elderly. The effect of each one is related to, and contingent upon, the level of the others.

Because living arrangements are the end product of a process, the effects of intervention strategies are likely to rebound through the system. Programs providing direct cash subsidies to the family with which an older person resides may undermine, for example, the preference of older persons to live in their own households. Hence, previous research strongly suggests that efforts to modify existing patterns of living arrangements will be successful only if they reflect a comprehensive life-course perspective.

REFERENCES

Adams, B. Isolation, function, and beyond: American kinship in the 1960s. *Journal of Marriage and the Family*, 1970, *32*, 575–597.

Aizenberg, R., & Myers, G. C. *Residential mobility and living arrangements*. Paper presented at the Annual Meeting of the Gerontological Society, San Francisco, Calif., November 1977.

Aldous, J. Intergenerational visiting patterns: Variations in boundary maintenance as an explanation. *Family Process*, 1967, *6*, 235–251.

Barney, J. L. The prerogative of choice in long term care. *Gerontologist*, 1977, *17*, 309–315.

Beyer, G. H., & Woods, M. E. *Living and activity patterns of the aged* (Research Report No. 6). Ithaca, N.Y.: Center for Housing and Environmental Studies, Cornell University, 1963.

Blenkner, M. Social work and family relationships in later life with some thoughts on filial maturity. In E. Shanas & G. Streib (Eds.), *Social structure and the family: Generational relations*. Englewood Cliffs, N.J.: Prentice-Hall, 1965.

Brody, E. M. Seeking appropriate options for living arrangements. In E. Pfeiffer (Ed.), *Alternatives to institutional care for older Americans: Practice and planning*. Durham, N.C.: Duke University Press, 1973.

Brody, S. Poulschok, J. S. W., & Masciocchi, C. F. The family caring unit: A major consideration in the long-term support system. *Gerontologist*, 1978, *18*(6), 556–561.

Chevan, A., & Korson, J. H. The widowed who live alone: An examination of social and demographic factors. *Social Forces*, 1972, *51*, 45–53.

Comptroller General. *Report to the Congress: Home health—the need for a national policy to better provide for the elderly*. Washington D.C.: U.S. Government Printing Office, 1977.

Cumming, E., & Henry, W. E. *Growing old: The process of disengagement*. New York: Basic Books, 1961.

Estes, E. H., Jr. Health experience in the elderly. In E. W. Busse & E. Pfeiffer (Eds.), *Behavior and adaptation in later life*. Boston: Little, Brown, 1969.

Gans, H. J. *The urban villagers: Group and class life of Italian Americans*. New York: Free Press, 1962.

Hill, R. B. *The strengths of black families*. New York: National Urban League, 1972.

Karasik, S. The economic status of older women. Durham, N.C.: Center for the Study of Aging and Human Development, Duke University, 1973. (Mimeographed)

Kart, C. S., & Beckman, B. L. Black-white differentials in the institutionalization of the elderly: A temporal analysis. *Social Forces*, 1976, *54*, 901–910.

Kerckhoff, A. Nuclear and extended family relationships: A normative and behavioral analysis. In E. Shanas & G. Streib (Eds.), *Social structure and the family: Generational relations*. Englewood Cliffs, N.J.: Prentice-Hall, 1965.

Kiser, C. V., Grabill, W. H., & Campbell, A. A. *Trends and variations in fertility in the United States*. Cambridge, Mass.: Harvard University Press, 1968.

Kitagawa, E., & Hauser, P. M. *Differential mortality in the United States, a study of socioeconomic epidemiology*. Cambridge, Mass.: Harvard University Press, 1973.

Litwak, E. Occupational mobility and extended family cohesion. *American Sociological Review*, 1960, *25*, 9–21. (a)

Litwak, E. Geographic mobility and extended family cohesion. *American Sociological Review*, 1960, *25*, 385–394. (b)

Lopata, H. Z. *Widowhood in an American city*. Cambridge, Mass.: Schenkman, 1973.

Maddox, G. L. Families as context and resource in chronic illness. In S. Sherwood (Ed.), *Long term care: A handbook for researchers, planners, and providers*. New York: Spectrum, 1975.

McKain, W. C. *Retirement marriages* (Agriculture Experiment Station Monograph 3). Storrs, Ct.: University of Connecticut, 1969. (Mimeographed)

Murray, J. *Living arrangements of people aged 65 and older: Findings from the 1967 survey of the aged* (Report No. 4 from the Social Security Administration Survey of the Aged, 1967). Washington, D.C.: U.S. Government Printing Office, 1973.

Murray, J. *Family structure in the retirement years* (Report No. 4 from the Social Security Administration Retirement History Study). Washington, D.C.: U.S. Government Printing Office.

Myers, G. C., & Soldo, B. J. *Variations in living arrangements among the elderly: Final project report.* Durham, N.C.: Center for Demographic Studies, Duke University, 1977. (Mimeographed)

National Center for Health Statistics. *Cohort mortality and survivorship: U.S. death-registration states, 1900–1968 (Series 3, No. 16).* Washington, D.C.: U.S. Government Printing Office, 1973.

Newman, S. *Housing adjustments of older people: A report of findings from the second phase.* Ann Arbor: University of Michigan, Institute for Social Research, 1977. (Mimeographed)

Reiss, P. J. Extended kinship system: Correlates of and attitudes on frequency interaction. *Journal of Marriage and the Family*, 1962, 24, 333–339.

Retherford, R. *The changing sex differential in mortality.* Westport, Ct.: Greenwood Press, 1975.

Riley, M. W., & Foner, A. *Aging and society* (Vol. 1). *A compendium of research findings.* New York: Russell Sage Foundation, 1968.

Rosenmayr, L. Family relations of the elderly. *Journal of Marriage and the Family*, 1963, 30, 672–674.

Ryder, N. Notes on the concept of a population. *American Journal of Sociology*, 1964, 69, 447–463.

Schorr, M. . . . thy father and thy mother. . . . A second look at filial responsibility and family policy. SSA Publication No. 13-11953. Washington, D.C.: U.S. Government Printing Office, 1980.

Shanas, E. *The health of older people: A social survey.* Cambridge, Mass.: Harvard University Press, 1962.

Shanas, E. Living arrangements and housing of old people. In E. W. Busse & E. Pfeiffer (Eds.), *Behavior and adaptation in later life.* Boston: Little, Brown, 1969.

Shanas, E. Social myth as hypothesis: The care of family relatives of old people. *Gerontologist*, 1979, 19, 3–9.

Shanas, E. Older people and their families: The new pioneers. *Journal of Marriage and the Family*, 1980, 42(1), 9–15.

Shanas, E., Townsend, P., Wedderburn, D., Friis, H., Milhøj, P., & Stehouwer, J. *Old people in three industrial societies.* New York: Atherton, 1968.

Siegel, J. S. Some demographic aspects of aging in the United States. In A. M. Ostfeld & D. C. Gibson (Eds.), *Epidemiology of aging.* Washington, D.C.: U.S. Government Printing Office, 1975.

Soldo, B. J. *The determinants of temporal variations in living arrangements among the elderly: 1960–1970.* Unpublished doctoral dissertation, Duke University, 1977.

Soldo, B. J., & Lauriat, P. Living arrangements among the elderly in the United States: A log-linear approach. *Journal of Comparative Family Studies*, 1976, 7, 351–366.

Soldo, B. J., & Myers, G. C. *The effects of lifetime fertility on the living arrangements of older women.* Paper presented at the Annual Meeting of the Gerontological Society, New York, October 1976.

Stehouwer, J. Relations between generations and the three-generation household in Denmark. In E. Shanas & G. Streib (Eds.), *Social structure and the family.* Englewood Cliffs, N.J.: Prentice-Hall, 1965.

Streib, G. Intergenerational relations: Perspectives of the two generations on the older parents. *Journal of Marriage and the Family*, 1965, 27, 469–477.

Sullivan, D. *Conceptual problems in developing an index of health* (National Center for Health Statistics, Series 2, No. 17). Washington, D.C.: U.S. Government Printing Office, 1966.

Sweet, J. The living arrangements of separated, divorced, and widowed mothers. *Demography*, 1972, 9, 143–157.

Swenson, W. Attitudes toward death. *Journal of Gerontology*, 1961, 16, 49–52.

Townsend, P. The effects of family structure on the likelihood of admission to an institution in old age: The application of a general theory. In E. Shanas & G. Streib (Eds.), *Social structure and the family.* Englewood Cliffs, N.J.: Prentice-Hall, 1965.

Treas, J. Family support systems for the aged: Some social and demographic considerations. *Gerontologist*, 1977, 17, 486–491.

Troll, L. E. The family of later life: A decade review. *Journal of Marriage and the Family*, 1971, 33, 263–290.

Wolk, S. & Telleen, S. Psychological and social correlates of life satisfaction as a function of residential constraint. *Journal of Gerontology*, 1976, 31, 89–98.

II
Characteristics
of the Housing Environment
for Subgroups

5

Housing for the Black Elderly— The Need Remains

EDWARD C. WALLACE

INTRODUCTION

How many times and in how many fora has the following objective statement from the Older Americans Act of 1965 been repeated: "To assist our older citizens to secure full and free enjoyment of suitable housing, independently selected, designed and located with reference to their special needs, and available at costs they can afford"? Certainly governmental officials, legislators, housing planners and developers, and the American public at large support that objective without reservation. Yet 13 years and countless conferences later the plea is still made for "suitable housing, independently selected." To be sure, much has been done. As of 1972, 464,000 of the 1.3 million occupied public housing units were occupied by persons aged 65 or older. As of September, 1974, approximately 75,000 units of housing were completed under the Section 202 and 236 programs, with others under other specialized programs. But this is only a drop in the bucket when compared to the 120,000 units per year that were seen as the requirement as long ago as the White House Conference on Aging in 1971. However, even these sorry statistics do not reveal the plight of the black elderly. In fact, there are no reliable housing statistics that fully reveal the plight of the black elderly because the U.S. Department of Housing and Urban Development (HUD) either does not receive or does not compile its data on elderly housing with specific breakdowns by race. HUD does not know the intensity of that need. As was stated by a staff member of the House Select Committee on Aging with respect to the minority elderly—HUD does not know who they are, how many there are, or where they are.

One thing is known, however, on the basis of the partial data that are available from limited surveys; except for public housing, elderly blacks have been virtually excluded from federally financed elderly housing, that is, Sections 202, 236, and 231 housing. The irony of the situation is that they are the ones who need that help most, now and in the future.

The statistics are perhaps over-familiar. In 1972 the median annual income for all families aged 65 and over was $5,053 while the median annual income for black families over age 65 was $3,282.

Even worse, over time that income differential is increasing. In 1975 18.9% of whites aged 65 and over had annual incomes of less than $2,000, and 37.6% had annual incomes of less than $3,000. During the same year, 32.3% of blacks aged 65 and over had annual incomes of less than $2,000, and a staggering 64.7% had incomes of less than $3,000 a year. Of the total black population aged 65 and above, 36% live below the poverty level, while 13.4% of whites of the same age group live in poverty (U.S. Bureau of the Census, 1976).

Homeownership among the white elderly is high—71% of the 7.1 million housing units occupied by families headed by persons aged 65 or older were owner-occupied in 1970. But of that number, 53% of the homes were valued at less than $15,000 and 30% at less than $10,000. Moreover, of all housing units occupied by the elderly, whether owner-occupied or rented, 35% of those occupied by blacks lacked basic plumbing facilities as compared to 15% for whites.

Yet the specialized housing programs tend to exclude the very groups that need them most—the minority elderly. Nor is there any effort being made from the federal level to help older persons who, through emotional attachment to their homes, wish to remain in them but cannot afford the cost of the necessary repairs to bring them up to code requirements.

PROPOSALS FOR CHANGE

In order to begin to meet some of the housing needs of minorities, some specific proposals may be suggested.

Research

There is a need for research in the area of federally financed housing for the minority elderly. As stated earlier, data are not available to show the number of black residents of federally subsidized housing for the elderly; in fact, there is a gaping void. HUD is charged with the responsibility of ensuring that federal laws guaranteeing equal access to federally financed or subsidized housing are complied with. Yet, nowhere in that department is there data that shows the racial or ethnic background of the tenants of Sections 202, 236, or Section 8 housing.

The HUD regulations that govern submission of proposals for development of elderly housing under those sections require the inclusion of an "Affirmative Fair Housing Marketing Plan," which spells out in detail the projected racial composition of the development. The sponsors are even required to list the radio, television, and newspaper media with a predominantly minority target population through which the managers of the development will advertise. But once having done this, there is no requirement for periodic reports to HUD to show that elderly members of minority groups have, in fact, been successfully recruited. Nor is there any periodic inspection or other follow-up by HUD to ascertain the extent of compliance by managers with their own affirmative action plans.

HUD needs to rewrite its instructions to require such reporting on a regular and routine basis and must direct the appropriate division within the department to review, evaluate, and follow up those reports as necessary. The department should also commission a comprehensive study of all federally financed or supported housing projects to compile badly needed data on the housing requirements of the minority elderly; the extent of the recruitment efforts for minority tenants; the actual occupancy by minority elderly persons; attitudinal factors among the sponsors, managers, white occupants, current minority occupants, and prospective minority occupants; and the effect of project location on minority occupancy.

Such a study was called for by Lawton and Krassen in their study on federally subsidized housing not for the elderly black, which was published in 1973. But to this day, as far as could be determined, HUD has not undertaken or commissioned any such study.

Developments in Black Neighborhoods

There should be more Section 202-Section 8 developments in black neighborhoods. Although detailed research on the subject has been inconclusive, there have been some efforts at determining why there are so few blacks in Section 202 housing. In the most notable of these efforts (Lawton & Krassen, 1973), the researchers speculated that, in addition to "deliberate exclusion because of color" (p. 69), older blacks may be showing a preference for their own neighborhoods and social groups. There is some validity to that speculation. In spite of this, however, HUD and many urban planners actively discourage the location of elderly housing projects in ethnic neighborhoods, so-called "impacted areas." But such developments would do much to upgrade those areas and provide the minority elderly the opportunity both to move into modern, comfortable housing and to remain in their own neighborhoods. While white sponsors and developers have been reluctant to build in predominantly minority neighborhoods, minority groups would do so and should be provided with incentives for this action.

Therefore, HUD should increase its funding of black and other minority sponsors and developers to enable them to build adequate housing that would be attractive to their older people. This action would also counteract the effects of the subtle and sometimes not-so-subtle racially exclusionary practices of many current sponsors and managers.

Housing Rehabilitation

Upgrading homes owned by the minority elderly is of the utmost importance. HUD should undertake a massive program to finance the repair or rehabilitation of seriously deteriorated homes that are owned by the elderly. Often no amount of urging will persuade an elderly widow or couple to leave their home to move to a modern development. Over the years of struggling and saving at low-paying jobs to get the down payment and then to meet the monthly notes and pay the real estate taxes, they have developed an emotional attachment to their home. That home is now a part of themselves. If it is paid off, and it often is, even though it is 40 years old, badly in need of repair, and valued at less than $10,000, it is theirs and is usually their only asset of any value. To give it up would be like giving up a part of themselves. This emotional attachment to a house should be recognized, and rather than force the elderly to move, they should be assisted to upgrade the house so that they can live out their lives in comfort. There is currently no federal program that will assist elderly people in such a situation.

Prior to 1974, the Urban Renewal Program provided for rehabilitation loans under Section 312 of the Federal Housing Act and for rehabilitation grants under Section 115. Under Section 115, a poor person, regardless of age, whose annual income did not exceed $3,000 annually, could obtain grants of up to $3,500 that could be applied toward the actual cost of repairs or improvements necessary to bring a home up to the property rehabilitation standards for safe, decent, and sanitary housing. In 1974, with the passage of the Community Development Act, the Section 115 program was phased out. The rationale for elimination of the grant program was that adequate funds were being provided to the local governments from which they could finance such grants if they felt the need was sufficiently great to warrant it. The number of telephone calls that are being received in HUD offices that administer the Section 312 Rehabilitation Loan Program (which was not eliminated) is evidence that either the poor elderly are not aware of the provision for rehabilitation grants under the Community Development Block Grant Program or that local governments are not awarding such grants.

The poor elderly, black or white, find it difficult to obtain Section 312 rehabilitation loans because of their inability to repay. Since the local governments are not offering rehabilitation grants in sufficient numbers, the only solution to the program is a revival of the Section 115 grant program at the national level. It is possible that such a proposal would not be welcomed by the Administration or be resisted by many members of the Congress. However, the need for it is so great that advancing the proposal should not be deterred. The full support of the aging community should be mustered behind it to obtain reinstatement of the Section 115 grants.

Housing Options

The black elderly should be provided a choice of housing. Affluent middle-aged blacks are free to choose whether they will live in an apartment house, a town house, or a single-family dwelling. Should not the elderly black also have a choice? The late Hobart C. Jackson, founder of the National Caucus on the Black Aged and Executive Vice President of the Stephen C. Smith Geriatric Center, spoke to the caucus at its annual conference in October 1972, and called for such housing options for the black elderly (1972). He stated,

> There are a few black elderly who may want to enter existing housing, nursing homes, and geriatric centers in predominantly white situations. They should have that opportunity. But there are also those who, for whatever reasons, want to remain in their own communities. Such a choice should not be penalized by inadequate services, discriminatory practices, and open hostility. It should be simply one choice that they should be free to make.

Those who are committed to improving the lot of the elderly must exert great efforts to ensure that the government lives up to its moral obligation. In the area of housing, the National Caucus and Center on Black Aged is most assuredly devoting a major share of its resources to assure that decent, affordable housing is provided for the elderly black citizens of this country.

REFERENCES

Jackson, H. C. Presidential address presented at the annual meeting of the National Caucus for the Black Aged, Houston, Texas, October 1972.

Lawton, M. P., & Krassen, E. Federally subsidized housing not for the elderly black. *Journal of Social and Behavioral Sciences*, 1973, *19*, 65–78.

U.S. Bureau of the Census. *Current Population Reports* (Series P-60, No. 103). Washington, D.C.: U.S. Government Printing Office, 1976.

6
Black and Spanish Elderly: Their Housing Characteristics and Housing Quality

SALLY L. HOOVER

Among the vast array of services, programs, and concerns that contribute to the betterment of the lives of our nation's elderly, the ideal of providing adequate and secure housing is one of primary importance. While advances have been made toward providing elders with better quality housing, there is still much work to be done. In 1971 it was estimated that about 6 million elderly lived in substandard housing (U.S. Senate, 1971). Most definitions of substandard housing refer to the structural quality of the housing unit as well as the presence and quality of basic facilities. In 1950 the Department of Housing and Urban Development (HUD) defined a substandard housing unit as one that was rated by a Census enumerator as dilapidated and/or lacking a private bath, private flush toilet, or hot running water. Other researchers have taken a broader perspective on housing quality and have used room density (the number of persons per room) as an indicator of substandard housing. Depending upon the research purpose, ratios between 1.01 and 3.01 persons per room have been used to indicate crowded and, therefore, substandard units. Still others have felt it necessary to include quality of the immediate environment in their definition of substandard (Baer, 1976; Marcuse, 1971; Sutermeiser, 1969; U.S. Bureau of the Census, 1967).

As the elderly are not a homogeneous group there may be large differences in the proportion of any subgroup of this population that lives in substandard housing or has need for housing improvements. For example, rural housing dwellers are more likely to suffer from broader negative environmental conditions. In regard to urban dwellers, research has indicated that blacks and other minority groups tend to live in older, deteriorating, high-crime areas where housing quality is poorest (Congressional Research Service, 1974; Ettinger, 1965; Glazer

& McIntire, 1960; Grigsby, 1971; Rose & Rose, 1965; U.S. Bureau of the Census, 1973b).

As a group, then, elderly minorities are more likely to live in substandard housing. Their lower than average income, lower level of education, minority status, and other correlates of these characteristics tend to increase the chance of their experiencing unsatisfactory housing conditions. Lower income along with minority status may act to limit the availability of choices in housing location, size, and quality. Living on small and fixed incomes, a large proportion of community-dwelling minority elderly have neither the extra money needed for home improvement nor the option of moving to better housing. As the elderly minority person is less educated than the average elderly person and less assimilated into the mainstream of the American way of life (Hill, 1971; U.S. Bureau of the Census, 1973a), it is possible that he or she is less knowledgeable than the average elderly person about the housing services available and the means by which the services can be accessed. The multiple disadvantage of being both elderly and of a minority group (Hill, 1971; National Council on the Aging, 1972; U.S. Senate, 1971) should justify special attention to the housing needs of the minority elderly.

More substantive data pertaining to the quantity and quality of elderly minority housing is required in order to adequately assess their present condition and provide for their future needs. The purpose of this chapter is to aid in the documentation of the current housing conditions of black and Spanish elderly. A detailed analysis of the characteristics and quality of housing for these minorities includes comparisons of their housing with that of their white counterparts, utilizing not only the 1975 Annual Housing Survey (AHS) data but also 1970 Census of Housing figures (U.S. Bureau of the Census, 1973b). The Annual Housing Survey, commissioned by the U.S. Department of Housing and Urban Development (HUD) and conducted by the U.S. Bureau of the Census, is designed to provide detailed information on the nation's households, including data on characteristics of the occupants, indicators of housing and neighborhood quality, and the characteristics of recent movers for each year beginning with 1973 and continuing through the 1980s.

In 1975 data were collected for a sample of approximately 61,000 occupied housing units located in cities and counties throughout the entire nation. Each housing unit was weighted so that this sample represented all of the 70,831,000 occupied housing units in the United States.

A subset composed of those housing units whose household head was 65 years old or older was used for analytic purposes. This elderly sample consisted of approximately one fifth of the total sample or 12,000 households; it represented 12,647,000 elderly white households, 1,257,000 elderly black households, and 330,000 elderly Spanish households. For the purposes of this chapter "Spanish" includes Mexican American, Chicano, Mexican, Mexicano, Puerto Rican, Cuban, Central or South American, and other Spanish. Therefore, it should be noted that the figures mentioned here are based upon the total population distributions.

BLACKS AND NONBLACKS: 1970 AND 1975

Utilizing 1970 Census of Housing data it is possible to analyze the changes that have occurred between 1970 and 1975 in the housing situation of older Americans (U.S. Bureau of the Census, 1973b). The data were organized in such a manner that it is only possible to represent data for households headed by blacks aged 65 or over, and households headed by whites and all others, thus limiting the discussion of 5-year change to these two groupings of households. The 1970 data did not aggregate Hispanics in a way that allowed comparison with the later AHS data.

In 1970 there were slightly more than 1 million households headed by an elderly black person and approximately 11,400,000 households headed by all other persons aged 65 or over.

By 1975 the number of households headed by an older black person had increased by over 250,000 households to 1,266,000, while the number of all other households had increased to over 13 million. This was an increase of 25% for black households as compared with 16% for all other households.

If housing-related social service needs differ by race, and the data presented here suggest that this is the case, then it is important to determine the extent of these differences for future policy and planning efforts at the national level. Even if the proportion of households headed by an older black does not continue to rise, the absolute number of older blacks eligible for housing-related services will continue to increase.

Homeownership by blacks aged 65 and over increased by 3.5% from 1970 to 1975. By comparison, homeownership by whites and all other races increased by 2.6% for the same period. However, even with the greater gain in homeownership by blacks, the proportion of black homeowners in 1975 remained significantly below that of all other races, 57% as compared with 71%.

Older renters have housing problems and program needs that

differ significantly from older homeowners. Older renters often live in the poorest quality housing. Some current programs are targeted for one group or the other on the basis that their service needs are different. For example, future program developments could include government assistance with mortgage payments. A nationwide home-repair program is another example of a service that would benefit older homeowners. Yet these programs would be of no benefit to the millions of elderly renters. If homeownership is used as a criterion for program participation, then a disproportionately large number of older blacks will be unintentionally discriminated against. Care must be taken to direct a fair proportion of the available resources to the service needs of older renters.

Number of Persons

The increase in the number of all elderly-headed households is related to the increase in single-person households and households containing only two people. With the exception of elderly black homeowners, there was a trend between 1970 and 1975 toward an independent living situation. According to the 1970 census, 68% of the black and 85% of all other owner-occupied households contained either one or two persons (U.S. Bureau of the Census, 1973b). By 1975 the proportion of elderly nonblacks residing in this type of household had risen slightly to 88%; the proportion of black owner-occupied households remained the same. However, for blacks there was a definite increase in the proportion of single-person households, while a decrease occurred in the proportion of two-person households. The net effect was to mask this proportionate change that occurred for black owner-occupied units between 1970 and 1975.

For renter-occupied units, the trend toward smaller-sized households was very much more apparent for both groups. In 1970 approximately 79% of the renter households headed by blacks were occupied by either one or two persons; this figure increased to 87% in the 5-year time period. Elderly white renters were similar to elderly black owners in that the increase in smaller households that occurred between 1970 and 1975 was totally attributable to the increase in single-person households; there was actually a decrease of about 4% in the proportion of the two-person households.

As more older persons choose to live independently rather than with family members other than a spouse, there will be an increasing need for both formal, government-based and informal, neighborhood-based support networks and programs. This trend toward independence will probably continue with its far-reaching implications for the housing market unless a national effort is made to encourage creative house-sharing options. Presently few such incentives exist. For example, current tax laws penalize households that take an older relative into the home.

Household Composition

As might be expected, the majority of two-or-more-person owner-occupied households in 1970 consisted of a married couple living with or without other relatives. About 65% of households headed by older blacks and 80% of all other households headed by a person aged 65 and over included a male head with wife present. Close to twice as many older female blacks as all other races were the head of a multiperson household: 37% versus 14%.

For older renters, household composition differed significantly from that of older owners. In 1970 49% of the older blacks and 58% of all other households headed by an older person were single-person households. Within the two-or-more-person category there were fewer traditional male-headed, wife-present households among renters than among owners.

By 1975 the proportion of two-or-more-person units decreased and that of single-person households increased for all races. Additionally, there were slight proportionate shifts in the type of two-or-more-person households; by 1975 there was an even larger proportion of all households with an older black female as head, while the proportion of older white owner and black renter couples increased slightly.

Value of Unit

In 1970 older blacks were consistently more likely than older whites to own homes that were of lower value; about 1.5 times as many blacks (55%) as whites (34%) owned units valued at less than $10,000. Conversely, twice as many older whites (32%) as blacks (16%) owned units valued at $15,000 or more.

Although the proportion of both groups living in lower valued units (less than $12,500) had decreased by 1975, the same housing pattern was present; older blacks lived in units of lesser value (and by implication, lower quality), older whites lived in units of greater value ($20,000 or more). (The next higher dollar category, $10,000–12,499, was included in the 1975 definition of lower value housing based upon the shift in the proportion of both whites and blacks who fell into this category. Ideally, the 1975 housing values should be standardized to 1970 figures in order to better compare the proportion of older blacks and whites in each category.)

There is growing interest in converting home equity into income available for daily living expenses. Because such a large proportion of older persons do own their own homes free and clear of any mortgage, there is potentially a large market for a program that would convert the value of the dwelling into usable cash while allowing one to remain in the unit. Although Struyk (1979) demonstrated that a substantial proportion of low-income elderly-owned homes valued at $20,000 or more in 1976 would certainly benefit from home-equity liquidity programs, it is apparent from the data presented here that a sizable proportion of poor, older blacks, one of the subpopulations that would benefit most from extra monthly income, own homes that would neither be attractive to the managing financial institutions nor provide a significant income increase if accepted for an annuity program.

Value-Income Ratio

The value-income ratio is computed (for owner-occupied housing only) by dividing the value of the housing unit by the total money income of the family or primary individual. The difference between the value-income ratio for black and nonblack households in 1970 was minimal, with an average difference of 1% between the two groups for each category. However, by 1975 the proportion of nonblack households with a value-income ratio of 1.4 or less had decreased more than the proportion of black households. The increased proportion of households in the higher value-income ratio categories may be due to a more rapid rise in property values for homes owned by nonblacks, while average incomes for the two groups did not change in a proportionate manner.

As inflation and other economic trends drive property values even higher, an increasing proportion of older persons may find themselves living with low, fixed incomes and increasingly higher property taxes. The choice may then be to sell the property unwillingly or to cut back still further on the amount spent for life's other necessities. There is some irony to the fact that in this instance, poor older black owners may be less vulnerable to this insidious phenomenon simply because they live in less desirable neighborhoods.

Gross Rent

Amount paid for rent can be used as an indicator of the quality of the dwelling unit. In 1970 three quarters (75.3%) of black elderly renters paid less than $100 a month for gross rent (i.e., contract rent plus utilities); this figure does not include the proportion of households that paid no cash rent (7.1%). The proportion of white elderly households that occupied these lower rent units was slightly more than half (54%). Because of inflationary factors, it is difficult to define for 1975 a rent comparable to the 1970 rent of $100 or less. In spite of actual inflation costs, there was still a significant proportion of each group living in these low-rent ($100 or less) units in 1975: 60% of the elderly black renter households and 34% of all other elderly renter households.

For the low-income older renter, the availability of low-rent apartments is critical; nonetheless, older persons should not be forced to live in decrepit dwellings simply because they may be the only affordable units.

Gross rent as a percentage of income provides an estimate of housing cost for renters and an indicator of real spendable income. By common acceptance, and as built into the Brooke Amendment to the 1966 Housing Act, a rent-income proportion of 25% represents the maximum housing-expense burden tolerable for American renters. In 1970 somewhat more than two thirds (71.2%) of rent-paying older black households were paying 25% or more of their incomes for rent and utilities. The proportion of all other households paying more than the maximum recommended proportion of income for rent was 67.1%. For low-income older persons, once the rent is paid, there may be little left for food and medical expenses. By 1975 both the number and proportion of all older persons who were paying 25% or more for rent and utilities had decreased; however, the proportionate decrease was greater for older blacks than all other older persons: 12% versus 5.5%, a change that resulted in blacks being in a slightly more favorable position than other groups because a slightly lower proportion was paying 25% or more of the household income for rent.

Both the high proportion of older persons living in units renting for $100 or less and the high proportion of all older renters who must allocate a large proportion of monthly income for rent (leaving little left for low-income renters to spend on other life necessities) indicate a substantial and continuous need for Section 8 rental subsidies as well as a need for renovation and conversion of more existing units to this type of housing.

Dwelling-Unit Characteristics

The data indicate that significant changes in dwelling-unit characteristics have occurred during the 5-year interval for both groups. First, the number of units in the structure has changed. Between 1970 and 1975 two shifts took place in regard to the number of units in the structure where older persons resided. For owner-occupied units, in 1975 a slightly higher percentage of both groups lived in mobile homes or trailers. The percentage of nonblack households that had chosen this option in 1975 was just over 5%. For renter-occupied units, the number of households residing in buildings that contained 20 or more units increased by 4.5% for elderly black households and 3.5% for all other households from 1970 to 1975. This means that about 18% of the black and 29% of all other households were living in large, multi-unit complexes.

Older whites seem somewhat more inclined to consider housing options that require less time and energy for upkeep, such as larger apartment buildings. Mobile-home dwellings also provide access to secondary household services without requiring great effort on the occupants' part.

The second change is the age of the dwelling. A larger proportion of both owner and renter blacks occupied older dwelling units in 1970 as well as in 1975 than nonblacks. For example, in 1975 nearly two thirds (66%) of the minority-renter households resided in dwellings that were built in 1949 or earlier as compared with 58% of the nonblack households. An even higher percentage of black-owner households lived in units that were over 25 years old—72% versus 61% of the white-owner households. While older units are not always in greater obvious disrepair, their age does increase the likelihood of more structure-related problems, and as was mentioned above, based upon the age of the structure, older renters are just as likely as older homeowners to have need for home-repair services.

The third change is the year moved into the unit. Black households were more likely than nonblack households to have resided in their current dwelling unit for a longer period of time. This finding was consistent regardless of tenure or year of enumeration. In 1970 74% of the black and 71% of all other households had lived in their housing 10 years or more. In 1975 the proportion in the 10-years-or-more category remained the same for nonblack households, but for blacks it rose to 78%. The larger proportion of black households that remained in the same dwelling might be the result of fewer perceived residential opportunities for this group.

Because older people tend to age along with their dwelling, the broader residential environment can be negatively influenced by the presence of numerous deteriorating structures. A neighborhood conservation approach might be most effective in a neighborhood populated by aging homeowners and renters.

Finally, plumbing facilities have changed. As mentioned earlier, completeness of plumbing facilities has often served as an indicator of housing quality. However, its effectiveness as an indicator has lessened along with the diminishing number of units that have this flaw, although notable exceptions do exist. In 1970 approximately one fourth (24%) of the households headed by black elderly lacked some or all of the designated plumbing features. By 1975 the percentage of black households that would be categorized as poor quality by this measure had dropped to 18%, but this figure was still 4.5 times that for all other elderly households.

It is alarming that at a time when only 3% of all U.S. housing lacked complete plumbing facilities and could be judged as poor in quality by this measure, nearly one fifth of all older black households occupied units lacking basic plumbing features.

Summary of 1970 and 1975 Changes

It appears, then, that some changes in the characteristics of the housing of households headed by older persons did occur between 1970 and 1975. These include a trend toward fewer persons living in the unit and a greater preference by whites for units such as mobile homes or large apartment complexes where less maintenance effort by the older person is required.

Older people continue to be less mobile as indicated by the length of residence in their unit, therefore, they tend to age along with their dwelling. Unfortunately, this may result in the unit beginning to require more and more money and effort to maintain it just at the time when the residents are becoming less able to provide either the money or energy for home maintenance.

Although the numbers have changed somewhat between 1970 and 1975, a number of discrepancies still remain in household and housing characteristics between black and all other households. Blacks continue to live in generally older housing stock and, as indicated by the only measure of housing quality available here, dwellings of lower quality.

BLACKS, WHITES, SPANISH: COMPARISON OF HOUSING AND NEIGHBORHOOD QUALITY, 1975

In this section, 1975 AHS data on characteristics of housing and indicators of structural quality are presented for the mutually exclusive groups of households headed by older whites, blacks, or persons of Spanish origin. Persons of other races are excluded from the analysis. As was apparent from the data previously presented for the 1970 and 1975 comparisons, the housing conditions and environment of the black elderly are both quantitatively and qualitatively different from those of the white majority. What follows is a more elaborate comparison of data for the three racial/ethnic groups to further clarify these differences. For this section, the 1975 AHS public-user tape was the primary source of data.

In 1975 there were approximately 1,257,000 black and 220,000 Spanish surname households with heads of 65 years old or older, together constituting about 11% of the total households headed by an older person. Table 6.1 shows basic information by subgroup.

All older homeowners were more likely to live in the southern region of the country—about one third (32.3%) of the older whites, two thirds (64.9%) of the older blacks, and two fifths (43.4%) of the older Spanish who were homeowners at the time of the survey. Older white renters were slightly more likely to live in the Northeast, as were older Spanish renters. The majority (52.5%) of older black renters lived in the South, while about one third of the older Spanish renters lived in the West. Both older blacks and whites were proportionately less likely to live in this region of the country.

Older homeowners and renters are not uniformly distributed across the nation. Even within a racial or ethnic group the locational patterns are different for owners and renters. If program allocations on the regional level are to be provided based upon some criterion as homeownership, then it is important to make adjustments to the formula based upon such additional characteristics as race or ethnicity.

A much smaller proportion of minority than white persons owned their own homes—57% of the black and 53% of the Spanish households

TABLE 6.1
Characteristics of Households and Housing Units Occupied by Whites, Blacks, and Spanish Aged 65 and Over

	Whites				Blacks				Spanish Origin			
	Owner		Renter		Owner		Renter		Owner		Renter	
	Number[a]	%	Number	%	Number	%	Number	%	Number	%	Number	%
Region of Country												
North East	1,967	21.5	1,191	33.9	93	13.0	97	18.0	13	7.2	50	32.4
North Central	2,793	30.6	914	26.0	112	15.7	91	16.8	18	10.3	16	10.2
South	2,950	32.3	825	23.5	464	64.9	315	58.2	76	43.4	40	26.3
West	1,427	15.6	584	16.6	46	6.4	38	7.0	69	39.1	48	31.1
Household Composition												
Male head, wife present, no non-relatives	4,873	53.6	882	25.1	294	41.6	142	26.4	95	54.2	68	44.2
Other male heads	248	2.7	68	1.9	37	5.2	19	3.5	13	7.3	9	6.1
Female head	779	8.6	267	7.6	139	19.7	89	16.5	24	13.4	22	14.5
Primary individual	3,199	35.1	2,294	65.3	236	33.5	288	53.5	44	25.1	54	35.3
Year Moved into Unit												
Since April 1970	1,357	14.9	1,692	48.1	75	10.4	233	43.0	32	18.2	85	55.4
1965–April, 1970	1,272	13.9	724	20.6	81	11.3	132	24.4	26	14.8	39	25.6
1960–1964	1,040	11.4	443	12.6	102	14.3	73	13.5	32	18.2	7	4.6
1950–1959	2,032	22.2	319	9.1	185	25.9	54	9.9	43	24.4	9	5.5
1949 or earlier	3,436	37.6	336	9.6	272	38.1	50	9.2	43	24.4	14	8.8
Year Structure Built												
Since April 1970	465	5.1	381	10.8	20	2.8	45	8.3	6	3.6	10	6.3
1965–April 1970	757	8.3	419	11.9	31	4.3	29	5.4	20	11.3	15	9.7
1960–1964	648	7.1	334	9.5	41	5.8	31	5.7	8	4.7	9	5.6
1950–1959	1,683	18.4	363	10.3	105	14.7	76	14.1	43	24.6	19	12.0
1940–1949	1,233	13.5	325	9.3	136	19.0	77	14.3	27	15.4	22	14.3
1939 or earlier	4,350	47.6	1,692	48.1	382	53.4	282	52.1	71	40.3	80	52.1

[a]Numbers in thousands

Source: Annual Housing Survey, 1975, public-use tape.

as compared with 72% of the white households. Therefore, Spanish like blacks may be subtly discriminated against in federal, state, and local program advantages that selectively reward homeownership, such as income-tax deductions.

Spanish, white, and black homeowners were all more likely to be living in a household where both the husband and wife were present. Close to two thirds (65.3%) of the older white and half (53.5%) of the older black renters were living alone. Because the average renter has less control over housing repairs and maintenance, and single persons might be less motivated to pursue the correction of a housing-related problem, a greater proportion of both black and white renters may endure a wider range of housing faults.

Older black homeowners appear to have a slightly lower mobility rate; 64% were living in the same home that was purchased 25 years or more before 1975, as compared to 60% of the white and 49% of the Spanish property owners. It appears, then, that a major proportion of each group is "aging in place." As the dwelling ages it is more likely to need repairs or maintenance; as the homeowner ages it is more likely that he or she will be financially or physically unable to attend to the housing-related problems.

Older renters had a reverse pattern of length of residence; the largest proportion of each group (43% of the blacks, 48% of the whites, and 55% of the Spanish) had moved into the current residence since 1970. Although length of residence is related to age of the structure, there were some notable variations among the three groups. Older white- and Spanish-owner households were approximately twice as likely as black households to live in newer, more modern units. Only 7% of the black elderly owners lived in housing that was built between 1965 and 1975. The comparable figure for all-age U.S. owner-occupied households was 27%, or 4 times the proportion of black elderly households that lived in units less than 10 years old (U.S. Bureau of the Census, 1977). The lower proportion of all elderly households that lived in newer and perhaps more problem-free units might be attributed to both the lower mobility rate of the elderly and the higher cost of new housing units.

Although all elderly are more likely to be living in an older unit located in an aging neighborhood, older blacks are somewhat more susceptible to problems associated with declining areas. Access to a telephone in one's home can be particularly significant to an older person. Not only does it serve as a primary social facilitator for older individuals who might be less physically mobile than they once were but it also serves as a security provision. Only 10% of U.S. households of all ages were lacking access to a telephone in their homes in 1975 (U.S. Bureau of the Census, 1977). By comparison, 13% of elderly white, 22% of elderly Spanish, and 27% of elderly black households do not have access to this vital mode of communication.

Elderly whites are the most likely of the three groups to have access to a telephone; however, there is certainly not equal access within this group. For example, single older males are far less likely than their female counterparts to have a telephone (Hoover, 1978). Great effort should be made both to promote availability of a low-cost telephone "life-line service" rate and to identify these older individuals without telephones who are more isolated than those with telephones. Without a phone, it is difficult either to utilize a "dial-a-ride" service or become part of an informal support network of older persons who call each other daily.

Number of Living Quarters

About 5% more older black than white homeowners lived in one-unit structures: 89.4% versus 84.6%. A slightly lower proportion (82.7%) of Spanish surname homeowners lived in either detached or attached one-unit houses. The difference between older blacks and the other two types of householders may in part be due to older blacks' lack of access to mobile homes or trailers (which are less likely to be located in urban settings); only 1.4% of the older black homeowners resided in this type of unit as compared to just over 5% of older whites or Spanish.

Older black renters were even more likely than their white or Spanish counterparts to live in one-unit structures: 44.7% as compared to 24.7% and 29.9%, respectively. Conversely, older white renters were the most likely to live in large (50 or more units) residential structures; close to one fifth (18.2%) of older white renters chose this type of multi-unit building.

Those older persons who rent houses rather than apartments have maximized their housing-maintenance responsibilities while foregoing the traditional benefits associated with homeownership, including access to home-maintenance programs for older homeowners. Older white and Spanish renters living in large, multi-unit buildings are more likely to be living in a unit that both meets their spatial needs and offers access to such services typically located in apartment buildings as laundry, security controls, and outdoor maintenance.

Number of Bedrooms

The number of bedrooms per residence may be a better indicator of whether a sizable proportion of older persons is "overhoused," that is, living in housing that has more rooms than are necessary for the number of persons living there. Because many older persons have expressed a desire for a second bedroom to be used both as a guest room and workroom, it is assumed here that even a single older person living in a two-bedroom unit is not overhoused. The older white and black owners were far more likely than older renters to be living in homes whose size might be more suitable for a younger household. However, given the average length of residence for older owners, it is probable that they bought these large structures when they needed the space. About 44% of the older white, 48% of the older black, and 38% of the older Spanish owners lived in units with three or more bedrooms. All older renters were more likely to be living in smaller units; however, within this tenure category about half as many older white (8.8%) as older black renters (16.3%) lived in homes with three or more bedrooms. About 15% of the older Spanish renters lived in these large units.

Even if it is assumed that the criterion for overhousing is four or more bedrooms for older persons, there were over 1 million elderly-headed households in 1975 that could be categorized as living in dwellings that were both potentially less suitable for their spatial needs at that age and required greater upkeep effort.

Value of the Housing Unit

When comparing the value of the housing unit for the three groups, it can be noted that only 15% of all U.S. homeowners estimated that the value of their home was less than $15,000 in 1975 (U.S. Bureau of the Census, 1977). Over 1.5 times as many older whites (24%), 3 times as many older Spanish surname persons (47.3%), and 3.5 times as many older blacks (52.5%) estimated that their owned dwelling was worth this low amount or less. It appears, then, that older Spanish, like older blacks, would be proportionately less likely to be eligible for such programs as housing annuity, designed to provide monthly income based upon the value of the dwelling while allowing the older person the right to remain in the unit itself.

As might be expected from the data presented in Table 6.2, younger persons are more likely to live in more expensive homes. About 35% of all homeowners in the U.S. estimated their unit to be worth

TABLE 6.2

Financial Charcteristics of Housing Units Occupied by
Whites, Blacks, and Spanish Aged 65 and Over

	Whites Owner[a] Number	Whites Owner %	Whites Renter Number	Whites Renter %	Blacks Owner Number	Blacks Owner %	Blacks Renter Number	Blacks Renter %	Spanish Origin Owner Number	Spanish Origin Owner %	Spanish Origin Renter Number	Spanish Origin Renter %
Value of Unit (homeowners)												
Less than $10,000	758	11.0			202	34.5			36	25.7		
10,000 to 14,999	885	13.0			105	18.0			30	21.6		
15,000 to 19,999	1,050	15.3			84	14.3			14	10.2		
20,000 to 24,999	878	12.8			54	9.2			14	10.1		
25,000 to 29,999	855	12.5			57	9.7			20	14.5		
30,000 to 34,999	703	10.3			29	5.0			11	7.9		
35,000 and over	1,722	25.1			56	9.4			15	10.1		
House Cost as % of Income												
Less than 25%	4,648	75.6			337	62.3			82	68.3		
25 to 34%	748	12.2			84	15.6			16	13.2		
35% or greater	756	12.3			119	22.0			22	18.4		
Gross Rent (Specified renter)												
Less than $100			1,151	33.5			310	60.0			43	28.5
$100 to $149			838	24.5			103	19.9			43	28.4
$150 to $199			606	17.7			40	7.8			26	17.2
$200 or more			565	16.5			17	3.3			28	18.5
No cash rent			269	7.8			47	9.0			11	7.4
Gross Rent as % of Income												
Less than 20%			634	19.3			117	23.6			35	23.5
20 to 24%			490	15.0			68	13.7			16	10.9
25 to 35%			639	19.5			96	19.3			32	21.7
35% or more			1,237	37.8			169	34.0			53	36.3
Not computed			274	8.4			47	9.4			11	7.6
Live in Public Housing			371	10.6			110	20.3			17	11.0
Other Government Subsidies			121	3.4			12	2.2			1	0.6

[a] Numbers in thousands

Source: Annual Housing Survey, 1975, public-use tape.

79

$35,000 or more in 1975. This compares to about one fourth of the homes of older whites and only one tenth of the homes owned by the minority groups.

Housing Cost as Percentage of Income

Like gross rent as a percentage of income, housing cost as a percentage of income is a good indicator not only of relative expenditures but also of what proportion of income is left for all other living expenses. [Selected monthly housing cost is the sum of payments for mortgage, real estate taxes, property insurance, utilities (electricity, gas, water, and sewage disposal), fuel (oil, coal, kerosene, wood, etc.), and garbage and trash collection.] Less than a fifth (18%) of all U.S. homeowners in 1975 reported that they spent 25% or more of their total family income for housing-related costs. This compares to about 23% of older whites, 32% of older Spanish, and 38% of older blacks. Therefore, a large proportion of the older population had to manage with both a reduced income level and higher housing costs.

Although there is evidence that, on the average, homeowners' annual housing expenses are less than those of renters in comparable housing, it is apparent from these data that a large proportion of all older homeowners, but especially older minorities, have little flexibility in their budgets to cope financially with unexpected expenses.

Gross Rent

Although low rents are necessary if a low-income person is to have sufficient money left over for other necessities, the monthly rent of an apartment or house, on the whole, reflects the estimated quality of the unit. Those units that rented for $100 or less in 1975 are considered here to be more likely to have housing deficiencies. About one third (33.5%) of older white renters lived in dwellings that rented for $100 or less per month; the proportion of older black renters was about 50%. Fewer older Spanish renters (28.5%) inhabited the lower-priced units; nonetheless, one should not assume that a lower proportion were living in dilapidated housing. It is possible that older Spanish renters may be either paying higher than fair market rent or may need to live in larger, higher-priced units because they are more likely to live with other family members (Hoover, 1978). Conversely, older Spanish persons were slightly more likely to live in the more expensive ($200 or more per month) rental units than were whites or blacks: 18.5% as compared to 16.5% for whites and only 3.3% for blacks.

Gross Rent as Percentage of Income

In addition to absolute amount paid for rent and utilities, it is important to consider the amount of gross rent as a percentage of total family income. Even though a larger proportion of older black renters were living in the lower-cost units, there was little difference among the three groups in regard to the proportion paid for gross rent. For example, about 38% of the older whites, 34% of the older blacks, and 36% of the older Spanish were paying 35% or more of their incomes for rent and utilities. An additional one fifth of each group was paying 25% to 34%. Although it would appear that a slightly lower proportion of older blacks were paying a disproportionately high amount of their income for rent, considering the lower average income level of blacks, as a group they had relatively less money left over each month if they were paying 25% or more for gross rent.

Public or Government Subsidized Housing

According to 1975 AHS data, there were approximately 1,843,000 households of all ages living in public housing projects and an additional 522,000 households with other government subsidies (U.S. Bureau of the Census, 1977). Within the older population, about twice as many older black renters (20.3%) as older white renters (10.6%) or older Spanish renters (11%) reported that they lived in public housing. However, even though older blacks are proportionately more likely than all other elderly to live in public housing, older whites are the most likely to be receiving other types of government rent subsidy for community-based housing: 3.4% as compared to 2.2% of older black renters and only 0.6% of older Spanish renters. Older whites, then, seem somewhat more successful in utilizing government aid, which allows them to not only avoid public housing but also to remain in the community, possibly in their original rental unit, as in Section 8 housing subsidies in place.

Older blacks may be placed in public housing units more often than older whites in part because blacks' original neighborhoods were more susceptible to urban renewal projects. Public housing units may be the most readily available, certified-sound housing. The same general neighborhood conditions that trigger urban renewal programs also reduce the chances that local rental units are structurally sound enough to be designated as eligible for Section 8 rent subsidies.

Structural Deficiencies

The AHS was designed to collect detailed information on the current state of each unit's interior attributes (see Table 6.3). These included plumbing, kitchen facilities, heating equipment, electrical wiring, the basement, floor, walls, and ceiling. Additionally, information was collected on the breakdown of such major housing-related systems as heating, water, and sewage.

When compared on the basis of several key indicators, the housing of older minority group members was consistently of lower quality. For example, only 3% of the older white homeowners reported that their unit did not contain complete plumbing facilities; this was about the same proportion as all U.S. households, half the proportion of older Spanish (6.5%), and one fifth the proportion of older black home-owners (15.5%) who had a housing deficit as defined by this traditional housing-quality measure. About equal proportions of older white and Spanish renters did not have access to complete plumbing; however, over three times as many older black renters (20.5%) lived in units with this serious deficiency.

If a living unit has an installed sink, a range or cookstove, and a mechanical refrigerator, then it is considered to have complete kitchen facilities. Additionally, the facilities must be for the exclusive use of the occupants of one housing unit. Lack of access to complete kitchen facilities is a definite problem for older renters; about 16% of the black renters, 10% of the black owners, and 5% of the white renters had to cope with substandard facilities. Although it is not possible to know which kitchen feature these older persons were missing, each one is necessary if adequate meals are to be prepared.

Approximately 92% of all U.S. households had their homes heated by the more efficient and reliable types of heating equipment (warm air furnace, steam or hot water, built-in electric units, floor, wall, or pipe furnace, and room heaters with a flue); the same proportion of all households headed by an older white person resided in units that were equipped with a type of heating system that could better meet their greater physiological need for a constant, moderate temperature.

If the type of heating equipment is compared by race or ethnicity of household head, then great disparities emerge for households headed by older persons. Whereas only 8% of the white owners and renters depended upon one of the more inefficient and potentially dangerous heat sources (room heaters without a flue, fireplaces, stove, portable heaters, or none), close to one third of all black owners and renters, one fourth of Spanish surname owners, and one fifth of the Spanish renters had one of the less desirable methods as their primary heat source. However, a Catch-22 situation exists here: Older whites may live in units with more desirable built-in or central heating systems, but they may be more vulnerable to the rising cost of heating fuel. For example, they are less able to utilize such conservation measures as closure of rooms, which would help conserve fuel (Hoover, 1979).

Roof and basement leaks were particularly prevalent, possibly because of the large proportion of older people who lived in older structures. If not corrected readily, both types of leaks can dramatically and negatively effect other housing structures and systems. Cracks or holes in the ceiling and broken plaster, although less acute as problems, were fairly common and detract from a positive home environment.

Electrical problems such as exposed wiring and lack of working wall outlets were generally more likely to be present in black homes, but just about as likely to affect homeowners as renters. These problems go beyond aesthetics and may increase the chances of home fires or even electrocution.

Finally, the need for an exterminator service was critical in the case of dwellings occupied by blacks. About one fourth of black homeowners (25.9%) and renters (28.1%) reported signs of rats or mice. About half as many Spanish and one third as many whites had to contend with this potential health hazard.

With an occasional exception such as basement water leaks, both older white homeowners and renters were residing in units that had fewer structurally related problems as compared to older minority homeowners or renters. On the average, older Spanish origin persons lived in better housing than did older blacks. Yet, from the data presented above, it is apparent that a large proportion of all elderly are in need of a local home-repair service.

A substantial minority of each group rated their housing unit as only fair to poor: about 11% of the white owners, 22% of the white renters, 28% of the black owners, 43% of the black renters, 17% of the Spanish owners, and 28% of the Spanish renters.

Neighborhood Environment

Because the mobility of an older person may be more limited than that of a younger person, the older person may spend proportionately more

TABLE 6.3
Indicators of Housing Quality in Units Occupied by Whites, Blacks, and Spanish Aged 65 and Over

Quality Indicators	White				Black				Spanish Origin			
	Owner		Renter		Owner		Renter		Owner		Renter	
	Number[a]	%	Number	%	Number	%	Number	%	Number	%	Number	%
Lack of Complete Plumbing--Private Use	279	3.0	226	6.4	111	15.5	111	20.5	12	6.5	9	6.0
Type of Heating Equipt.												
Warm air furnace	4,621	50.6	979	27.8	182	25.5	63	11.6	48	27.3	22	14.6
Steam or hot water	1,573	17.2	1,277	36.3	102	14.3	146	27.0	11	6.3	47	30.4
Built in elec. unit	437	4.8	281	8.0	15	2.1	35	6.5	9	4.8	13	8.4
Floor, wall or pipe furnace	883	9.7	348	9.9	73	10.3	24	4.4	41	23.4	24	15.5
Room heater with flue	821	9.0	351	10.0	85	11.8	74	13.7	20	11.3	16	10.2
Room heater without flue	473	5.2	155	4.4	179	25.1	124	22.9	38	21.5	19	12.2
Fireplace, stove or portable heater	319	3.5	105	3.0	77	10.7	72	13.4	6	3.7	9	5.9
None	10	0.1	18	0.5	2	0.2	2	0.4	3	1.7	4	2.8
No Complete Kitchen--Private Use	116	1.3	185	5.3	71	9.9	84	15.5	5	2.9	4	2.8
No Phone	366	4.0	451	12.8	79	11.0	145	26.7	22	12.7	33	21.5
Roof Leaks	380	4.2	243	7.9	113	15.8	91	18.8	8	4.4	16	11.1
Non Concealed Wiring	156	1.7	65	1.8	44	6.2	46	8.4	4	2.0	3	1.8
Cracks or Holes in Ceiling	165	1.8	221	6.3	72	10.1	108	20.0	6	3.7	11	6.9

Holes in Floor	39	0.4	61	1.7	36	5.0	61	11.3	5	2.7	1	0.5
Broken Plaster	142	1.6	162	4.6	38	5.3	71	13.1	6	3.5	9	5.7
Basement Water Leaks	1,204	25.1	270	19.0	58	23.2	23	17.7	4	9.9	4	10.2
Non-Working Wall Outlets	416	4.6	126	3.6	109	15.3	93	5.0	8	4.8	5	3.3
Rats or Mice Present	813	9.0	232	7.0	183	25.9	144	28.1	23	13.7	18	12.5
Firmly Attached Stair Rail												
No	556	93.0	1,921	93.8	39	89.5	175	86.0	12	83.7	68	92.2
No	18	3.0	84	4.1	2	3.6	14	7.0	0	0.0	4	6.0
No stair railings	24	4.0	42	2.1	3	6.9	14	7.0	2	16.3	1	1.9
House Rating												
Excellent	3,781	41.6	991	28.5	179	25.2	74	13.9	55	31.1	22	14.6
Good	4,320	47.6	1,734	49.8	331	46.4	229	42.7	92	52.3	87	57.4
Fair	919	10.1	638	18.3	177	24.9	173	32.2	25	14.5	37	24.6
Poor	61	0.7	119	3.4	25	3.5	60	11.2	4	2.1	5	3.3

aNumbers in thousands

Source: Annual Housing Survey, 1975, public-use tape.

time at home. Hence, both the home and immediate neighborhood environment may have a more significant effect on an older person's well-being.

The AHS provides extensive data on perceived local neighborhood conditions (e.g., streets in need of repair, presence of street lights, and incidence of crime). All homeowners were more likely to report problems related to inadequate city services, that is, a consistently higher proportion of owners reported such troublesome conditions as streets in need of repair, impassable streets, inadequate street lighting, and presence of trash or litter. It is possible that homeowners either have higher expectations about these features or that these problems are related to geographic location of the homes (e.g., outside metropolitan areas).

A consistently higher proportion of all renters reported the presence of industrial activity in the neighborhood. More importantly though, a higher proportion also reported the presence of crime in the neighborhood. Regardless of whether the actual crime rate was higher in the neighborhoods of older renters, the mere perception of such would affect an older person's lifestyle and well-being. Over one fifth of older white renters (21.2%), older black renters (23.1%), and older Spanish renters (23.3%) responded that they perceived crime to be a problem in their neighborhoods.

Both homeowners and renters, regardless of race or ethnicity, reported both heavy street traffic and street noise to be a problem. These two problems may be noticed more by an older person who is at home during the day when street traffic and noise may be maximized.

Only two neighborhood characteristics seem to be more problematic for older blacks than older whites or Spanish. Both older black homeowners and renters more often reported the presence of abandoned structures or run-down houses in the neighborhood. This observation was corroborated by the interviewers, who were instructed to note whether or not they saw abandoned buildings on the street. According to this measure, both older blacks and Spanish may actually be less aware of abandoned buildings in the neighborhood; older whites' perceptions seem closer to that of the interviewers.

It is apparent from the high proportion of older residents who live in the problematic neighborhoods that a holistic approach to housing preservation is necessary. Increased effort should be made to encourage such programs as Neighborhood Housing Services and Historic Districting (Myers, 1979) in neighborhoods with a high proportion of elderly owners and renters, while protecting them against opportunistic rent and tax increases.

Neighborhood Services

Regardless of the type of neighborhood-based service, older home-owners were more likely than older renters to consistently perceive the service as inadequate. Public transportation was perceived to be less than adequate by all older persons, but particularly by older home-owners; about 42% of the whites, 36% of the blacks, and 37% of the Spanish felt that the transportation system that served their neighborhood was inadequate. Lack of adequate neighborhood shopping facilities was mentioned next most often by older homeowners. It, too, was a problem for older renters, but a lower proportion of each racial or ethnic group mentioned it.

These findings underscore the need for national support of better public transportation systems for the benefit of all age groups. Until that time, service providers should continue to look for alternative systems such as dial-a-ride to insure that older persons are not limited to inadequate neighborhood shopping facilities or medical services.

Neighborhood health care clinics and facilities are most often perceived as inadequate by older Spanish homeowners; about 18% of the respondents answered in this manner as compared to about an equal proportion of whites (13%) and blacks (12.4%)

Finally, police and fire protection were again more likely to be perceived as inadequate by homeowners; however, far fewer total respondents felt that these services needed to be improved.

SUMMARY AND CONCLUSIONS

Although there are fewer older black than white homeowners, it appears that the blacks are more likely to remain in a home once it is purchased; therefore, as a group they may be slightly more likely to experience the tangential problems of overhousing and structural deterioration.

A structure that has more rooms than needed can be an escalating economic and maintenance burden to an older person. For example, higher fuel bills, greater maintenance costs, and higher property taxes can put a great strain on the total household income, which may be initially low. For example, in 1975 the average household income for all older owner-occupied units was about $8,300 as compared to $16,600 (U.S. Bureau of the Census, 1977).

The exact age of a housing unit cannot be determined from these survey data because the final category is "1939 or earlier"; however, as mentioned above, the age of a unit is related to the amount of maintenance necessary to keep it in optimal condition and older blacks are slightly more likely than older white homeowners to have to cope with the result of the aging process of a structure.

Older Spanish persons are less likely to be either property owners or long-term residents if the property is owned. At present there does not seem to be a trend toward greater participation in homeownership. Therefore, their social service needs are different from those of older whites; older Spanish persons, like older blacks, may be disproportionately excluded from programs that only apply to homeowners.

Older blacks, for reasons that cannot be determined here, seem either less interested in or less able to move to both mobile homes or large apartment complexes, each of which can offer lower maintenance levels. Older whites seem to have a growing interest in both types of housing; older Spanish seem to be closer to older whites in their housing-type preference.

If various indicators of structural quality such as value of the unit, gross rent, condition of plumbing, heating equipment, roof, or electrical wiring are examined, with few exceptions a consistent pattern emerges: Older white owners live in relatively better structures; older black owners live in units that have the most structural deficiencies; and older Spanish owners live in structures that are neither as sound as those of whites nor as deficient as those of blacks. (Because the Spanish group includes so many diverse ethnic groups, it is difficult to draw any conclusions about the "average" Spanish heritage older person.) Older black renters, however, are far more likely than any other group to live in problematic housing.

Problems associated with the neighborhood seem to cut across racial and ethnic lines. This finding would lend support to the further development of government programs that recognize the importance of a more comprehensive approach to home improvement, which cannot be divorced from neighborhood rejuvenation.

REFERENCES

Baer, W. C. The evolution of housing indicators and housing standards: Some lessons for the future. *Public Policy*, 1976, 24, 361–393.

Congressional Research Service, Library of Congress. *Critique of housing in the seventies*. Washington, D.C.: U.S. Government Printing Office, 1974.

Ettinger, A. C. Color differentials in housing and residential patterns. *Journal of Intergroup Relations*, 1965, 4, 240–252.

Glazer, N. & McIntire D. (Eds.). *Studies in housing of minority groups* (Special report to the Commission on Race and Housing). Berkeley: University of California Press, 1960.

Grigsby, W. J. *Housing and Poverty.* Philadelphia: University of Pennsylvania, Institute for Urban Studies, 1971.

Hill, R. B. A profile of the black aged. In *Minority Aged in America.* Detroit: Institute of Gerontology, University of Michigan—Wayne State University, 1971.

Hoover, S. L. *Housing characteristics and quality of multigenerational households.* Paper presented at the annual meeting of the Gerontological Society, Dallas, Texas, November 1978.

Hoover, S. L. *How the energy crisis will affect the elderly: Assessing their heating equipment and fuel situation.* Paper presented at the New Jersey Department of Energy Conference, Newark, N.J., October 1979.

Marcuse, P. Social indicators and housing policy. *Urban Affairs Quarterly,* 1971, 7, 193–217.

Myers, P. *Neighborhood conservation and the elderly.* Washington, D.C.: Conservation Foundation, 1979.

National Council on the Aging. *Triple jeopardy: Myth or reality?* Washington, D.C.: Author, 1972.

Rose, A., & Rose, C. B. (Eds.). *Minority problems: A textbook of readings in intergroup relations.* New York: Harper & Row, 1965.

Struyk, R. J. *The housing and income needs of older Americans.* Paper presented at Conference on Unlocking Home Equity, Wisconsin Bureau of Aging, Madison, Wisc., May 1979.

Sutermeiser, O. *Inadequacies and inconsistencies in the definition of substandard housing in housing code standards: Three critical studies* (National Commission on Urban Problems, Research Report No. 19). Washington, D.C.: U.S. Government Printing Office, 1969.

U.S. Bureau of the Census. *Measuring quality of housing: An appraisal of the census of statistics and methods* (Working paper No. 25). Washington, D.C.: U.S. Government Printing Office, 1967.

U.S. Bureau of the Census. *Social and economic conditions of the black population in the U.S.* (Current Population Reports, Series P-23, No. 48). Washington, D.C.: U.S. Government Printing Office, 1973. (a)

U.S. Bureau of the Census. *Census of housing: 1970 subject reports HC(7)-2, housing of senior citizens.* Washington, D.C.: U.S. Government Printing Office, 1973. (b)

U.S. Bureau of the Census. *Annual Housing Survey.* Current Housing Reports Series H-150-754. Washington, D.C.: U.S. Government Printing Office, 1977.

U.S. Senate, Special Committee on Aging. *Developments in aging.* Washington D.C.: U.S. Government Printing Office, 1971.

7

Federally Assisted Housing Programs for the Elderly in Rural Areas: Problems and Prospects

PAUL F. NOLL

Most Americans have a romantic image of rural life. Calendars picture idyllic rural scenes. Television's rural American family is self-reliant, living in comfortable, if modest, surroundings. The Sunbelt retirement communitites of Florida and the Southwest represent to many a movement to less crowded "rural" areas. But these are carefully selected images designed to reinforce that romantic image. A second look reveals that there is another, very different but very real rural America.

This rural America is unvisited by most Americans, who now drive the throughways rather than the byways; it is neglected by the media, who find it easier to depict poverty and its attendant problems through nearby urban scenes; it is often unnoticed by elected representatives in the state and federal legislatures. Rural people often suffer in silence as eyes fall easily on urban problems.

Great numbers of elderly people make their homes in rural America. Although these elderly have much in common, they resist stereotyping. From the semiretired fisherman to the disabled, retired miner, to the elderly farmworker—pensioned and unpensioned, married and alone—their needs are as varied as the people themselves and the places they call home.

The rural elderly are not highly mobile, and are not likely to move to bigger cities in order to improve their quality of life. The exodus to larger cities by youth and young adults seeking white- or blue-collar employment has created a rural population that is predominantly elderly. Although they often own land or own their homes, they are rarely either well off or well housed.

Further, the power drawing young adults to urban areas means that rural areas are usually poorly served by doctors, nurses, social workers, and other professionals who could be providing services needed by the elderly. Far worse, it often means that older citizens are hundreds of miles from their children and their much-needed support. Indeed, the rural elderly are often forgotten Americans.

The 1970 census (U.S. Bureau of the Census, 1973) provides us with many grim facts about the rural elderly:

Income

81% have incomes below $4,000 per year.

61% have incomes below $2,000 per year.

3% have no reported income.

Housing

82% own their homes.

60% live in homes at least 40 years old.

$8,000 is the median value of the owned units.

More than 20% of the units lack complete plumbing.

Average rent is more than 30% of income.

Transportation

30% of the elderly have no automobile available.

In comparison to those in urban areas the rural elderly suffer from twice the incidence of substandard housing, 15% lower incomes, and much older housing that is valued at 50% of urban housing values—if it is marketable at all.

Senior citizens who live on fixed incomes are the group hardest hit by inflation. Most of these elderly require housing subsidies, or without them must deprive themselves of other necessities because housing requires so much of their income. Thus when we look for programs to improve their housing, we must turn to federal or state government subsidized programs. The few well-to-do among the elderly can be served by the private market suppliers of housing, but the greater proportion will achieve decent housing only through a government program.

Comparing housing needs of the nearly 1 million elderly living in substandard housing with the public efforts to provide them decent housing shows us that although the United States has had housing assistance programs since the 1930s and has fostered significant numbers of housing units, a much more crucial task still lies ahead.

This chapter first reviews current federal housing programs used for the elderly and examines their performance in filling the needs of the nonmetropolitan elderly. It will conclude with a discussion of national policy issues.

The U.S. Department of Housing and Urban Development (HUD) and the Farmers Home Administration (FmHA) of the U.S. Department of Agriculture have the major responsibility for housing programs for the elderly in rural areas. The Community Services Administration and the Department of Health and Human Services (HHS) also fund housing-related programs and/or social services that support independent living in this housing.

THE FARMERS HOME ADMINISTRATION

The origins of the FmHA may be traced to the Resettlement Administration (RA) of the Emergency Relief Act of 1933. In 1938 the RA was renamed the Farm Security Administration and in 1947, in a consolidation of various agencies that helped farmers, the FmHA was born. Within 2 years it had programs of direct and insured loans for the improvement of farm housing. In 1961 nonfarm residents were made eligible for its housing programs.

FmHA's homeownership programs from 1950 onward had special provisions for senior citizens. In 1963 the Section 515 Rural Rental Housing Program began. Since the inclusion of nonfarm residents in 1961, the size of service areas eligible for FmHA programs has progressively increased, from towns of less than 5,500 persons to towns of less than 20,000 persons, provided the town is in a nonmetropolitan county. Today a small percentage of FmHA's housing is for those engaged in farming.

FmHA also conducts community facilities loan programs under which nursing homes, intermediate care facilities, health facilities, and recreation centers, including senior centers, can be built. FmHA also conducts business and industrial loan programs to increase employment in rural areas. Although the name is misleading, FmHA is a full partner with HUD in its responsibilities for housing for the rural elderly.

Section 515 Rural Rental Housing Program

This FmHA program provides both subsidized and unsubsidized loans for multifamily rental projects. Approximately one third of the units constructed under this program are built for elderly occupancy. The balance are for rural families. The program has seen rapid growth in the last 5 years. In 1972 $20 million of loans provided for the construction of 3,868 units. In 1977 $544 million was authorized for the construction of 32,056 units, of which 8,809 were for the elderly. This program produces more units annually than the Section 202 Program. (See Table 7.1.)

With each passing year, Section 515 is seeing more widespread use, particularly in states where it had been dormant. The fiscal year (FY) 1979 budget recommendation of the White House asked for $868 million for Section 515, a more than 2,000% increase over 1972, or enough to build approximately 45,000 units.

Section 515 developments average fewer than 20 units per project and more than 90% are subsidized. The subsidy mechanism is an interest credit, with the tenant paying rent based on his income with a mortgage interest rate ranging from 1% up to the market interest rate (8.5% to 9.5% in 1978). A project's rents are based on market-rate interest charges (e.g., $200 per month). However, if the money is borrowed at a 1% rate, the rent would be only $120 per month. If the developer is a nonprofit organization or a housing authority, the tenant would pay the $120 per month and the federal government would provide the remaining $80.

Borrowers and Eligible Activities. Eligible borrowers include public or nonprofit corporations, public bodies, consumer cooperatives, and for-profit and limited-profit organizations, individuals, or partnerships. If the applicant is nonprofit, eligibility requirements include a provision that a majority of the members must reside in the community where the housing will be located, and that not less than five of the directors be leaders of community civic, governmental, fraternal, or religious organizations. Public housing authorities are also eligible for Section 515. Section 515 projects for senior citizens are open to all people aged 62 or over, regardless of income.

There are various financing plans, but the most common one for nonprofit organizations (Plan II) is a loan for the full development cost of the project to be paid back over a period of up to 50 years.

The Section 515 program funds can be used to construct new

TABLE 7.1
Farmers Home Administration Section 515 Program Activity
by Fiscal Year, 1969–1975

(Dollars in thousands)

Fiscal year	Number of Sec. 515 loans	Number of Sec. 515 units	Amount of Sec. 515 loans	Amount of Sec. 515 subsidized loans
1969	390	2,075	$ 17,335	$
1970	510	2,995	28,441	
1971	422	2,624	26,789	n.a.
1972	515	3,868	40,118	
1973	730	8,839	105,063	
1974	879	12,590	173,314	134,743
1975	1,153	20,903	292,356	242,576
1976 & TQ	1,539	31,466	499,983	432,765
1977	1,336	32,056[a]	544,954	512,971
TOTAL 1969–1977	7,474	117,416	$1,728,353	$1,323,055[b]

[a] preliminary figure

[b] excludes pre-1973 subsidies

housing or repair existing housing and related facilities such as a lounge, recreation center, central cooking and dining, laundry, and emergency care rooms. Offices and living quarters for a resident manager may also be provided.

Opportunity for Congregate Housing. On October 12, 1977, President Carter signed into law the Housing and Community Development Act of 1977. The Act modified the Section 515 program to permit the construction of congregate housing for the elderly and handicapped. Where previously each housing unit constructed had to contain a private bath and full kitchen facilities, the Act authorized units that may or may not have complete kitchens, but are served by a central dining facility. The regulations incorporating this program change are expected to take effect by the fall of 1978.

Use of the Section 515 Program in Combination with HUD Section 8.   Section 515 financing may be used for projects to be assisted under HUD's Section 8 rent subsidy program. Under the June 1976 HUD/FmHA Memorandum of Understanding, FmHA alone processes applications of sponsors of rural rental housing seeking to use Section 8, and makes all required certifications to HUD (contract rent, site standards, environmental assessments, etc.). For new Section 515/8 projects, FmHA automatically provides 1% interest credit below market rate (e.g., from 8% to 7%) and provides a 2% interest rate reduction if necessary to lower the contract rent below HUD's fair market rent (FMR) for the area. If necessary, HUD can increase the rent to 120% FMR. For-profit developers may participate, but only at market rate.

In FYs 1977 and 1978 HUD made available to the FmHA 10,000 Section 8 units, to be applied to rental housing produced under FmHA's Section 515 program. The service area for Section 515 crosses metropolian lines and includes communities of up to 20,000. Although HUD and FmHA had concerns both about the approval process and the monitoring of the program, it was nevertheless fully utilized, and proved unable to meet the demand reflected in the applications. The bulk of the units went to just 10 states, and the program produced units for the elderly almost exclusively. Without this set-aside, it would probably have been difficult for HUD to meet the nonmetropolitan share requirement (at least 20% of the Section 8 program) in the law. Although formal action had not yet been taken, it was expected that HUD would continue this set-aside in 1979. A continuing problem was that the HUD set-aside allocated mostly family units, while FmHA requests were for elderly units, despite FmHA national office's instructions to seek out and encourage family-unit developments.

Use in Combination with FmHA Rental Assistance.   In November 1977 FmHA began implementing the Rental Assistance Program to further reduce the rents paid by the tenants of the Section 515 program projects. This program applied to new projects, projects in planning, and to all projects previously constructed under the Section 515 program. The amount of assistance received depended on the financing plan chosen. If it was a Plan II project, the rental assistance covered the differences between 25% of the person's adjusted income and the approved basic rent for the unit. Formerly, the maximum subsidy was to reduce the rent from the market to the basic rent. In the example given earlier where the basic rate was $120 per month, a tenant with an adjusted annual income of $5,760 or less had to pay the basic rent, regardless of what proportion of income it represented. Under the Rental Assistance Program, if an elderly person had an adjusted income of $2,000 per year, the monthly rent the tenant would pay would be set at $41 per month including utilities, with the government paying the difference. In 1978 FmHA hoped to convert 15,000 existing units to this program and to apply an additional 5,000 rental assistance payments to new projects. The Rental Assistance Program will probably be funded at this rate until all the eligible tenants in existsing 515 housing have been converted to this subsidy program.

FmHA Section 502 Homeownership Loan Program

Section 502 is FmHA's basic homeownership program of direct loans to low- and low moderate-income families who cannot get credit elsewhere. There are no speical provisions in the program for senior citizens, although they are eligible.

The loans may be used for new construction, purchase of existing housing, or repairs on already-owned houses.

The loans carry an interest-credit subsidy, so that the loan terms to the borrower can be as low as 1% interest rate on the full market value of the home, for a period of 33 years. The purchaser is expected to make a minimum contribution of 20% of adjusted income toward the mortgage, taxes, and insurance.

Although more than 10,000 units per year have been approved under this largest of the FmHA programs, only approximately 3,000 loans per year have been made to senior citizens. This is not a quota. Were more elderly to apply, the share of loans to the elderly would undoubtedly increase. Any elderly person or family living in an FmHA service area is eligible and may apply directly to an FmHa office for a loan. At present it is the only government-funded homeownership subsidy program helping senior citizens.

FmHA Section 504 Very Low-Income Repair Loan and Grant Program

FmHA's Section 504 Repair and Rehabilitation Program provides loans and (for senior citizens only) grants to very low-income homeowners to remove hazards to their health and safety. It is not necessary to make all the repairs necessary to bring a home up to code. Repairing roofs, replacing heating systems, storm windows and doors, insulation, new bathrooms, and correcting structural faults are typical of the purposes for which the loans and grants are made. The loans are for 20 years at a 1% interest rate. The maximum loan is $5,000.

Since 1977, FmHA has been making grants to senior citizens that can be used to reduce the amount to be repaid under a loan. The grant and loan combination may not exceed $5,000. Before 1977, an average of 4,000 loans totaling $5 million were made in a year. When the grant provisions were finally funded in 1977, program demand jumped (see Table 7.2). The full $5 million in grants appropriated for 1977 was spent. The demand for the initial $5 million in 1978 was so intense that a request for a supplemental $4 million was made very early in the year 1978. The $4 million was included in the Supplemental Appropriations bill before Congress; thus the total 1978 program was to be $9 million.

At the end of FY 1977, FmHA had 7,398 Section 504 grant and loan applications on hand, compared with only 1,514 at the end of 1976. These applications requested approximately $17 million in grants and $24 million in loans, allowing approximately 16,000 homes to be repaired.

Only a handful of states have recorded heavy use of this program, while others appear unable to generate any significant amount of loan activity. Kentucky, Texas, and Mississippi have used the program most heavily, with each receiving more than 10% of the program's appropriation. Other high-activity states are Missouri, New Mexico, North Carolina, and Alabama. In Kentucky over 500 loans and grants were approved in 1977; in California only a single loan was approved in 1975, but after the grant program was initiated, 50 were approved in 1977. This indicated renewed demand for the program, with the grants encouraging more widespread use in the future.

This program was one for which there was a high ratio of FmHA staff time to the dollar amounts loaned, and the program always had a low priority. Community action agencies (CAA), nonprofit organizations, and even state agencies have acted as catalysts to increase program activity in their areas. The FmHA allows "gratuitous personnel" to be placed in its offices by other agencies. These persons are earmarked for certain programs of special interest. Section 504 is one program the use of which has been greatly increased by these gratuitous personnel. Salaried by the Comprehensive Employment Training Act (CETA), the CAA, or by the state, personnel have done outreach, packaging, and initial processing. CETA labor has also been used to do the repair work itself.

TABLE 7.2

Farmers Home Administration Section 504 Program Activity
by Fiscal Year, 1969–1975

(Dollars in thousands)

Fiscal year	Number of loans	Number of Sec. 504 grants	Amount of loans	Amount of Sec. 504 grants
1969	5,514	-	$ 5,799	-
1970	4,750	-	5,244	-
1971	4,741	-	5,482	-
1972	3,803	-	5,340	-
1973	3,078	-	4,515	-
1974	2,635	-	4,429	-
1975	2,554	-	4,808	-
1976 & TQ	3,799	-	8,289	-
1977	3,505	1,989[a]	7,886	$5,000[a]
TOTAL 1969–1977	34,389	1,989	$51,795	$5,000

[a] First year for which grants were funded.

Pennsylvania, Rhode Island, and New Mexico are three states that have provided gratuitous personnel to FmHA. In New Mexico the staff of various community action agencies did the outreach and initial processing for FmHA for a number of years. These catalysts were so successful that the state legislature initiated a loan processors program and took over the costs of these additional people.

The Rural Demonstration Program, providing housing and community development assistance to remote rural areas, is funded jointly by HUD and the U.S. Department of Agriculture (USDA). Gratuitous personnel to generate loan and grant applications are the keystone in each of the states where the demonstration is being conducted (California, Colorado, Illinois, and West Virginia).

THE U.S. DEPARTMENT OF HOUSING AND URBAN DEVELOPMENT

HUD and its predecessor agencies have held the primary responsibility for meeting the housing needs of the poor since the enactment of the Housing Act of 1937, from which the low-rent public housing program began. Since 1956, elderly persons have been specifically noted as eligible recipients of public housing. Since then, more than a half million units have been produced for the elderly, but only a very small share of these are located in rural areas. Similarly, in 1959, the Section 202 program of rental housing for low moderate-income elderly was enacted, but of the approximately 50,000 units produced by 1974, only 3,500 were in small towns and rural areas.

To help rural areas achieve a more fair share, the 1974 Housing and Community Development Act designated that at least 20% of the funding of HUD's subsidized housing programs must be allocated to nonmetropolitan counties. While this target was higher than past experiences, housing allocated on the basis of true need would require 30%–35% of HUD program funds for rural areas.

HUD currently has two active programs that provide housing for the elderly in nonmetropolitan areas. These are the Section 8 Housing Assistance Payments Program and the Section 202 direct loan program for rental housing for the elderly and handicapped. HUD has numerous other smaller subsidy programs that are not described here.

Section 8 Housing Assistance Payments Program

Section 8 is HUD's major subsidy program. In the past 3 years the subsidy has been applied to some 346,000 tenants in substantially rehabilitated, newly constructed, or existing standard housing. Approximately 20% of these units are located in nonmetropolitan counties, and the recent data on the program showed that the elderly's share of the program was about 28%. Reservations have been made on an additional 300,000 units, and Congress has continued to fund the program at approximately 400,000 units per year.

HUD's Section 8 program provides a rent subsidy to owners of new, rehabilitated, or existing housing units occupied by eligible low-income tenants. The tenant pays 15% or 25% of his or her income as the contribution toward rent. HUD pays the property owner (which can be a public, private, nonprofit, or cooperative entity) the difference between the tenant's contribution and the HUD-approved contract rent for that area.

Under Section 8, eligible rental housing includes single-family units, multifamily apartments, congregate housing, and new mobile homes. The owner of new or rehabilitated units generally receives housing assistance directly from HUD, while the owner of existing units usually receives the payments from a local public housing agency that uses HUD funds.

Eligible Recipients.   A family eligible for assistance under Section 8 must have an income below 80% of the median income for the area. On a national average, at least 30% of the assisted families must be very low-income (i.e., having incomes below 50% of the median income for the area). The term "family" includes the elderly.

Under the Section 8 existing-housing program, the family applies to the Public Housing Authority (PHA). Upon determining that the family is eligible, the PHA issues a certificate of family participation with which the family can try to find a suitable unit and enter into a lease with the owner. The family can also use the certificate for housing it already occupies if the housing meets HUD's property standards and if the family is paying more than 25% of its income toward rent.

Under HUD's Section 8 new-construction and substantial-rehabilitation programs, a prospective tenant must apply directly to the owner, who determines whether the family is eligible.

As previously noted, a Section 8 subsidy may be used in combination with the FmHA Rural Rental Housing Program or with HUD's Section 202 rental housing program.

For rural areas the major advantage of the Section 8 program over the traditional housing program is that Section 8 does not require the prior establishment of a local (or state) housing authority. Public entities, such as a department of social services or welfare, a Community Action Agency, or a regional council of governments can serve as a local public housing agency and seek reservation from HUD for certificates of participation for its client population. Nearly 50% of the rural counties in the United States do not have an active housing authority, and those that do most often have small projects located in usually only one or two towns in the county. These above two features enhance the potential of this program to serve the rural elderly.

In addition, these certificates can be used in place, that is, elderly now paying exorbitant rents could have the rent in their present dwellings reduced to 25% of adjusted income under Section 8, with the federal government providing the balance to the landlord.

Program Performance.   Actual production figures for Section 8 are available only through FY 1977. A total of 913,697 units were reserved through the first 3 years of the Section 8 Program.

It should be emphasized that the production figures represent approvals, and not actual housing units built or existing households assisted. Some of the units approved failed to materialize even in the existing-units category. For instance, of the 913,697 units approved by the end of 1977, only 459,568 were eligible for Section 8 payments (i.e., occupied). The overwhelming share of these were in the existing-units category, including financially troubled projects with HUD-insured or HUD-held mortgages. Of the 382,281 approved for either new construction or substantial rehabilitation, only 140,641 were actually started and none were completed.

The estimates for FY 1978 activity show that the program remained a strong producer of subsidized units. HUD estimated that an additional 320,000 units would become eligible for Section 8 payments by the end of that year, and expected construction starts on 125,000 units.

With the exception of the start-up year 1975, the nonmetropolitan share of reservations has consistently fallen between 20% and 25% each year. Actual occupancies in nonmetropolitan areas fall well below the 20% share since there is a much heavier reliance on new construction in these areas. There is a 1- to 2-year lag between the reservation and actual occupancy.

Figures released in 1978 show that 80,518 units were reserved in nonmetropolitan areas in 1977. This number represents 24.8% of total Section 8 reservations. Estimates of the percentage of nonmetropolitan activity in new construction in the various program set-asides have shown that 78% of the FmHA Section 515/Section 8 units, 35% of the public housing, 26% of the state housing finance agency reservations, and 15% of the Section 202s were in nonmetropolitan counties.

Section 202 Rental Housing Program for the Elderly and Handicapped

The HUD Section 202 housing program provides direct loans to nonprofit sponsors to construct new or substantially rehabilitated housing for the elderly and the handicapped. Section 202 loans provide both construction and permanent financing and are restricted to those projects that will use Section 8 rental assistance payments. A successful project applicant for Section 202 funds is guaranteed that sufficient Section 8 subsidies are available to cover the number of Section 202 units requested. National nonprofit corporations may apply for Section 202 loans on behalf of a local nonprofit borrower. The borrower is responsible for developing and managing the project. The housing financed by Section 202 loans may include space for services not normally allowed in nonelderly programs.

Section 202 loans are amortized over 40 years. The interest rate for 1978 was $6\frac{7}{8}$%, although $\frac{1}{2}$% higher during construction. HUD requires the sponsor to provide a minimum cash contribution not to exceed $10,000 "to assure HUD of the borrower's continued commitment to the development, management, and operation of the project." The sponsor's investment is held for 3 years to help pay operating expenses or deficits; any funds remaining after that period are returned.

The Application Procedure. HUD's national office is responsible for notifying the public when proposals will be accepted for Section 202 loans. The nonprofit sponsor responds to this invitation and submits to HUD's national office a proposal for the reservation of Section 202 funds. Successful applicants then apply to the appropriate HUD area office for the Section 8 assistance that has been set aside for Section 202 projects. As with all other HUD programs, 20%–25% of the assistance is mandated for nonmetropolitan areas; HUD has indicated that its approvals or loan reservations will reflect this distribution. HUD also provides interest-free loans for planning Section 202 projects. HUD's Section 106(b) loans are available to cover up to 80% of planning costs incurred in developing the elderly/handicapped housing project.

Program Performance.   In FY 1977 24,791 Section 202 units were placed under reservation, utilizing the full budget authority of $850 million. A total of 54,648 units had been reserved in the program since the revised regulations were published in 1975. Yet only 3,414 units were under construction and none were completed, although HUD estimated that some 1,500 would be completed during 1978.

The Section 202 program continues to have a strong urban bias, although preferences have been stated for rural locations in 1979 and 1980 guidelines. In the initial program from 1959 through 1974 less than 8.5% of the funds went to towns of less than 10,000 persons. For example, by 1972, Florida had 29 projects, Georgia had 7 projects, and the rest of the South, from Virginia to Louisiana, had only 13 projects. While California had 42 projects, 14 mostly rural states had only 2 or 3 projects, and 9 states had 1 project each. In the revised program since 1974 there has been some movement to correct this urban emphasis, but the rural share continues to be inadequate. For example, in 1977, of the 16 projects approved in New York State only 1 was in a non-metropolitan county and in North Carolina only 1 of 6 was in a nonmetropolitan county. Overall, approximately 15% of the units were reserved for nonmetropolitan locations and as before, many rural parts of states had yet to receive a single approval.

The program continues to hold problems for the rural sponsor. Groups with limited experience have difficulty being funded because HUD's criteria for project selection require previous housing experience and are met more fully by larger sponsors in metropolitan areas. Control of the land at the time of application also remains a problem. Although housing authorities and limited-dividend corporations are eligible by law, Congress excluded them in appropriation language and thus eliminated the only capable housing developers in many rural areas. The alleged similarity between the FmHA Section 515/Section 8 and the HUD Section 202/Section 8 programs also inhibits Section 202 activity in rural areas.

Program demand remains extremely high. In FY 1976 HUD received applications for over 230,000 units and funded only 10% of them. In 1977 applications were received for 1,300 projects, containing 230,000 units and requiring $5.6 billion in funding; only 206 were approved. It is difficult to understand HUD's reluctance to expand the program in the face of this unprecedented demand and need for subsidized housing of the elderly and handicapped.

Despite the problems, the Section 202 program is a major source of funds for the new construction under the Section 8 program.

DEFICIENCIES IN NATIONAL HOUSING POLICY
FOR RURAL AREAS

Government Responsibility

There is a lack of agreement as to which government agency bears the ultimate responsibility for providing housing and services to the elderly. This has resulted in a scattering of programs across the bureaucratic landscape, and in social service programs that are only casually related to the housing programs, if at all. At least four federal agencies are involved in the full spectrum of housing types and programs, from independent living to nursing homes: the Department of Health and Human Services (HHS), HUD, the USDA, and the Community Services Administration (CSA). Most of these have multiple programs, which often appear to provide similar benefits. For example, in the FmHA programs, rental housing for the elderly can be funded under the Section 515 housing program, the Community Facilities Program, or with a business and industry loan if the business is to operate housing for the elderly. Under HUD programs, it is possible to rehabilitate housing for the elderly under the Community Development Block Grant Program, Urban Development Action Grants, Section 312, Section 8, and through the traditional public housing programs. Weatherization funds could come from FmHA, CSA, or the Department of Energy, and the Department of Labor could cover the labor costs through CETA.

Social services are not provided by these housing agencies, and the housing program regulations discourage small projects. The HUD Section 8 program, particularly in its existing housing component, contains no provision for supporting services. Most rural public housing agencies have no social service staff, and can do little more than referral. Thus many social services simply do not reach remote areas.

Inadequate Delivery Systems

Rural areas lack the necessary local components of the delivery system required to facilitate the use of publicly assisted housing programs. Most government programs are passive. They do not aggressively generate activity according to a plan, but rather respond to requests submitted by interested parties. Because many rural areas lack housing sponsors (public, nonprofit, and private), financial institutions, builders, and other professional skills, they often do not get a fair share of the federal housing programs available.

Residents of large cities take public housing authorities for granted. Yet a study by the Housing Assistance Council completed in 1977 found that in 1,233 of the nation's 3,103 counties there was no public housing; 1,056 of these 1,223 counties are nonmetropolitan. While only 7% of the nation's metropolitan population lives in counties without public housing, 29.4% of the nonmetropolitan residents live in such counties. Nearly 16 million people have no access to public housing.

Where public housing authorities in rural areas exist, they have a much smaller share of the housing relative to their need. Metropolitan areas have 1 public housing unit for every 5 units of substandard housing, nonmetropolitan areas have 1 public housing unit for every 17 substandard units, and the nonmetropolitan elderly have but 1 public housing unit for every 34 substandard elderly-occupied units. Even the HUD Section 8 program—created to overcome the absence of a housing authority by allowing any public agency to serve as a facilitator of rent subsidies—has had limited success in delivering units into previously unserved counties.

The government network to deliver this assistance also provides additional hardships for rural areas. HUD offices can be found in only one or two of the largest cities in each state. Many decisions on applications are made at the HUD regional office, whose remoteness from many rural areas precludes adequate communication between the potential sponsor and the HUD administrators.

Urban Bias

Programs are developed from an urban perspective. Their use in rural areas is severely limited. In some federal housing programs, the minimum number of units required to make a project feasible is often more than the demand for such units in a small town.

Site criteria ignore rural realities. A town that is but one block wide, parallel to the highway and railroad, and with no capacity to extend its water and waste system will fail to meet site selection criteria. Yet persons living there need to be provided with adequate housing without being forced to relocate to another town.

Regulations in Urban Development Action Grants and Small Towns Program of the HUD Community Development Block Grant Program have requirements that are more restrictive for smaller towns than for towns just under the upper limit of eligibility.

Even the HUD Minimum Property Standards (MPS) pose problems. In northeast California, where many low-income families can acquire free firewood from the numerous mills, home woodburning heating stoves are not permitted. A public housing project of Northern Pueblo Enterprises was held up for years because the homes were to be constructed of adobe, a material on which the MPS are silent. Because of concern as to whether or not the material would last, HUD required a "slump" test. Despite the existence of 300-year-old adobe structures, the project was not approved until the appropriate tests were done. In 1977, the FmHA at last accepted adobe construction of housing.

Even in housing research, rural differences are ignored. In an Urban Institute study on the management of local housing authorities, (Sadacca, Loux, Isler, & Drury, 1974) the sample was drawn from only those authorities with more than 100 public housing units. Those authorities with between 100 and 500 units were labeled "small" authorities, 500 to 1,250 "medium," and those over 1,250 "large." Unfortunately, over 1,300 housing authorities, nearly half of the nation's total number, were excluded from the sample by virtue of being too small. Yet conclusions reached from sampling authorities with up to 250 units have been extended by assumption to authorities with 10 units.

Inadequate Subsidies

Subsidies often do not go deep enough. Programs based on reducing mortgage interest rates simply do not provide large enough subsidies to serve many of the elderly poor. The Section 236 and Section 202 programs of HUD, and the Section 515 program of FmHA all had this limitation. To overcome this, the programs have been used in tandem with other deeper subsidy programs such as the HUD Rent Supplement, the Section 8 Programs, and the FmHA's Rental Assistance Program.

In rural areas, a deep-subsidy homeownership program is a must. Congress adopted a rural low-income homeownership program for FY 1979 on a test basis for 16,000 units. This program was designed to assist those too poor to qualify for the existing homeownership programs with interest subsidies.

Underfunding and Disproportionate Distribution

Many programs are underfunded and distributed disproportionate to need. HUD Section 202 elderly housing is a prime example of an underfunded program. Despite applications requesting $5.6 billion for the construction of 230,000 units, the program was held at the $750 to

$850 million range from 1976 to 1979, enough to fund only 25,000 units per year, and experienced only moderate improvement for 1980.

The FmHA allocates its Section 515 funds according to demand rather than need. While over 100 projects for the elderly are approved each year in Iowa, in neighboring states such as Nebraska fewer than a dozen projects are approved. At the extremes, southern states such as Georgia, Alabama, and Louisiana, are allocated less than $250 annually for housing programs per family living in substandard housing, while in Idaho, Utah, Maine, and New Jersey, the annual allocations exceed $2,500 per family.

Additional barriers inhibit the national effort to accomplish its housing goals. These include federal staff shortages that limit the number of applications processed and hide the actual program demand, and the lack of outreach, which keeps programs from being used to their fullest potential in rural areas.

These barriers perpetuate a never-ending cycle of underfunded programs. For example, because many rural people and organizations are unaware of certain programs and do not apply, the staff requirements of the federal agencies remain low. Since there is limited staff, backlogs develop, and loans in excess of the funding maximums cannot be processed. Congress feels little pressure to increase the amount appropriated for these programs. Because all the appropriated funds are used, there is no perceived need to promote more public awareness of the program.

In the larger context, even when Congress is fully aware of the need, housing programs must be measured against all other budget requests. In an era of high inflation and moves to reduce the role of the federal government, housing programs yield to other more pressing national responsibilities. Federal outlays for housing programs are less than 3% of our national budget.

Proposed solutions to the variety of problems include federal action to simplify and modify present programs and to develop new programs. There is also a need for deeper subsidies and for more funding. Governmental reorganization plans should also consider establishing a single responsible agency that can provide the elderly with housing and all the necessary service supports. At the state and local level, there is need for supplemental programs and a responsive delivery mechanism to broker the necessary services to maintain an independent lifestyle for the elderly.

As long as this limited commitment to housing programs is tolerated, rural housing problems will be unsolved.

REFERENCES

Sadacca, R., Loux, S. B., Isler, M. L., & Drury, M. J. *Management performance in public housing.* Washington D.C.: Urban Institute, 1974.

U.S. Bureau of the Census. *Census of housing: 1970 subject reports HC(7)-2, housing of senior citizens.* Washington, D.C.: U.S. Government Printing Office, 1973.

8
Housing-Related Needs of the Suburban Elderly

MICHAEL GUTOWSKI

Over 4 million households headed by a person over 65 years of age currently live in suburban areas of Standard Metropolitan Statistical Areas (SMSAs). These suburban households represent nearly 30% of all elderly households.

While central cities still claim a larger share of urban elderly households, the balance is slowly shifting toward the suburbs. The large number of earlier suburban developments that began sweeping the country following World War II have matured and retained many of their initial residents who are now elderly or pre-elderly families. Suburban areas are also experiencing a net in-migration of older residents. In 1974 alone over 250,000 elderly households moved into suburban areas of SMSAs. The suburban elderly tend to have higher incomes, larger proportions of homeowners, and fewer minority members than their central-city counterparts.

Does this changing location pattern of the elderly population suggest alteration of the type and structure of housing and social services designed to meet the needs of the elderly population? Do the characteristics and needs of the suburban elderly suggest new or different approaches to service delivery? This chapter will discuss the factors associated with the rapid growth of the suburban elderly population, assess broad differences in their characteristics, and suggest possible policies or programs that can be developed in order to focus on the unique needs of the elderly in suburbia.

THE GROWING SUBURBAN ELDERLY POPULATION

The projected explosion in the elderly population will not bypass suburbia. Suburbia is growing older. In 1950 only 12% of the population aged 65 and over was located in suburban portions of urbanized areas.

By 1970 the proportion of the elderly in suburban areas increased substantially to 21% of the elderly population (Golant, 1975). Golant further points out that intrametropolitan moves tend to reinforce this pattern. Between 1965 and 1970 only 6% of the elderly moving within a metropolitan area moved from the suburbs to the central city, while 14% of such moves were from the central city to the suburbs. While mobility patterns reinforce the suburbanization of the elderly population, they are not the dominant factor.

Elderly households do not have a strong tendency to relocate. Current location patterns reflect in large part prior decisions based on past income levels and the journey to work. In 1973 more than half of the elderly population had moved into their current dwelling unit prior to 1960. The current location pattern of elderly households is not closely related to the values of current economic variables. Income has typically fallen well below the level during peak earning years when the housing choice was made and the journey to work is no longer relevant for most elderly households. The desire to maintain the same residential location is more closely associated with noneconomic phenomena, such as the desire to remain in a familiar neighborhood, the strength of friendships and informal social networks, and inertia. These factors are strong enough in many cases to generate a housing disequilibrium situation where the elderly household continues to consume housing with space and costs appropriate for an earlier time when family size and income were higher.

Concentrations of elderly households are thus closely related to the age of the housing stock in particular areas. This hypothesis was tested for Montgomery County, Maryland, a suburban area of the Washington, D.C. SMSA (Gutowski & Field, 1979). A multiple linear regression relating the proportion of elderly residents, Y to the proportion of the housing stock built prior to 1950, X_1 and a dummy variable set equal to 1 if more than 50% of the dwelling units in a census tract were multifamily units, X_2 was run for the Montgomery County area. Units of observation were the 125 census tracts with 1970 populations over 500. One census tract was excluded from the data set because it primarily included a recently developed private retirement community. After dropping this tract from the data set the resulting regression equation was

$$Y = 2.54 + 0.112X_1 + 4.50X_2 \qquad R^2 = 0.40; \ n = 124$$

$$(t = 7.4) \quad (t = 5.2)$$

where Y is the proportion of population over age 65, X_1 is the proportion of the housing stock built prior to 1950, and X_2 is a dummy variable equal to 1 if more than 50% of housing units in census tract are multifamily units.

Given the complex set of factors that determine location choice, it is somewhat surprising that 40% of the variation in the proportion of elderly in census tracts is explained by the age structure of the owner-occupied housing stock. The relation between age of residents and age of residential structures would probably be more pronounced if only owner-occupied housing structures were included. The positive relation between X_2 and the proportion of elderly residents suggests that this relation would be weaker for residents of multifamily structures, who are primarily renters.

Montgomery County's elderly population is concentrated in the older, more densely developed sections of the county. In Montgomery County as well as in most suburban areas of SMSAs the older, more densely populated portions of the suburban area tend to be those closest to the central city and along the early suburban growth corridors in outlying areas. Further testing of the hypothesis that the relative size of the elderly population is determined by the age of the housing stock in a particular area should be developed for other SMSAs. Casual inspection of the data suggests that the hypothesis can be supported in most older large metropolitan areas.

Twenty years ago these inner suburbs were scrambling to build the urban infrastructure needed to provide educational and recreational facilities for a growing school-age population. These same areas are now faced with declining school-age populations, school closings, and increasing demands for facilities, housing, and housing-related services to meet their expanding elderly population.

Outlying suburban areas currently faced with pressures to build schools and youth- or family-related facilities will also face an aging housing stock and population in the future. The dynamics of location patterns of the elderly should be considered in developing service strategies for the elderly. The current concentration of the elderly in central cities may suggest greater relative concentration of program efforts in the central city. The programs cannot, however, ignore the problems of the current suburban elderly, which may be less intense but just as acute for individual elderly households. Over time a shifting concentration of program resources to suburban areas should be anticipated in response to the dynamics of intrametropolitan location of the elderly population.

CHARACTERISTICS OF THE SUBURBAN ELDERLY

In very broad terms, the suburban elderly are generally conceded to be better off than their central-city counterparts. While the suburban elderly typically have higher incomes and higher rates of homeownership, it is a mistake to consider the suburbs as a monolithic area where all residents including the elderly are solidly entrenched in the middle class.

The problems of the central-city elderly are certainly more acute. Niebanck and Yessian (1968), for example, contend that "by the 1980s a substantial portion of all households in our older central cities may be headed by impoverished elderly Negroes" (p. 123). While a larger share of the elderly population in central cities and rural areas has very low incomes, the older Americans residing in the suburbs are not immune from poverty. Table 8.1 compares the proportion of the elderly population with incomes below the poverty level in the central city and the suburbs for selected SMSAs.

While the proportion of the elderly population below the poverty income level is higher in the central city for each of the SMSAs in Table 8.1, there are substantial numbers of impoverished elderly living in the more affluent suburban areas. The poor central-city elderly are a natural focal point for public policies and programs because of the higher proportion of poor households and their greater visibility given the higher population densities and relatively greater spatial concentrations of elderly households. While the intensity of the problem may be more acute in central cities, the problems faced by the poor suburban elderly are as real as those faced by the poor central-city elderly. The poor suburban elderly are less visible and dispersed over a much wider geographic area, placing a greater premium on an effective outreach and service distribution strategy.

When the income distribution of elderly households in central cities and the suburban areas of SMSAs is examined, owner-occupant elderly families are seen generally to have higher incomes than renters in both central-city and suburban areas of SMSAs (Annual Housing Survey, 1973, special tabulations, public-use tapes). The median income of elderly households is about 19% higher for suburban than central-city households.

One of the major differences between suburban and central-city elderly households is the rate of homeownership. Nearly 74% of the eldery suburban households resided in owner-occupied housing in 1973, while only about 55% of the central-city residents were owner occupants. The median value of the owner-occupied homes was

TABLE 8.1
Comparison of Population Over 65 Years of Age Below Poverty Level
in Central City and Suburbs of Selected SMSAs

	Population over Age 65 (Thousands)		Percent of Elderly Population Below Poverty Income Level	
	Central City	Suburbs	Central City	Suburbs
Boston	82	229	18.6%	14.1%
Buffalo	61	74	25.3	17.4
Detroit	173	167	22.5	15.2
Los Angeles/ Long Beach	334	319	18.2	15.9
Portland, Oregon	57	53	22.6	19.9
Washington, D. C.	71	101	19.8	12.3

Source: 1970 Census of Population and Housing, public-use tapes.

$24,248 for the suburban elderly and $19,029 in the central city. Another sharp difference between the central-city and suburban elderly populations is the relative concentration of black households. Only 3.3% of the owner occupants and 5.6% of the renters in suburbia are black. The corresponding percentages in the central city are 15.2% and 26.1%.

Only about 40% of the central-city elderly have a private automobile available for their use, while 55% of the suburbanites can rely on this form of private transportation. The need for an automobile in suburban areas is much more pressing given the lower density and generally poorer public transportation systems. Only 59% of the suburbanites considered the public transportation services to be adequate in their area, as compared to 85% of the central-city residents. Transportation and transportation-related services are critical needs for the suburban elderly.

A recent study of the elderly citizens in Montgomery County, Maryland provides a case study of some of these national trends in the suburban population (Burkhardt, Annan, & Dietz, 1977). Montgomery County, one of the most affluent counties in the United States, represents a large portion of the Washington, D.C. suburbs. Between

1970 and 1976, the population over 60 years of age in Montgomery County increased from 50,080 to 70,100. This represents a 40% increase compared to an overall county population growth of 11.4%.

The larger portion of the elderly population resides in the older, densely developed sectors of the county closest to the central city. The elderly population is growing older. Of the population aged 60 and over, 40% were 70 years old or older in 1970. By 1977 this percentage increased to 52% over 70 years of age. Associated with the increasing age of the elderly population was an increase in the proportion of elderly living alone; 27% in 1976 as opposed to 19% in 1970.

Although the median personal income of the elderly was $11,300 in 1975, 18% of the elderly population had incomes below $4,000. Nearly half of the elderly population in Montgomery County has more than a high school education. Since the generally high income and educational attainment of the county's population reflects its status as one of the nation's most affluent large counties, it cannot be viewed as typical of most suburban areas. But even in this high-income suburban area there are substantial numbers of very low-income elderly.

When major problems perceived by the elderly in Montgomery County were ranked in terms of the percentages naming them as such, income-related problems stood out as the most significant, with nearly 20% of the elderly having some problems with income. Transportation, crime, isolation and loneliness, and health care are other areas where at least 10% of the elderly have problems. Most other areas showed less than 5% acknowledging problems (including home repair, homemaker services, and housing).

Do the problems and needs of the suburban elderly differ significantly from the central-city elderly? Should attempts be made to sharpen the structure of service delivery to specifically meet the most pressing needs of the elderly in specific locations?

A ranking of social service priorities by survey respondents over 60 years of age in Wayne County, Michigan was obtained (Michigan Department of Social Services, 1976). Seventy percent of the elderly population resides in the Detroit central city. While the specific categories of services represented and the survey questions differ from the Montgomery County sample, a clear difference in the pattern of service needs is evident.

Health-related needs emerged as the dominant social service priority in Wayne County (64%), with mental health and rehabilitation (45%) also ranking highly as a separate service category. The second and third highest priorities were education and training (60%) and employment-related services (52%). Housing-improvement needs were voiced by 47% and chore services by 21%. Education and employment, in contrast, fell far down the list of problem priorities in suburban Montgomery County.

These data suggest in rather sketchy terms that there may be critical differences in the patterns and types of services required to address the housing and social service needs of the elderly in different types of urban neighborhoods. What is clearly needed is a more thorough understanding of differences in the characteristics and needs of the elderly population in differing residential settings.

Are transportation-related problems, social isolation, and information and referral needs more acute in suburban areas given the greater dispersion and lower concentrations of elderly households? Should more emphasis be placed on home repair and chore services given the substantially higher rates of homeownership in suburban areas? Should greater focus be placed on development of more alternative types of housing for the elderly in suburban areas? Given the predominance of single-family housing in suburban areas, the elderly often have few housing options available if they desire to remain in or near their current neighborhoods. Movement to congregate, multifamily arrangements, or some other alternative to a single-family home in reasonable promixity to the current location of the suburban elderly household is often severely constrained by the unavailability and by zoning or urban development plans that restrict such housing to specific areas in the suburbs.

In order to develop effective housing-related programs that address the differing needs of the elderly in alternative residential locations, priority should be placed on thorough assessment of the differences in the characteristics, needs, and structure of current programs in these areas. The current delivery system for housing and housing-related services is fragmented and disjointed with no consistent central mechanism for assessing the total structure of service needs by area.

The housing needs of the elderly cannot be viewed in isolation from a broader range of social services that enable the elderly to remain in their own homes or improve their housing situations. Improvement of existing housing programs and development of new housing programs and policies to serve the elderly can be made more effective by attempting to integrate delivery of these services along with provision of the physical housing structure.

A variety of federal, state, and local programs have been mounted to meet the housing and broader housing-related needs of the elderly ranging from HUD housing assistance programs to Title XX social services, Community Development Block Grants, and state or local property tax circuit breakers. Funding distribution and assessment of needs is dispersed throughout all levels of government. Some mechanism is needed to integrate the wide range of existing programs with the future program initiatives. Such a comprehensive, integrated program structure must address the differing needs of the elderly households in central city, suburban, and rural areas.

POLICY INITIATIVES TO ASSIST
THE SUBURBAN ELDERLY HOMEOWNER

While the impoverished elderly in our nation's central cities, rural areas, and to a lesser but still significant extent, suburban areas should be the focal point of housing and social services programs for elderly households, there are several low-cost policy options that can directly attack serious problems facing the relatively affluent elderly homeowner.

A large segment of this elderly homeowner population is confronted with what can be described as a housing disequilibrium situation. Their current residential location reflects past income levels, family structures, and employment situations. The onset of retirement with associated income decline along with the departure of grown children often results in an imbalance between the need for housing services and the financial resources necessary to operate and maintain the housing.

In most cases only a portion of current retirement income is indexed for inflation, resulting in continuing declines in real income with age. Operation and maintenance costs of the house, particularly energy costs, continue to mount despite the decline in real income. The elderly household faced with this housing disequilibrium may be forced to move from the current residence in order to supplement current income with the proceeds from the equity in the home.

Owner-occupied housing equity is the dominant asset available to elderly households. More than half of the total wealth of households headed by a person over 65 years of age is represented by this equity. Almost 70% of all elderly heads own their own homes and most of these, 84%, have no outstanding debt on their homes (Projector & Weiss, 1966). Since the elderly frequently have no substantial assets to liquidate other than their own homes and loans are difficult to obtain, "undermaintenance is perhaps the most widely used method of dissaving" short of selling the residence for elderly homeowners

(Guttentag, 1975). That is, by foregoing essential maintenance expenditures, the elderly homeowner "dissaves," or finances current consumption, by allowing the value of the housing equity to fall.

As the housing stock in a particular neighborhood ages, the proportion of elderly homeowners increases and the potential for undermaintenance in a large proportion of the housing stock to correct the housing disequilibrium of older homeowners grows. To a large extent the blighted and decayed areas of central cities began their decline through this same process. The growing suburban elderly population and its concentration in many of the older neighborhoods adjacent to the central city suggests a concentrated effort to stem the extension of blight into suburban neighborhoods. Thus attention to urban problems should have an ultimate impact on the suburbs.

A program could be mounted specifically to address the undermaintenance response in aging urban neighborhoods. At present, publicly supported rehabilitation and maintenance programs are targeted to already decaying and blighted areas through the Community Development Block Grant and Model Cities Programs. Housing-related services including chore, homemaker, home management, housing, and services to enable people to remain in the home are available to a growing proportion of the elderly population under the Title XX Program, but the program focus and availability of such services differs widely between states and within individual states. Nearly two thirds of Title XX service expenditures for the elderly in North Carolina are for these housing-related services. In New York and Oregon only about one third of the Title XX expenditures for the elderly are directed to these housing-related functions (Gutowski, 1978).

A concentrated program to provide housing maintenance, repair, and chore services for elderly homeowners in aging urban neighborhoods can play a powerful role in preventing more serious problems of blight and decay from spreading to older neighborhoods in the older suburbs and outlying areas of central cities. A modest current investment in "urban maintenance" directed toward elderly residents can result in significant savings of future outlays to arrest urban blight and decay in later stages.

It can be argued that a specific program targeted to neighborhoods that are not currently in serious trouble can be handled through existing FmHA home improvement loans. For the elderly homeowner, however, undermaintenance represents a conscious attempt to dissave and correct a housing disequilibrium situation. Can additional funding for maintenance and preservation of older neighborhoods be considered in urban neighborhoods that are predominantly middle class even if the externalities associated with prevention of urban blight are recognized? Any additional program funds for the elderly might be more closely targeted to the impoverished elderly and already-blighted or decaying neighborhoods.

Two possible approaches to providing expanded maintenance services to these aging neighborhoods without requesting additional funding may be suggested. The first is to couple the home-maintenance needs of the elderly with cyclical needs for public employment expenditures. When a cyclical downswing in the economy results in the unemployment rate reaching a critical level, funding for jobs programs or public employment is normally sought. By setting up the mechanism for channeling this type of employment to assess and provide maintenance and chore services specifically for elderly homeowners at minimal or no cost would provide a clear focus for public employment programs during cyclical downswings in the economy.

The program trigger would be the general level of unemployment, unemployment rates in the building trades area, specific area unemployment rates, or the level of housing starts in the economy. In periods when excess labor capacity exists in the building trades, public service employment can be automatically channeled into the productive activity of assisting in the maintenance and preservation of aging neighborhoods. The undermaintenance of owner-occupied homes by elderly households is a long-term and continuous problem. Periodic initiatives timed to coincide with cyclical downswings in housing and construction activity can make strong inroads to the problem while providing a demonstrable productive outlet for public service employment.

This type of program could be developed to gain the support of labor in the building trades industries, since it could moderate substantial swings in employment opportunities. This type of program can be viewed as an increase in funding specifically addressed to counterswings in cyclical economic activity rather than as a request for additional program funding for the elderly. A much broader base of political support can be generated by merging the specific needs of the elderly with broader economic concerns. It is, however, essential that the mechanism for implementing such a program be developed soon. By waiting for the next downswing in economic activity to develop support and define the operating mechanism for such a program, valuable program development time would be lost, resulting in delay of implementation until after the economic recession has abated and demands for the types of labor needed for the activity are accelerating in the private market for housing and development activity.

A second related policy initiative currently gaining support is the housing annuity program, often referred to as a split equity or reverse equity mortgage program for elderly homeowners (Chen, 1970; Guttentag, 1975). In a housing annuity program, the elderly homeowner would essentially transfer title to his or her home to a savings and loan association in exchange for an annuity and the right to continue tenancy in the home for life or some specified number of years. The program would essentially enable the elderly homeowner to supplement current income with annuity income derived from the equity in his or her home. The potential users of such a program would be concentrated in suburban households because of their higher rates of homeownership and more substantial levels of housing equity.

The amount of annuity income the elderly homeowner could expect from such a plan would depend on the homeowner's life expectancy, expectations concerning property appreciation and interest rates, and a complex set of actuarial considerations. As a rough rule of thumb the annual income payment to the elderly homeowner would equal the current value of the home divided by life expectancy in years. Thus an elderly owner of a $24,000 home with no debt outstanding and a life expectancy of 12 years would receive an annual income payment in the vicinity of $24,000/12 = $2,000. The amount of the annuity would be further adjusted depending on sex, whether benefits are to continue for a surviving spouse, and a host of other factors.

The government role and additional budget resources necessary to introduce such a program could be limited to program regulation and the supervision and development of the procedures for a housing annuity program. The housing annuity would be a much more complex financial instrument than a home mortgage. While it has potential to serve the needs of the elderly, there is also great potential for program abuse. Determination of the fair market value of a home and expected rate of price appreciation should be under close surveillance by the public sector to assure equitable assessment of the annuity. Guttentag (1975) notes that "we have ample experience to indicate that when one party to a contract participates once in a lifetime while the second party is in the business, freedom of contract means that the second party writes the contract and the potential exists for 'small print abuse'" (p.19). He suggests a possible role for the federal government in specifying the basic format of standard contracts and specifying a limited number of optional procedures to limit the potential for program abuse.

Two specific features of the housing annuity program could generate significant differentials by neighborhood location in the net annuity income to program participants. Program participants in declining urban neighborhoods would receive lower net returns compared to a property of the same value in a more stable neighborhood because of higher anticipated maintenance costs and a differential in expected price appreciation of the property.

The financial institution purchasing the reverse equity mortgage has a vested interest in adequate maintenance and insurance of the property. The elderly homeowner would have no clear incentive to maintain the value of the home to be transferred to the financial institution in the future. The elderly homeowner could be made responsible for the burden of fixed amounts of maintenance and insurance activities. Guttentag (1975) suggests that the best arrangement would be for the financial institution to assume responsibility for expenses and to deduct a fixed maintenance fee from the equity payment. As a large-scale institutional buyer of services, the financial institution would be in a stronger market position to purchase lower cost services and could guard against excessive payments, overmaintenance, and contracting abuses in the home repair and maintenance industry.

An extensively used housing annuity program would thus also serve the secondary objective of assuring that elderly homeowners participating in the program do not correct their housing disequilibrium position through undermaintenance of owner-occupied properties. The deduction of expected maintenance costs from the annuity would, however, mean a lower net income payment to elderly program paticipants in older decaying neighborhoods where expected maintenance costs would be higher.

Another factor that would yield relatively greater returns to program participants in the more stable suburban and outlying central-city neighborhoods is the expected rate of price appreciation. A key determinant of the size of the annuity for the individual is the expected value of the home at time of transfer to the financial institution. All other things being equal, a $20,000 home expected to double in value within the life expectancy of the homeowner will yield a much larger annuity value than a property with similar current market value located in a declining urban neighborhood with potential for price decline. A housing annuity program with federal involvement limited to regulation and control would thus yield greater relative returns to elderly homeowners in stable or growing urban neighborhoods.

To some extent the federal government could correct this area differential by taking a more active role in the program. For example, the federal government could directly provide or finance maintenance costs for lower income households in declining areas or absorb the costs of declines in property values permitting higher annuity payments. These types of program adjustment would, of course, entail a more substantial federal government budget commitment.

Unless the federal government takes an active role in providing income assistance to lower income elderly households, or assumes some of the risks borne by financial institutions, the budget impact would be minimal. The increased current income flowing to elderly households would essentially stem from an intergenerational transfer of assets. The elderly household would increase current income by reducing the value of the estate remaining to heirs by the value of their homes. Since owner-occupied housing represents the major form of asset held by elderly households, the program could yield significant declines in intergenerational transfers of assets. Introduction of the housing annuity program would also generate competing claims for the supply of long-term loanable funds. If savings and loan associations, for example, participate in the program, it would entail a reduction in the supply of mortgage funds available to younger home purchasers and upward pressure on mortgage interest rates. The potential effect on the availability of mortgage funds may generate some concern on the part of the housing industry.

Whether the program will attract elderly homeowners in reasonable numbers is questionable. It depends crucially on the relative assessment of the needs for current income and the desire to preserve an estate for their heirs. The program can provide a major option to the elderly homeowner for correcting their current housing disequilibrium situation. Given the higher rates of homeownership, higher home values, and the potential for greater annuity payments given lower maintenance costs and expected price appreciation, such a program would probably be concentrated in the more stable urban neighborhoods in suburban and outlying central-city locations.

The two specific policy options discussed would be available to all elderly homeowners, but would have significantly greater potential impact in suburban areas. Recognition of differences in the concentration, characteristics, and needs of the elderly in central-city, suburban, and rural areas should become an integral component of developing new policy initiatives to serve the elderly. The appropriate size and location of senior citizen centers, the type and structure of transportation or outreach services, the mix of services provided in an area, and the allocation of service funds by area are other questions where location-specific data and a thorough understanding of the differences in the needs and characteristics of central-city suburban elderly can enhance the policy decision process.

REFERENCES

Chen, Y. P. Making a theory work: The case of homeownership by the aged. *Aging and Human Development*, 1970, *1*, 9–19.

Burkhardt, J. E., Annan, S. O., & Deitz, S. K. *The status and needs of Montgomery County's senior citizens.* Office of Community Development and Division of Elder Affairs, Area Agency on Aging, Office of Human Resources, Montgomery County, M.D., 1977.

Golant, S. M. Residential concentrations of the future elderly. *Gerontologist*, 1975, *15*, 16–23.

Gutowski, M. F. Integrating housing and social service activities for the elderly household. *Occasional papers in housing and community affairs* (Vol. 1). Washington DC: U.S. Department of Housing and Urban Development, 1978.

Gutowski, M., & Field, T. *The graying of suburbia.* Washington, D.C.: Urban Institute, 1979.

Guttentag, J. M. Creating new financial instruments for the aged. *The Bulletin for the Center for the Study of Financial Institutions*, New York University, Graduate School of Business Administration, 1975. (Bulletin 1975-5)

Michigan Department of Social Services. *Michigan annual title XX social services plan.* Lansing, Mich.: Office of Planning, Budget and Evaluation, Michigan Department of Social Services, 1976.

Niebanck, P. L., & Yessian, M. R. *Relocation in urban planning: From obstacle to opportunity.* Philadelphia: University of Pennsylvania Institute for Urban Studies, 1968.

Projector, D. S., & Weiss, G. S. *The survey of financial characteristics of consumers.* Washington, D.C.: Board of Governors, Federal Reserve System, 1966.

III
Neighborhoods and Service Systems for the Community Resident Aged

9
Costs of Home Services Compared to Institutionalization

THOMAS J. WALSH

It has long been recognized that the absence of community-based home-delivered services may result in the premature or unnecessary transfer of an older individual to an institution. The past decade has been characterized by a growth of the search for community alternatives to institutionalization. All too frequently, however, this search has proceeded in the absence of data regarding basic issues such as the availability of services, their costs, and the gains and losses associated with different types of services and sources of service. This chapter describes a study of a large metropolitan area designed to determine the level of impairment of older people in the community and in institutions, the types of services received, the source of the services, and the costs of the services received by people of differing impairment levels.

To assist in understanding the analysis, the chapter is divided into the following three sections: the methodology and results section showing how the analysis was done, the cost comparison section comparing the cost of maintaining a person in a home to that of maintaining a person in an institution, and the predictors of institutionalization section identifying the number of people who are as impaired as most older people now in institutions and who do not have a family and friend to support them.

METHODOLOGY AND RESULTS

The information in this chapter is based on extensive data developed in Cleveland, Ohio. The study gathered information on the characteristics

Much of the contents of this chapter was published in a report to the Congress from the General Accounting Office entitled *Home Health—The Need for a National Policy To Better Provide for the Elderly* (HRD-78-19). Washington, D.C.: U.S. General Accounting Office, 1977.

of a random sample of 1,609 people aged 65 years and over living in Cleveland.

A questionnaire developed by the Duke University Center for the Study of Aging and Human Development was used (the OARS Multidimensional Functional Assessment, Pfeiffer, 1975). It contains questions about an older person's status in the following areas of functioning: social, economic, mental, physical, and activities of daily living.

The older person's responses to questions during the interview were used to categorize his or her physical status as being excellent, good, mildly impaired, moderately impaired, severely impaired, or totally impaired. For example, the older person's physical health status was placed in the appropriate category on the following scale after considering responses to 22 detailed questions on physical health:

1. *In excellent physical health.* Engages in vigorous physical activity, either regularly or at least from time to time.
2. *In good physical health.* No significant illnesses or disabilities. Only routine medical care such as annual checkups required.
3. *Mildly physically impaired.* Has only minor illnesses and/or disabilities that might benefit from medical treatment or corrective measures.
4. *Moderately physically impaired.* Has one or more diseases or disabilities that are either painful or require substantial medical treatment.
5. *Severely physically impaired.* Has one or more illnesses or disabilities that are either severely painful or life-threatening or require extensive medical treatment.
6. *Totally physically impaired.* Confined to bed and requiring full-time medical assistance or nursing care to maintain vital bodily functions.

Each of the other four areas of functioning was similarly rated on the basis of varying numbers of questions.

Although separate ratings were made for each of the five areas of human functioning, the five were combined to form an overall impairment-level scale as follows:

Impairment Level	Description Based on Five Areas Included in Duke University OARS Questionnaire
Unimpaired	Excellent or good in all five areas of human functioning.

Slightly impaired	Excellent or good in four areas.
Mildly impaired	Mildly or moderately impaired in two areas or mildly or moderately impaired in one area and severely or completely impaired in another.
Moderately impaired	Mildly or moderately impaired in three areas and or mildly or moderately impaired in two areas and severely or completely impaired in one area.
Generally impaired	Mildly or moderately impaired in four areas.
Greatly impaired	Mildly or moderately impaired in three areas and severely or completely impaired in another.
Very greatly impaired	Mildly or moderately impaired in all five areas.
Extremely impaired	Mildly or moderately impaired in four areas and severely or completely impaired in the other or severely or completely impaired in two or more areas.

Impairment Level

Comparison of the data gathered in Cleveland with similar data gathered in Durham County, North Carolina showed the two samples to be similar in demographic characteristics and on scores in the five individual functional areas (Pfeiffer, 1975). Further, the status and distribution by impairment level of older persons in Cleveland and Durham were similar. About 21% were unimpaired, 21% slightly impaired, 18% mildly impaired, 17% moderately impaired, and 23% in the four most impaired categories. Other analyses showed that impairments were less frequent among younger people, whites, and those with higher incomes and more education. By contrast, among the institutionalized of Durham, 76% were extremely impaired, 11% greatly impaired, and 4% generally impaired, or 91% in the four most impaired categories.

Services and Their Costs

The questionnaire and service information was used to determine the services each person received, the source of each service, the average frequency of use of each service made by people at each of the eight impairment levels, and an average cost for each service, based on information obtained from 27 federal, state, local, and private agencies in Cleveland. These average costs appeared reasonable when compared to similar data from Chicago (compiled by the Mayor's Commission on Aging) and Durham.

To calculate service costs for each impairment level the four data elements were combined: cost or value of each service, average frequency of use of each service per month, percentage receiving each service from an agency, and percentage receiving each service from family or friends. The cost assigned to services provided by agencies and families and friends was calculated individually for people at each impairment level.

The agency cost was calculated in terms of an average monthly cost per individual. This process was repeated to determine the value of services provided by families and friends. In the absence of family and friends, any services received would have to be from an agency. Therefore, the same cost was assigned to family and friend services.

The two service costs (agency, family and friends) were added to determine the total cost or value of services provided for people at each impairment level (Table 9.1). At the most impaired levels, home-service costs increased rapidly and the proportion of care provided by families and friends also increased. Table 9.1 shows that the family and friend's portion was significantly higher than the agency's portion at all impairment levels and that the average proportion provided by family and friends increased from 59% for the unimpaired to almost 80% for the extremely impaired.

COST COMPARISON BETWEEN NONINSTITUTIONALIZED AND INSTITUTIONALIZED

The costs for the noninstitutionalized and the institutionalized groups were compared to determine at what impairment level the total cost to keep an older person at home (including the value of the service provided by family and friends) equals the cost to institutionalize the person.

Noninstitutionalized People

Several factors contribute to a person's ability to exist outside an institution. One is the level of impairment. People who are more impaired receive more services than people who are less impaired. Data not included here show that transportation, checking, and social and recreational services are received by the less impaired. At the more impaired levels, social and recreational services are relatively infrequent, while nursing care, personal care, and continuous supervision increase significantly as impairment increases. Eventually the most severely impaired people require almost constant care.

TABLE 9.1
Average Monthly Costs of Services Provided by Friends/Family
and by Agency for Different Impairment Levels

Impairment Level	Family/Friends	Agency	Total	Proportion Family/Friends
Unimpaired	$ 37	$ 26	$ 63	.59
Slightly impaired	63	47	110	.57
Mildly impaired	111	65	176	.63
Moderately impaired	181	78	259	.70
Generally impaired	204	100	304	.67
Greatly impaired	287	120	407	.71
Extremely impaired	673	172	845	.80

An important aspect of institutional care is that a person receives a package of services. Home care also requires a package of services and the care needed by the greatly or extremely impaired living at home is very similar to that needed by those in institutions. For example, an arthritic person may need physical therapy twice a week but may also need help in getting out of bed or preparing meals. As a person becomes more impaired, more services will be added to the package and the person's use of these services will increase.

Institutionalized People

Cost data for Ohio's medical nursing homes from January to February 1977, including intermediate care and skilled nursing facilities, showed that the average total cost for long-term institutionalization reimbursed under its Medicaid system was $597 per month per individual. However, offsets from Social Security, pensions, and other income from those individuals reduced the average cost to $458 per month per individual. Although these costs are based on Ohio data and will vary in other states, they were representative when compared to national averages.

Nursing-home costs include room and board, laundry, medical equipment and supplies, over-the-counter drugs, personal care, nursing care, supportive rehabilitative services, and social activities. Physicians' fees, prescription drugs, and other medical costs are not included in either the costs of institutionalization or home services because medical expenditures are generally related to particular physical conditions and should be similar for people with the same condition, whether they live in institutions or in their homes.

Break-Even Point

Figure 9.1 compares the cost of home services with institutional services. The horizontal line at $458 represents the net average cost of institutional care, assumed to be invariant with level of impairment. The cost data for services from family and friends and from agencies in Table 9.1 are plotted by impairment level. As shown, there is a point in the impairment scale when home-service costs, including the value of services provided by families and friends, equal institutional costs. Thereafter the cost of home services increases significantly over the cost to institutionalize. This point falls in the greatly impaired level.

About 10% of noninstitutionalized older people fall in the area above the break-even point. However, on the average, it would still cost the public more to institutionalize these people because agencies are spending less per person for home services than for institutional care. Families and friends provide over 50% of the services received at all impairment levels. At the greatly impaired level where the break-even point falls, families and friends are providing over $287 per month for services for every $120 being spent by agencies.

PREDICTORS OF INSTITUTIONALIZATION

Two major differences emerged when institutionalized and noninstitutionalized people were compared. One is level of impairment. Older people in institutions are much more impaired than those not in institutions. For example, as shown in Table 9.1, 87% of the institutionalized people in Durham were greatly or extremely impaired, while only 14% of the noninstitutionalized had the same impairment levels (Pfeiffer, 1975).

It is of interest to estimate the percentage of the total elderly population that is institutionalized for each impairment level separately, and to compare these percentages with the percentage distribution by impairment level of the total older population (i.e., community residents plus the institutionalized). Because the characteristics of the Cleveland and Durham populations were similar, they were combined. For the two geographical areas the greatest probability of

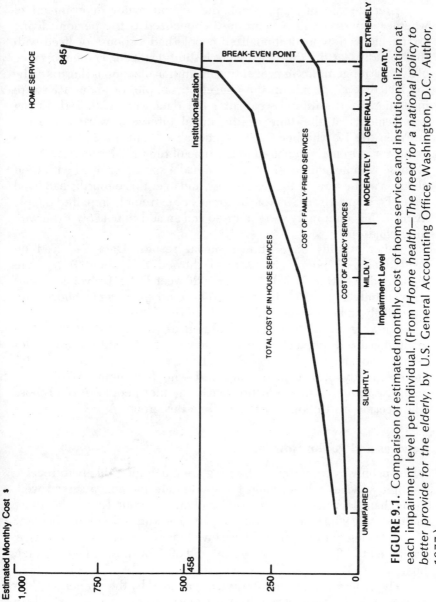

FIGURE 9.1. Comparison of estimated monthly cost of home services and institutionalization at each impairment level per individual. (From *Home health—The need for a national policy to better provide for the elderly*, by U.S. General Accounting Office, Washington, D.C., Author, 1977.)

131

institutionalization exists at the extremely impaired level, where 37% are in institutions.

After degree of impairment, the second major determinant of whether a person will become institutionalized is the person's living arrangement. Few institutionalized people had a spouse or lived with their children at the time they were institutionalized. The importance of living arrangements in preventing institutionalization is illustrated by the fact that 17 people in the Cleveland sample, or about 1%, were institutionalized within 1 year after our data were gathered. Living arrangements at the time of the initial interview were compared between the 17 who became institutionalized and the 217 who were greatly or extremely impaired at the time of the initial interview. None of those who became institutionalized had a spouse or lived with their children at the time of the first survey, and over three fourths had lived alone. By comparison, 29% of the greatly or extremely impaired people living in the community were married and an additional 25% lived with their children.

Other studies have shown similar results. Data gathered on institutionalized people in Durham showed that about 90% were unmarried (Pfeiffer, 1975). Further, a 20-year Duke University longitudinal study showed that those who have no spouses or children are more likely to be institutionalized (Palmore, 1970).

Knowing these two major differences, the status of the non-institutionalized population was examined to identify those older people who have a high probability of being institutionalized—the 31% of the greatly or extremely impaired who live alone. While they comprise about 5% of noninstitutionalized older people, 76% of those who became institutionalized were from this group.

Services and Public Housing

Older people living in public housing are much more likely to receive multiple services which could be appropriate to their assessed well-being than older people who own their homes or rent. Examining those in the sample who were generally impaired or worse, we found that 84% of those living in public housing received four or more types of service, compared to 53% of those who rent and 39% of those who own their homes.

The difference lies in the services provided by the agencies. Older people in public housing received as many services from their family or friends as those not in public housing. However, more than half (58%) of those in public housing received three or more services from an agency compared to only 5% of those not in public housing.

Multiple services were available primarily at public housing sites. However, about 9% of the sample, a projected 5,718 older people in Cleveland, were not living in public housing but could benefit from multiple services and were not receiving them. Conversely, many older people in public housing may not need multiple services—27% of our sample who lived in public housing, a projected 1,284 people, were unimpaired or only slightly impaired.

One way to make multiple services available to those who need them most would be to expand the eligibility criteria for public housing to give preference to older people who could benefit the most from multiple services. Currently, eligibility is based primarily on economic consideration. Also, a way could be developed to provide multiple services to older people who do not live in public housing.

Homeownership and Financial Help

Older people who own their homes were much less likely to be receiving financial services than those who rent. As an illustration, of those with less than $2,000 income, only 46% of the homeowners received financial services, compared to 87% of the renters. Also, of those with incomes between $2,000 and $4,000, only 12% of the homeowners received financial services, compared to 57% of the renters.

Homeowners were less likely to receive financial help from either their family and friends or from an agency. Of those with less than $2,000 income only 29% of the homeowners received financial services from their family and friends, compared to 51% of the renters. Of those with less than $2,000 income, only 20% of the homeowners received financial services from an agency, compared to 62% of the renters.

One possible explanation for this inequity is that many families and friends provide financial services to older people by encouraging the older people to move into their homes. Another could be that older homeowners are hesitant to accept financial services from agencies.

SUMMARY

About 60% of the elderly who are extremely impaired live outside of institutions. However, these people receive a wide array of in-home services such as personal care, meal preparation, nursing care, homemaker service, and continuous supervision. Other services are transportation, housing, and social and recreational. Because all of these services help to maintain people in their homes, they are called, for simplicity, "home services." These home services are provided in combination to help sustain health, activity, and independence. Both the combination and frequency of services varies depending on the level of impairment of the individual.

At all levels of impairment, the value of services provided by families and friends greatly exceeds that cost of services provided by public agencies at public expense. The total cost of these home services becomes greater than the cost of institutionalization for older people who are greatly or extremely impaired. About 17% of those aged 65 or over fall into these categories.

The relationships between people in Cleveland at different levels of impairment, the services they received, and how these services were delivered, were examined. The analysis showed that

- As expected, people who are more impaired receive more services than people who are less impaired.
- Public agencies are currently spending less per person for home services than is spent for institutional care regardless of the levels of impairment.
- 87% of older people institutionalized are greatly or extremely impaired compared to 14% of those at home.
- Care provided to the greatly or extremely impaired living at home is similar to institutional care.
- Family and friends provide over 50% of the services received by older persons at all impairment levels and over 70% of the services received by the greatly or extremely impaired.

REFERENCES

Palmore, E. (Ed.). *Normal aging*. Durham, N.C.: Duke University Press, 1970.
Pfeiffer, E. (Ed.). *Multidimensional functional assessment: The OARS methodology*. Durham, N.C.: Duke University Center for the Study of Aging and Human Development, 1975.

10

"Passing It On": The Senior Block Information Service of San Francisco

JULIO L. RUFFINI
HARRY F. TODD, JR.

Providers of services to the urban elderly typically work from a set of interrelated yet often tacit premises regarding the nature of their client population. These premises owe their origin to the gerontological literature and to impressions based on experience with certain segments of that population.

One such set of premises includes the following:

1. The urban elderly tend to have relatively few friends (fewer than they had when they were younger, and fewer than present-day younger populations).
2. The elderly belong to fewer voluntary organizations than others, and to fewer than they did when they were younger.
3. Life satisfaction for the urban elderly, as a result of these and other factors, tends to be low, but possibly would be improved if they could become more active in voluntary organizations and acquire more friends, particularly among age peers.

While the generality of these premises may be questioned, these deprivations are widespread enough to warrant a search for effective counteractants.

The research on the Senior Block Information Service was conducted as part of a study on the legal behavior of the elderly. That research was carried out in 1976–1978 and was supported by grant no. SOC76-11309 from the Law and Social Sciences Program of the National Science Foundation. The authors gratefully acknowledge the assistance of the Foundation in making this research possible. We further express our appreciation and gratitude to the staff and volunteers of the Senior Block Information Service and Geriatric Services of Community Mental Health District V of San Francisco, California.

The urban elderly are also seen as relatively unaware of available services and diffident about using those services. If the elderly became more conscious of being members of a category of people with shared interests and needs, by banding together they could learn about available services and lobby for increased services. On the basis of these premises, often inarticulated, gerontologists seek ways to help the elderly expand their social networks and activity. This chapter describes one such attempt in the Sunset and Richmond Districts of San Francisco, the Senior Block Information Service (SBIS), a unique and daring experiment in organization for the elderly.

THE SETTING

San Francisco is a city with a concentration of elderly higher than the national average. In 1970 the population of the city was 715,674. Of these, 101,676 (14.2%) were 65 years old or older. The Sunset District of the city, where the SBIS is most active, had an even higher concentration of elderly. Of a total population of 103,423 residing in this area, 17,029 (16.5%) were elderly. Three of the eleven census tracts within this district showed considerably higher (21%–23%) elderly populations, while an additional four ranged from 17% to 18% (Duffy, Attkisson, Ablon, & Harris, 1973).

The Sunset District lies in the west-central area of San Francisco. The Richmond District, smaller but similar, is to the north, separated from the Sunset District by Golden Gate Park. The Sunset District fronts the Pacific Ocean and extends about 40 city blocks inland, comprising approximately 500 square blocks in all. The area is relatively flat and its streets are laid out in a grid pattern. Dwellings are largely single-family units (70%), interspersed with multiple-dwelling units (30%) (Duffy et al., 1973). While the area is primarily residential, there are a number of major arteries running east-west through the district, which are thriving commercial complexes.

As of 1970 the modal family income for members of the general population of the Sunset was in the $10,000–$14,999 range. Of the employed males, 35% were professionals, 24% white-collar workers, and 44% blue-collar workers. For employed females, 23% were professionals, 60% white-collar workers, and 17% blue-collar workers. Ethnically the composition of the district has been undergoing radical change. In 1960 the nonwhite population comprised less than 2% of the district's total; in 1970 that figure had jumped to a little over 11%. Although no more recent figures are available, it is clear that this figure has increased sharply since that time with the influx of Chinese, Filipinos, Koreans, and other Asians. Persons with Spanish surnames were grouped with the white population in the census materials and comprised almost 19% of that population in 1970 (Shepard Associates, Inc., 1973).

Among the elderly population of the district, 89% also were white (including Spanish-American) in 1970. Thirteen percent were living below the poverty line, and 25% lived alone (Shepard Associates, Inc., 1973). While little else is known about the demographic characteristics of the elderly in the area, the district still displays a greater variation in living arrangements, ethnicity, income, and educational levels than any other area of San Francisco having as high a concentration of elderly residents. The Sunset District, indeed, is increasingly becoming one of the most heterogeneous districts in the city, one in which a wide range of ethnic and socioeconomic types are to be found.

The district contains a number of service organizations and facilities specifically geared to the elderly. These include at least seven church-sponsored senior centers, five publicly sponsored recreational senior centers, and other senior activity centers serving food, providing friendly visitors, day care, medical services, or legal advice.

ORGANIZATIONAL STRUCTURE OF GERIATRIC SERVICES

This elderly population is also served by Senior Services of the Council of Churches, of which the SBIS is a part. The Council of Churches has the contract to provide geriatric service to Community Mental Health District V, in which the Sunset and Richmond Districts are located. The head of geriatric services for District V is also in charge of the city-wide Senior Services Program of the Council of Churches. Most of these programs are housed together in a building in the Sunset District, while the SBIS is housed separately.

The programs of Senior Services include Retired Senior Volunteer Program (RSVP), SBIS, Telephone Reassurance, Senior Aides, and a number of senior activity centers. Council of Churches geriatric programs for District V consist of the Home Evaluation Unit (social workers and nurses who are backed up by psychiatrists and intervene in crisis situations), the Geriatric Day Treatment Center for elderly with psychiatric problems, and the Residential Care Home Program (staff consisting of social workers and recreation aides, which provides visits to elderly in the over 100 residential care homes in District V.

The elderly of the Sunset and Richmond Districts, then, are served by a dedicated group of professionals who accomplish much with limited funds. This chapter describes one of the key elements of this geriatric program—the Senior Block Information Service.

HISTORY OF THE SENIOR BLOCK INFORMATION SERVICE

The SBIS began in the fall of 1973. Senior Services of the Council of Churches undertook an outreach effort to contact elderly in the Sunset and Richmond Districts whom the staff considered to be isolated and hence uninformed of the available services for the elderly. This effort was carried out primarily by volunteer college students as part of their field placements.

The volunteers went door-to-door to locate elderly, to identify their needs, and to inform them of available resources and services. This was a difficult task as few elderly were willing to allow these volunteers into their homes. The students also distributed flyers that outlined a number of services. The flyers were distributed on the streets and placed under the doors of homes of the elderly who had been located in the initial outreach effort.

These flyers also contained requests for elderly volunteers, who were asked to become "senior block chairpersons" to canvass the elderly on their blocks and distribute a newsletter—at this time an expanded version of the flyer—on a monthly basis. This stage represented the beginning point of the formalization of the block outreach program.

The goal was to form or build upon block information networks. Since it was difficult for the staff volunteers to attain access to the elderly, the goal was to have the elderly themselves serve as volunteers. They would know the other elderly people on their blocks or could obtain access to them. They could then inform people of available services and attempt to help them with their problems. The primary role that these volunteers were to play was as middlemen mediating among the community, the staff, and service providers.

The initial appeal resulted in a total of about 30 elderly volunteers. Since then the ranks of volunteers have grown steadily to over 300. The monthly newsletter has also grown to 8 to 10 pages, and SBIS has a regular staff, funded jointly by the Council of Churches and the San Francisco Commission on the Aging (the area agency on aging).

SBIS TODAY

The goals of the program are (1) to provide information and referral for elderly residents of the districts through publication and distribution of a monthly newsletter and (2) utilizing the services of senior volunteers, to encourage increased interaction among the aged by developing block-based social networks. These two goals are being met in part by a third goal: encouraging the elderly to help each other. This is done through recruitment of senior volunteers (block chairpersons), whose duty it is to canvass the particular blocks that they volunteer to service (usually the one on which they reside and/or adjacent blocks); to compile a list of all persons (names, addresses, and telephone numbers) aged 60 and above on these blocks; and to assume responsibility for the distribution of the monthly newsletter to each of these individuals. While distributing the newsletters, the senior volunteers may engage in conversations with each elderly person on the block, thus directly providing information and referrals to help in problem solving. Problems that the volunteers are unable to handle themselves are referred to the program's staff.

The regular staff of SBIS has changed from time to time in composition and number. Presently there is a full-time director (whose college degree is in health education); a full-time secretary (whose degree is also in health education) with wide-ranging responsibilities; two part-time outreach workers; three part-time outreach workers funded by VISTA; and several part-time college students fulfilling their social work field placement obligations through their work with SBIS.

The staff is hard-working and conscientious, working diligently to obtain information of value to the elderly; compiling this information for inclusion in the monthly newsletter; referring those elderly who phone the office with various problems to the appropriate agencies; distributing the newsletter to the senior volunteers; taking training in such matters as tax preparation so that they can assist the elderly with these problems; and sponsoring numerous activities of interest to the elderly.

In order to be effective in providing useful information to the elderly population of the Sunset and Richmond Districts, the staff must diligently ferret out such information themselves from a wide variety of sources. In the process, SBIS has built up a network of contacts and resources and compiled a continually growing information and referral list. The staff is not content, however, with knowing about available resources; it actively solicits and recruits new services and contributors. The staff serves as a mediator, bringing together potential resources and the elderly. SBIS acts as a catalyst by suggesting to a variety of agencies that they should offer services to the elderly and inviting the elderly to utilize these newly available services. Much of the Staff's time, then, is devoted to maintaining and enlarging ties with the wider community of potential service providers.

The SBIS staff selects material from the total accumulated information it obtains for its monthly newsletter, which is distributed by over 300 elderly volunteers to approximately 6,000 sites. The newsletter contains information on senior services, social and recreational events, educational opportunities, tax assistance, social security benefits, health care, legal problems, and consumer protection.

The newsletter is written and edited by SBIS staff and printed by the Commission on the Aging. SBIS staff and elderly volunteers assemble and staple the pages. The newsletters are then gathered into bundles and delivered by staff and volunteers to the approximately 300 block chairpersons. Each bundle has a small slip of paper with the name, address, and phone number of each volunteer and the number of newsletters he or she delivers. Some volunteers are responsible for as few as 5 newsletters while others have 20 to 40. One very active volunteer distributes over 100 newsletters each month.

The number of newsletters that the Commission on the Aging can duplicate is limited. SBIS staff feels that they could (with their present staff) greatly expand the number of recipients and volunteers if they could afford to print more newsletters. While some batches of newsletters are delivered to public libraries, churches, and nutrition sites, the SBIS staff has generally preferred to distribute the newsletters largely through elderly volunteers, and thus to use the newsletter as a mechanism for increased interaction on the part of the elderly volunteers and the people to whom the newsletters are delivered.

The hope of the staff is that the volunteers will talk informally with people when they deliver the newsletter. In this way old friendships or acquaintances may be enhanced, or new friendships created. As we have noted above, this is not always an easy matter. Nevertheless, this goal is often achieved. As one volunteer stated:

> I've taken them [elderly on her block] to meetings. Sometimes there are the health meetings, and [meetings on] hearing and people that are deaf, and the other, the feet and various things. So I tell them, well, you get out there to that meeting. And you will hear what you want to hear and you will be taken care of. And it's all for free. So they get there.

Other volunteers have stated that their relations with neighbors have become closer since they began distributing the newsletters. While SBIS has achieved remarkable success in this area, this ideal model is not always easy to achieve, as the following excerpt from one of our interviews indicates:

Q.   And what do you do when you distribute the newsletters each month?
A.   Well, each month I just drop them in the mail box, but probably once a year I canvass to see if there are changes in the neighborhood. Many houses are sold and the elderly move out.
A.   Do you talk to the people getting them, or do you just put them in the mail box?
A.   That's right, just put them in.
Q.   Do you know most of the elderly?
A.   No, I don't know them; I really only know two.
Q.   And did you know those two before you started distributing the newsletters?
A.   One.
Q.   You knew just one. Do you think your relationship with any of the people that you deliver the newsletter to on that block has changed?
A.   Not really, because they aren't very, they really aren't very open when you drop by. They're very reluctant to open their doors.
Q.   Even for you?
A.   Yes, sure.

The opposite problem may occur:

Q.   Do you think your relationship with the elderly on your block has changed since you've been delivering the newsletter?
A.   Well, I have talked about it a little bit more. They talk about it, and I think a little bit, yes. They say, "Oh, you're the one that brings me those papers," or something like that. And sometimes they are lonesome and I try to get it in the box without them seeing me.

Another volunteer expressed a widespread attitude: "So I thought maybe she missed it [the newsletter]. So I gave her a note saying that there is a party, but I haven't seen her at the party. I don't like to intrude."

The recipients of the newsletter also tell the volunteers of problems they are having and the volunteers may make referrals or suggestions, or refer them to the SBIS staff. The staff does, in fact, receive many phone inquiries from volunteers and newsletter recipients. The staff either provides the required information or assistance or refers the caller to the appropriate agency. As one volunteer expressed it:

So I can help. Anything that just comes up, if I meet somebody who I think is in need of something and doesn't know where to go for help, then I would call them [SBIS] and ask them whatever I need....I'm always keeping in touch with the Senior Block almost, I would say, twice a week or so I would call. If there is anything... that somebody is worried about, or whether there is an agency that we could refer them to, or whatever, then I would call and discuss it with them.

The staff also spends considerable time in outreach efforts—to inform people of the existence of SBIS and to recruit volunteers. Outreach workers go door-to-door to let people know about the newsletter and to sign up volunteers. In the process, the outreach workers also canvass blocks to locate the elderly, providing direct services on these vists. Recently, for example, an SBIS outreach worker located a non-English speaking woman who was quite isolated and seldom left her home. The outreach worker arranged for the woman to participate in a senior day center where she has increased her social activities. SBIS also recruits volunteers through appeals in the newsletter, at senior activity centers, by personal referral, and on occasions when people gather for immunizations, blood pressure screenings, or other health services.

SBIS attempts to accomplish its goals of informing and organizing the elderly through a range of activities. Monthly meetings at a church in the Sunset District are designed to provide information for SBIS volunteers, but they are advertised and open to all. Refreshments are served and guest speakers give talks on a wide range of subjects of concern to the elderly: colo-rectal cancer screening, senior citizens' property tax and renters' assistance, heart disease, legal problems, cataracts and glaucoma, transportation, social security regulations and procedures, and many other topics. From time to time, police officers give talks on crime and crime prevention.

In addition to these regular monthly meetings, SBIS hosts a number of social and recreational activities. Recently SBIS sponsored a rummage sale. As the newsletter expressed it: "The idea of the sale isn't just to make a few dollars for our supplies, but more importantly, to encourage more community participation and interaction in our programs."

Each year SBIS sponsors a Christmas party that is very well attended and popular. Refreshments are served and entertainment is provided by elderly and nonelderly volunteers. Luncheons for SBIS volunteers are also held from time to time. Picnics at an ocean beach, complete with food and entertainment, were held during the summer of 1977.

On several occasions SBIS has invited the Complaint-Mobile of the San Francisco District Attorney's Office to visit SBIS functions. The

Complaint-Mobile is a part of the Consumer Fraud Unit and is designed to inform citizens of their rights and to mediate disputes. At one meeting, however, the speaker spent most of her time listening to the complaints of the elderly audience and declaring that her office could not handle those problems. The reaction of many in the audience was that this claim of lack of responsibility was the order of the day and typical of bureaucrats.

Much more satisfying to the elderly are the annual health fairs sponsored by SBIS. Hundreds of elderly come to these well-organized and coordinated displays of services offered by a wide array of health agencies. Booths and tables are set up for the representatives from community health, social service, educational, and recreational agencies who provide screening (e.g., hearing, vision, hypertension, podiatry, dental) and information. Entertainment and refreshments are also provided. At the recent health fair, 41 community agencies were represented.

The SBIS staff has recently attempted to encourage social networks and increased interaction through sponsorship of block parties in which the elderly residents of a block take turns hosting regular tea parties. In the process, in addition to serving social functions, the participants provide each other aid and support. Even though it is too early to evaluate the success of this project, it does appear to be an innovative approach to creation of age peer identification and solidarity.

PROPOSED EXPANSION OF THE PROGRAM

Because of the success of this program in the Sunset and Richmond Districts of the city, plans are presently being formulated for its expansion into other areas of San Francisco—particularly to the areas populated primarily by minority and ethnic groups (e.g., blacks, Latinos, and Asian-Americans). These groups have been traditionally underserved, and present a new challenge to the program in terms of the wide range of unique problems (as well as more generic problems that they share with the larger elderly population) that could be addressed by an organizational effort of this kind. The staff recognizes, however, that the model currently operating so successfully in the Sunset and Richmond Districts of the city—areas that comprise a primarily middle-class white population—cannot be lifted as a unit and planted in another area of the city for a population with different needs, problems, and perceptions, as well as different patterns of housing.

It is believed, however, that the general model can be adapted successfully for other areas of San Francisco, and that, with some structural and organizational changes, it can be just as successful in these other areas as it has proved to be in the Sunset and Richmond Districts in meeting the needs of specific population groups. The staff will continue its present function of obtaining information to disseminate to all participating in the program, but the organizational efforts will have to be adapted to particular environmental and community characteristics. For example, in neighborhoods characterized by high-density concentrations of elderly in hotels, the units of organization will be the hotels themselves or hotel floors, rather than blocks. The churches, especially in the black community, are expected to play an important role in the organizational efforts and in the recruitment of senior volunteers. The SBIS then may ultimately become a citywide effort, and will maintain a more or less unified character (with a centralized staff) in terms of information acquisition and dissemination; recruitment and community-building functions will vary according to the population served and will have to be adapted to local conditions and needs.

While the exact combination of factors that work will have to be decided on an individual basis, it would seem that the model created by SBIS would have a strong chance of success in a similar urban environment—one characterized by a large percentage of physically mobile elderly homeowners and apartment dwellers dispersed in an age-heterogeneous neighborhood.

The SBIS has proven to be a success in achieving its goal of informing the elderly. The monthly newsletter reaches 10,000 people, and monthly meetings and other functions bring in new people as volunteers. SBIS has succeeded in involving large numbers of the elderly as volunteers. It is too soon to know to what extent SBIS has succeeded in its goal of increasing social interaction on the blocks and district-wide.

Nevertheless, SBIS has at least created the conditions that should aid in fostering community building. It has accomplished a great deal in a short time and with a small staff. It has shown how much can be accomplished with very limited funds. While many aspects of the program would have to be modified to suit other conditions and settings, SBIS may prove to be an innovative model and inspiration for many other communities. Similar projects are underway in Oakland and other communities. While efforts of this sort are painfully slow in starting, once they are established, momentum may create significant results. An example is provided by an SBIS volunteer:

Q.   Do the people on your block ever ask you for information or help with their problems or for referrals?

A. It all depends. Now, as I say, about that rent thing [SBIS staff assisted elderly renters in obtaining refund money from the state]. I told one lady about it. I said, "For heaven's sake, all you have to do, you know, is get in touch with the state building, collect your rent receipts and all that." And I said, "You can't be hurt, you know, for trying. All they can say is no. But this thing [SBIS Newsletter] says so right here. You can read it for yourself. And it gives you the phone number to call and everything." And she said, "Would you help me?" and I said, "Well, I'll do anything you want me to do." So I helped her and then she told somebody else and you know how it is, go on and on, and then they're all wanting the newsletters. They all wanted to know. And I told her, "This is one way you can help them. You can do your thing. You know, what I did for you. You pass it on."

REFERENCES

Duffy, J., Attkisson, C., Ablon, J., & Harris, M. *Health District V of San Francisco: A comparative study of 1960 and 1970 Census data. Program Information Series*, Vol. 4, No. 4. San Francisco: Community Mental Health Training Program and Langley Porter Neuropsychiatric Institute (USCF) and District V Mental Health Center (SF), 1973.

Shepard Associates, Inc. *A comprehensive and coordinative plan for aging problems in San Francisco.* Prepared for the San Francisco Area Planning Agency for Aging, 1973.

11
Neighborhood Injustices: Aging in a Changing Urban Environment

HARRY F. TODD, JR.
JULIO L. RUFFINI

In recent years there has been increasing concern among geron-tologists and legal scholars with the legal needs and problems of older Americans. The literature on various aspects of this subject is growing rapidly (see, for example, the overview discussions of Antonucci, 1973; Bernstein, 1969; Cohen, 1967, 1974; Heyman, 1974; U.S. Senate, 1970, 1971). These scholars and researchers (many of whom have received legal training themselves), however, have tended to adopt an overly formal, legalistic definition of law—a definition that views law as "the law," framed in terms of statutes, ordinances, regulations, and court decisions. This definition contrasts with a broader, more encompassing perspective—evident particularly in anthropological approaches to the study of law—that views the law and the formal legal system as but one of many mechanisms that individuals have available for their use in attempting to resolve interpersonal conflicts, disputes, and grievances. Courts and lawyers, in this perspective, are but one aspect of a range of dispute-managing mechanisms available to individuals seeking relief, and are complemented by those available—and used—in the informal or unofficial system.

Thus by focusing too strongly on the relationships between the elderly and the law or formal legal institutions (courts, the bar,

The research on which this paper is based was carried out in 1976–1978 in San Francisco, California and was supported by grant no. SOC76-11309 from the Law and Social Sciences Program of the National Science Foundation. The authors gratefully acknowl-edge the assistance of the Foundation in making this research possible. We further express our appreciation to the staff of Geriatric Services of Community Mental Health District V of San Francisco; the faculty and students in the Gerontological Pro-Seminar and Medical Anthropology Program at the University of California, San Francisco; and to Ms. Gail Venti, for their thoughtful comments on earlier drafts of this paper.

legislative bodies, and governmental and quasi-public bureaucracies), those concerned with the legal problems of the elderly have neglected the whole of the informal legal arena. This focus, in turn, has led to a concentration of efforts in a relatively small number and limited range of specific problem areas—particularly criminal victimization and fraud (Anonymous, 1969; Brostoff, Brown, & Butler, 1972; Clemente & Kleinman, 1976; Denenberg, 1972; Forston & Kitchens, 1974; Gubrium, 1974; Sundeen & Mathieu, 1976; Rifai, 1976; U.S. Senate, 1965); guardianships, conservatorships, involuntary commitments, or other protective services for the elderly (Bennett, 1965; Burr, 1971; Fisher & Solomon, 1974; Hall & Mathiasen, 1973; Lehmann, 1962; Regan, 1972); and advocacy and policy questions centering around the delivery of legal services to the elderly (Collins, Flanagan, & Donnelly, 1972; Coppelman & Hiestand, 1972; Golick, Jennings, Kraus, & Weiss, 1971; Marlin & Brown, 1972; Nathanson, 1974; Terris, 1972; U.S. Senate, 1976). Since law impinges upon practically every other aspect of social life, one can further find in the literature articles on virtually every substantive area of the lives of the elderly—employment and job discrimination (Antonucci, 1973); retirement and income maintenance (Bernstein, 1969); health and medical care (Silver 1970); and housing (Wallin, 1972).

These scholars have concomitantly failed, however, to deal with a number of everyday disputes and grievances that exist at the neighborhood and community levels—the problems that we call "neighborhood injustices." For a number of reasons, many of these everyday disputes are not brought to the attention of or successfully processed within the institutions of the official legal system; the elderly are either required to seek resolution elsewhere, or to reconcile themselves to a lack of satisfaction.

Given that law—in its most general sense—is an attempt to establish a set of mutual rights and obligations, and given that the emerging field of legal gerontology is strongly geared to policy, planning, and advocacy objectives seeking to insure that these rights and obligations are available and enforced, serious implications arise when the whole area of neighborhood injustices is excluded from consideration.

Our purpose in this chapter, therefore, is to explore the range of interpersonal disputes and grievances within neighborhoods, on blocks, or in immediate living environments, which, according to our findings, appear to be a prime concern of many urban elderly. Here, we argue, the official legal system is ill-equipped to deal with a wide variety of neighborhood injustices that the aged face in this urban setting, and that the police, the bar, and legal and social service providers are, by and large, unaware of or are nonresponsive to these neighborhood grievances, or are ineffectual when they become involved in attempts to alleviate or resolve them. Further, we argue that this nonresponsiveness of the formal system results in a feeling of powerlessness and frustration on the part of the elderly in their own neighborhoods.

SETTING

The area in which this study was carried out was described in Chapter 10 of this volume. The data presented there that describe the research setting provide a picture of the district as a solid, middle-class community. This picture, however, is gradually changing, for the community is undergoing transition; and to many informants, it is changing for the worse.

Our elderly informants are unanimous in considering the district a good place to live. They regard it as convenient and peaceful, and relatively safe when compared with other neighborhoods. Most of them have lived there for the major portion of their adult lives (i.e., they are original homeowners who have raised their families in the district).

They are also unanimous, however, in feeling that the district has changed, and that it has, to some extent, deteriorated. This perceived deterioration is partially physical, for example, due to cutbacks in city finances, streets are not kept in as good condition or cleaned as often as informants feel they should be. The houses are older now, and some are not as well kept up as they were 20 years ago.

The elderly perceive their environment as deteriorating socially and culturally as well; however, these perceptions are largely related to the recent influx of new people whose behavior they often find offensive. To them, the district has changed from a quiet, relatively homogeneous area populated by families of similar backgrounds and values who have lived together for over a generation to a heterogeneous environment, populated by a wide range of groups and individuals, many of whom are alien to them. In this new setting, the elderly often feel ill-at-ease, uncomfortable, and unwanted. The behavior of those with whom they are forced into everyday contact is now less familiar, more unpredictable, and even hostile. Vandalism of both public and private property, and safety within the neighborhoods—traditionally low-crime areas—have now, for the first time, become issues for many informants.

These perceptions of neighborhood change find support in the demographic shifts that occurred within the district between 1960 and 1970, and that have continued, perhaps at an even more accelerated rate. In that period only the population in the 15–24 age group has paralleled the growth of the aged population, their numbers increasing from 11% in 1960 to 15.5% in 1970. In addition, the single (over 14-year-old) population of the district has increased since 1960, rising from 20.6% to the 1970 figure of 25.1%, while at the same time the married population has decreased from 66.4% to 59.2%. A report by a neighborhood association (Eichenberg, 1974) on the state of the district documents both these demographic and social transitions, and comes to several disturbing conclusions:

1. Families with children—the initial residents of the area—are rapidly disappearing.

2. The number of single-family homes decreased from 74.4% in 1960 to the 1970-level of 64.9%—a rate of decrease that was nearly five times the city average.

3. In the same period, there was a 60% increase in the number of housing units in apartments—despite the fact that the community lost 2% of its population.

These factors led the compiler of the report to conclude that

> The cumulative effect of these trends indicates to us that the community is in a period of transition. Families are growing up and moving out of the area. Home ownership is dropping, rentals are increasing, and the character of the neighborhoods is changing from single-family homes to box-like apartments. Key districts within our community are being transformed from stable, low-density, family-oriented neighborhoods into impersonal, transient, high-density areas. (Eichenberg, 1974, p. 2)

METHODOLOGY

The data reported here are exploratory and preliminary in nature; they result from a number of interrelated pilot, presurvey efforts aimed at providing an overview of the population, its legal problems, and its responses to these problems (i.e., a starting point for an ethnography of law for this elderly population).

The methods utilized in collecting these data ranged across a broad spectrum of traditional anthropological techniques, including those of participant-observation, and informal open-ended interviewing in a wide range of settings. In the course of the research, we questioned or talked informally with more than 150 informants about their legal problems. Settings included public gatherings, such as the monthly meetings of the Senior Block Information Service (SBIS) and the local chapter of the American Association of Retired Persons, senior picnics and hobby shows, or senior health fairs. In addition, structured, in-depth interviews, each lasting between 3 and 6 hours in length, were carried out with 25 key informants. Interviews were also conducted with a number of service providers in the district—in legal service programs, as well as in other geriatric programs serving the elderly of this area.

It must be noted, however, that the data collected from all of these sources are preliminary and provisional. They are suggestive only, and because of the nature of the sample and the exploratory nature of the initial phase of this research effort, they are insufficient for making any generalizations as to the plight of the elderly in this area. In spite of these limiting factors, however, we feel that the data reported on in this chapter are so striking and consistent, and shed so much light on an important area, that attention must be drawn to them. Further, despite their provisional nature, these data offer a rich, qualitative texture and depth that complements the traditional quantitative approaches and perspectives generally found in the gerontological literature, and provide a wealth of suggestions, hypotheses, and new ideas that can and should be tested utilizing these quantitative techniques.

THE CASE OF THE RECALCITRANT NEIGHBORS

The following case report derives from a 6-hour interview with a 67-year-old retiree who lives alone in her home in the study area. When she bought her home some 25 years ago, Mrs. Wilson (a pseudonym) selected it particularly because it was detached from her neighbors' homes. She had lived in an apartment for a number of years before that, and wanted a place that was relatively quiet. In 1971 a family consisting of a widowed mother with four teenage sons moved in next door. It was at this point that Mrs. Wilson's problems began.

"My main problem," she stated, "is noise: noise from the neighbors—neighbors with four teenage boys." Almost from the day they arrived, Mrs. Wilson reported, she was barraged with loud music at all hours of the day and night, with noise from drums, from motorcycles, and from parties that often spilled outdoors onto the sidewalks, with public drinking and boisterous behavior.

In seeking relief, Mrs. Wilson approached the boys' mother on several occasions; each time, however, she was unsuccessful, and the problem continued. The mother was at first indifferent to the requests for quiet, then became hostile.

As the boys grew older, Mrs. Wilson's concerns grew larger, for now she began to be faced not only with noise problems, but also with a much wider range of grievances against her neighbors. She complained of chicken bones and beer bottles being dumped in her garden; of harassment by the neighbor's children and by the mother and her newly acquired boyfriend; of the continuing beer parties on the sidewalks; of the boys and their friends breaking her windows, and urinating against and writing obscene graffiti on her fence; of cars and unknown, suspicious people continually coming and going at all hours of the day and night, of horns blowing, of car motors left running while their drivers ran into the house next door for 5 or 10 minutes; of the neighbors' boys and their visitors (including a live-in girlfriend) taking all the parking spaces in front of her house, and of parking in her driveway, of double parking, of parking across the sidewalk and in front of fire hydrants; of the boys' abandoning broken-down cars on the street for long periods of time; of loud motorcycles racing up and down the street; of the mother's boyfriend, a truck driver, who would park his rig in front of her house, come out "in his pajamas" at 5:00 A.M. to start the truck up, return to the house, and let the motor run for half an hour before finally coming back to drive it off.

After her initial attempts at direct negotiation failed, Mrs. Wilson drafted a letter to the mother of the household, stating that everyone has a right not to be bothered by other people's noise and activities. This letter was circulated among the other neighbors, some of whose signatures were collected to protest the neighborhood disruptions the family was causing. The letter was sent by registered mail to the mother—again without effect.

Mrs. Wilson then turned to the police, who came out on a number of occasions. "I tried to do it in a nice way," she said, "but they just wouldn't stop the noise. All they understand is force. They think that being nice is the same thing as being weak." Police intervention typically would stop the noise problem for a day or two at a time, but gradually the noise level would increase again. Mrs. Wilson began to realize that any help the police could—or would—give was at best temporary, and began to look elsewhere for additional help.

She joined a consumer action group, and went regularly to noise pollution meetings. She went to police-community relations meetings to voice her complaint. She sought help from both the District Attorney's and City Attorney's offices, from the Environmental Health Service, from a San Francisco supervisor's office, from a neighborhood improvement club, from the Assistant Director of Public Health in the district, and from a wide range of other community service agencies. She tried moving her bedroom to another part of her house, and installed special noise barriers. She tried to arrange a meeting between the offending neighbors and a "professional—a legal counselor or psychologist" through the District Attorney's office; she contacted a senior service information and referral program in the district, and talked with the principal of the nearby school—all to no avail. None of these approximately 20 different resources that she had contacted in the past 6 or 7 years was able to help her in gaining the relief she sought.

In a recent effort to solve her problems with her neighbors, Mrs. Wilson contacted a senior legal service organization. She arranged an appointment with a senior legal assistance attorney, and on arrival at the office, she was introduced to the attorney. Mrs. Wilson described their meeting as follows:

> I don't even remember her name, and she kind of jumped on me. In her way, she wanted to be helpful. She was also very sympathetic, but, you know, I was still in the stage where I couldn't be functional and alert enough in my usual way [because of a recent recurrence of the noise problem]. I was so flustered. All she wanted to do was write this letter and specify all the different problems. She just didn't give me the time. They don't have time enough to really sit down with you. And, at last, she ended up by saying, "Well, give me this [journal that Mrs. Wilson had been keeping of all disturbing activities connected with the offending neighbors], and I'll glance it over." I didn't want to do that, so I told her a few things that still happened. It is important to know what is happening now. At last I got through [to her that] since I called the police last week two days in a row, it hasn't improved. The hi-fi I've hardly heard any more. The only thing that still goes on, but has increased already a bit, is the cars coming and going. Well, so I said that cars are still coming and going, and she caught on right away. She says, "Aha, drugs." And this is my feeling too. But, if I think back, right now, this last week, I would say that things [i.e., the problems that had arisen with the neighbors] are always changing.

The legal service attorney suggested the possibility of bringing suit, to which Mrs. Wilson responded:

> I don't want to bring it to court, this noise thing; that was her set-up, the attorney's set-up, which is the logical thing. But I don't want to go through all of this. When you're younger, you can manage things. See, my problem is actually not a problem of the elderly. My problem—noise—is a problem of everybody. The only thing where the older people are coming in is it's harder to deal with it. This problem is ruining my life. I get so fed up with dealing with all these people. But, you see, I've got to go very careful about that, because I don't want to get this whole gang on my neck.

The attorney agreed to draft a letter that would be sent to the neighbor, but Mrs. Wilson insisted that the letter first be sent to her for approval before it was sent to the neighbor since it was to include an implicit threat of suit. Although at the time of the interview, Mrs. Wilson had received the draft letter, she was leaning strongly against sending it on to the neighbor because of her fear of reprisal.

RANGE OF PROBLEMS

This case report was selected because it provides a striking example of the plight of one elderly individual living in this age-heterogeneous environment. While a greater number of problems with neighbors were reported in this case than were reported by other informants, it is noteworthy that all informants interviewed in this pilot effort reported problems similar to those of Mrs. Wilson. Further, while many of the problems reported by our informants are undoubtedly not unique to the elderly, the impact of these problems, as Mrs. Wilson concluded, may assume greater importance or significance to this population. We note, further, that informants reported many more and a wider array of legal problems than the ones dealt with in this chapter. While many informants complained of the lack of government responsiveness (or the outright rudeness of bureaucrats with whom they were forced to deal), high taxes (homes purchased by informants for $4,000 in the 1930s and 1940s now carry tax assessments almost equaling the original purchase prices), consumer problems (e.g., home repairs that were done badly or work left unfinished, or purchase of defective merchandise), and many other problems that lie directly within the legal arena, we have chosen to exclude these additional problem areas from consideration here. Instead, we focus in this chapter on interpersonal disputes within the immediate living environments of our informants and with which informants must cope in carrying on the everyday business of living. This range of neighborhood injustices and the impact of these problems on the elderly in the study area are our primary concerns in this section.

In talking with our informants, we found that their problems were associated with three different yet interrelated aspects of their everyday living environment: (1) those associated with a deteriorating and increasingly unsafe and unsightly physical environment; (2) those associated with an increasingly hostile social environment; and (3) those associated with a changing and confusing cultural environment. In practice, most situations partake of elements in each category, although to varying degrees.

Physical Environment

The physical environment itself presents direct threats to the safety of the elderly individuals in their neighborhood. Many of these problems exist in the physical environment itself, and present particularly salient problems for the frail elderly. The physical environment, however, is also becoming increasingly dangerous for the nonfrail. Included here are problems encountered in boarding and riding public buses and streetcars, on which most of our informants depend.

Informants also complained about dogs running wild, off leashes, and of children rushing by them on foot, bicycles, or skateboards, coming dangerously close and putting them in fear of being knocked down. One informant commented, "There are many seniors living out here and there are so many kids with their bikes on the sidewalks and also their skateboards, and they have problems there. That is dangerous for other people and the kids, too. If you don't watch out, these kids come around the corner without looking."

Reckless driving and speeding through the neighborhood and failure to observe the rights of pedestrians in crosswalks were also cited frequently. "I don't see why they let all these kids drive cars," one informant complained. "I think in San Francisco they don't need all these cars. Especially when these kids 16 and 18 are going tearing around in cars up our street. It's just terrible. You take your life in your hands." Another commented, "I think that we have young people who drive cars, that are going too fast; they are going over the speed limit. They don't stop for people who need to cross the street, even though we have many, many stop [signs]."

Reckless and fast driving is a particularly important problem in congested shopping areas where visibility is impaired for both the elderly themselves and the drivers. These driving problems present clear and present dangers to the elderly, both to those on foot and to those who are able to drive.

Not all complaints voiced by informants with respect to the physical environment centered around the question of safety. Many of these problems dealt with the general issue of "visual pollution," and included complaints against neighbors who parked cars in front of informants' houses, leaving unsightly oil spills which many informants felt obliged to clean up themselves. Informants in situations such as these generally seem to prefer to adopt a "wait and see" attitude, opting to do nothing rather than to chance alienating a neighbor—even an offending neighbor. In some instances, however, they tire of waiting, and take action. One informant reported that she finally decided that she had to call the fire department to report the people who lived immediately behind her. "I had to call the fire department because it was a filthy back yard, all kinds of debris out there, dried trees and whatnot, and it was a fire hazard for everybody; and everybody in the neighborhood grumbled but nobody did anything, so I finally did it. Well, boy, we had all kinds of hell popping around there because of us; they got so furious . . . . Well, I didn't care. I figured I'd get that back yard cleaned up."

Litter and other debris thrown from passing cars or dropped by negligent passersby onto the streets and sidewalks was also seen to pose a visual pollution and health problem. Informants complained that "there is garbage that's dumped on the corners by people who don't or won't put it in the garbage cans, or pay for it [i.e., to have it picked up]. Every other corner is loaded with garbage." Another informant reported that "I'm always finding beer cans out here [in front of my house]," blaming it on "a bunch of kids." Still another informant noted that "we have these rats [because of the garbage situation] that we can't seem to get rid of, and we have this dog situation on the streets where we don't keep our streets clean." Another informant complained of "even grownups who take the dogs themselves, without a bit of shame, into your area."

The problem of parking in the neighborhood was also found to be a recurrent complaint that was generally voiced against "outsiders" (i.e., against people from outside the neighborhood). These parking complaints were particularly salient for those informants living along major transportation arteries that connect the district with the downtown business areas of San Francisco. Commuters from points south of San Francisco regularly drive their cars into the city, park them for the day on the streets along the major bus and streetcar lines, and take public transportation into the downtown areas in which they work. These daytime parkers not only increase traffic congestion in the neighborhoods so affected, but also frequently block informants' driveways or remove informants' access to parking spaces that would otherwise be available to friends or relatives who come to visit. The parking problem is further compounded on a short-term basis (particularly on weekends) for informants whose homes are located near activity centers (e.g., Legion Halls or shopping districts). In all of these instances, informants complained of a range of parking offenses, including parking across sidewalks and driveway entrances.

One additional class of disputes centering around the neighborhood and directly related to the housing situation included disputes between neighbors. These neighbor disputes were sensitive areas for most informants that they disliked talking about. Instead, when queried about them typical responses were, "We try to get along," or "I don't like to complain." Nevertheless, informants provided a number of specific instances of interpersonal disagreement, which often led to long-standing grudges between neighbors. Some of these complaints centered around responsibility for keeping fences separating lots in good repair (i.e., who was to pay for what). Others focused on recurrent activities on the part of neighbors in creating nuisances such as open burning of trash and the resultant soot and ash that was deposited on the neighbors' lawn and house. Still other cases involved minor infractions of building codes or ordinances such as the case in which an informant had built a glass enclosure over her rear stairway to protect it during rain. Her neighbor complained to the city offices that the structure infringed by a few inches onto her air space and the informant was forced by city officials to remove the enclosure.

Social Environment

Many of these aspects of the physical environment pose threats to the well-being, safety, and health—both physical and emotional—of the elderly population in the district. Further, many are aspects over which the elderly themselves have little, if any, control. The elderly reported having a similar lack of control, however, over several aspects of the social environment as well. Here, they tended to dichotomize the population of the district into "we" and "they"—the older population versus the younger generation—and to attribute the hostilities encountered in the social environment almost entirely to this younger generation. Particularly salient concerns here were threats to physical and psychological security, especially in the areas of noise, harassment, vandalism, and violence, that were generated by teenagers and children.

Informants consistently complained of problems with noise—phonographs, radios, and televisions blaring loudly into the late night hours. Mrs. Wilson's case is a prime example of this kind of problem. But they also complained about loud parties at neighbors' houses; of motorcycles and mufflerless cars being driven up and down their streets; of firecrackers; and of youngsters parking on the streets, with their car radios blaring. "We've got [a barking dog] in back of us now," one informant reported. "Six or six-thirty in the morning, they put him out and he howls all day. I don't do anything because, well, I've complained, and I've gone to the police. But you see, you cause hard feelings in the neighborhood; and I just hate fighting with people."

Several informants reported having windows broken in their homes by rocks or BB guns. "On Friday the 13th, the gang of them [neighbor's children] went out and two kids—I'm pretty sure it was two kids from their family—ran around the corner, broke my window at 11 o'clock and they thought it was cute, you know, Friday the 13th. That will fix the old gal. That will give her something to, you know...." Other informants experienced verbal abuse and threats and name-calling. One noted that "they just talked horrible. They call a woman like me most things beginning with 'f'." Other informants reported having dirt thrown into their houses when they answered the doorbell, or having raw eggs thrown at their homes and being unable to clean the resultant yellow stains off the front of the house, thus having to repaint the exterior.

Harassment may take the form of vandalism as in the instances of windows being broken out in homes or destruction of gardens. "I, myself, have [neighbors'] children who know my love to garden. So consequently, to irritate me, they like to pull my flowers out. Why?" one informant asked. Another reported that, "We had to do away with our lawn because it was just a little area and everybody walked on it and used it, and we couldn't keep anything decent, so we cemented it. The kids come along and they throw whatever you can—gum, candy, half-eaten sandwiches, garbage, old 7-Up cans. They break the bottles, and they're all over so that nobody else can walk, so that if anybody else came along and got hurt on those . . . I'm always out there cleaning and doing something, 'cause I don't want any trouble."

A range of other problems were also reported by informants, indicating the state of the social environment in the district. Some reported instances of cars being nicked or intentionally scratched with rocks, screwdrivers, or nails, or of having radio antennas snapped off parked cars. Several informants reported instances of lighted matches being dropped down their mail slots, and several others reported being barraged at bus stops or along the streets in front of their homes by water balloons thrown from passing cars by youngsters out on a lark. While many of these instances were not directed at particular elderly individuals, all serve to place them on guard while walking on the streets or waiting for a bus, and to generate a sense of fear when it comes to dealing with a younger, unknown, unpredictable generation.

Cultural Environment

This perception of the younger generation as an unknown, unpredictable quantity is nowhere more clearly indicated than in our informants' perceptions of their cultural environment, and in the array of psychological assaults or affronts to which they feel they may be subjected in their everyday existence. These assaults, again, are perceived as coming almost exclusively from the youth of the area (and those coming into the area to attend local schools). They consist principally of affronts to basic values, assaults on hitherto unthreatened ideas and accepted standards of behavior. "These kids live right around the corner from me," one informant reported. "And I don't know what they want of me, I really don't. The only thing they have against me is that I won't let them carouse all night on my porch so mother and dad can't see what they do. I have talked to them [the parents] and they seem to think I'm an old hag. That I've got to get used to their children. And to me, the way they're growing up.... But my daughter says, 'Mother, you may have to rent your place, and go get an apartment. Or something—get out of there. I think it would be good for you to get a new slant on life.' But I'm not going to let them take me."

Another informant put it this way: "The kids are always there. They live on the street. They'll go in for maybe 15 or 20 minutes, they have lunch, and out they come with a banana to eat, or something, throwing it [on the sidewalk]. They always live on the street."

Another example of this conflict between cultural values pertains to the increasing prevalence of graffiti, particularly, obscene graffiti, written on public places such as bus stops that the elderly use. "It bothers me because we constantly come into the area and read this. It's never nice things."

Another area of major concern is that of general neighborhood vandalism. "We never had broken windows in the school. Our school up the hill has got 16 windows broken out of it [now]." Speaking of problems in the neighborhood, another informant cited the "activity of some of the kids over there at the school, where they burned down the library and did a few other things, broke some windows, kind of vandalist kinds of things. It was pretty bad for a while. A lot of neighborhood children who went there were really afraid to go. My neighbor next door here, she walks to the school with her daughter and walks her home. She won't let her go alone. When my children went there, there were 1,100 in the school, and they all lived here. It was entirely different." Finally, one informant noted, "What I am frightened about are the children in our city. All these children are the ones that are causing problems."

To our elderly informants all of these aspects of everyday life with which they are forced into contact represent a different, alien set of cultural values—values that they associate strongly with a younger generation in which parental control is lacking, and over which any form of social control seems to be absent. Their acts are departures from the former predictability of life in an area in which most of our informants have resided for the majority of their adult lives, and serve to the elderly as clear symbols not only of neighborhood deterioration, but of cultural disintegration. They are the products of a younger generation that the elderly does not understand—a generation that also does not seem to understand the needs and values of the elderly. Their acts are assaults on the values of the older population—assaults on their rights to quiet and privacy, on the right not to be exposed to offensive materials, on the right not to be bothered.

Further, all these assaults are perceived as threats to well-being, both physical and psychological; all are by-products of urban life in a changing environment. They are generated by an environment over which our informants feel they are able to exercise less and less control. In short, these elderly see themselves as an embattled population struggling against an unpredictable, unremitting foe with whom they are unable to communicate and unable to make understand. As one informant summed up the situation of the elderly with respect to the young, "The minute you retire, you're a nothing. I had a family. They seem to feel that we've never been young, we've never been anything. We're just a big zero."

RESPONSES

The environment, then, engenders for the elderly an ever-increasing sense of frustration, anxiety, and fear in their own neighborhood. In seeking to cope with this environment, the elderly have developed a series of strategies or ploys. Some attempt to involve formal legal remedy agencies, particularly the police; others seem to prefer handling the matters for themselves, taking some kind of direct action; and still others—either before or after trying the two former alternatives—fall back onto a third coping strategy, avoidance.

Legal Remedies

Those elderly who try to invoke the help of the police or other official third parties learn relatively quickly that these official remedy agents are by and large unresponsive and ineffectual in dealing with such everyday legal problems. Informants note that the police hesitate to become involved in neighborhood disputes, claiming either lack of jurisdiction or inability to grant the desired relief. Even when they are called, their attitudes toward the elderly may affect their assessment of the situation itself. As one informant put it, "One policeman I had a little trouble with when I complained about the children [making love on her doorstep]. He asked me how old I was. I guess he thought maybe I had forgotten what love making meant, or maybe 'you old hag.' When I called him, he proceeded to ask me questions on how old I was, and I had the feeling if he wondered if I were a little nuts." Another informant, after having her purse snatched by a neighborhood teenage boy, called the police. "And do you know what happened?" she asked during the interview. "They put me on a machine . . . . The machine was answering, and I didn't even, I just stopped. It's awful. I mean, we are not protected. In no way are we protected. You call the police, and what happens?" When asked if she would call the police again if a similar incident happened, she responded, "I don't think so. I would just be annoyed to be hooked up with a machine." Later in the same year, this informant reported that she returned home to find a young burglar ransacking her apartment. She confronted the intruder, who threatened to kill her. However, she remained calm and did not scream, and thereby escaped harm. The burglar fled with the money he had found in her home. She did not report the incident to the police.

Even when the police respond to the calls of the elderly in the district, the violators may be unknown or the event may have occurred so quickly that the culprit has gotten away long before the police arrive. Commenting on police promptness, one informant remarked, "They're slower than the second coming."

Calling the police in these neighborhood situations may also have unwanted repercussions, a concern that was frequently verbalized by informants. "If you call the police about everything," one noted, "you get the reputation of being the neighborhood crab; and that's a miserable life because, right off the bat, the kids hear about it and make your life miserable. As soon as they find out that you [have complained] or the parents are talking about you and you've done something, right away, they do all kinds of things [to you]."

Recourse to lawyers and/or courts is also not practical in most of these problem situations. As Antonucci (1973) has noted, to lawyers the elderly may represent a devalued clientele, either because of personal preference for dealing with families and children or because of an unwillingness or inability to address many of the technical issues that affect the elderly, for example, tax and probate law (Terris, 1972). Marlin and Brown (1972) also point out the negative effects of heavy caseloads for poverty lawyers and a societal bias in favor of the young. To these listings we would add that many of these neighborhood situations themselves would be undesirable from the lawyer's standpoint because of the low fees they are likely to generate, the difficulty of proof involved, and the inability in many instances to show damages.

Even when free legal representation is made available, however, the result may be less than satisfactory, as Mrs. Wilson's report would indicate. Not only did she feel that insufficient time had been allowed for her interview and for the presentation of her case, but she felt also that she was offered insufficient options by the attorney. The lawyer could or would do little more for Mrs. Wilson than write a letter threatening suit, a suit in which Mrs. Wilson did not want to become involved. In this instance, the legal representative was responsive but ineffective because Mrs. Wilson was afraid that other aspects of the legal system—namely, the police—would be unable to protect her from retaliation. The help given in one area of the formal system, therefore, may be nullified or undone by the ineffectiveness or unresponsiveness in another area. Further, many of the middle-class elderly in the district have incomes that are high enough to disqualify them from obtaining free legal services from senior legal programs, yet are not sufficiently high to permit them to feel financially able to obtain consultation with an attorney for each instance or situation in which they feel aggrieved.

Direct Action

Thus the unresponsiveness or ineffectiveness of official remedy agents forces the elderly individual to fall back on other resources outside the formal system—on contacts and social control pressures that may be available in the informal or unofficial system. Mrs. Wilson, for example, first sought out the help of other neighbors in trying to get her problems solved. Neighbors, however, seem reluctant to become involved in problems that do not directly concern them, or in problems in which they are not inextricably involved themselves. And friends and relatives can apply even fewer social control sanctions against the offending party than can the police or even the victim. About the best one can expect from a neighbor in this situation is commiseration and advice— the kind of advice that the daughter of the informant noted above gave to her mother: move away. To this embattled informant, however, and to many others like her, this solution was not an attractive one. She had lived in her home for almost 40 years, and was not "going to let them take me."

Many elderly informants, like Mrs. Wilson, also look to neighborhood associations for information and assistance—again, generally, to no avail. A male informant reports:

> I went to a meeting not too long ago where a city supervisor... was telling us how to cope with the crime problem. And most of the people there, I was surprised to see, were older people. There weren't very many younger ones. The older people, some of them were extremely skeptical of the supervisor's remarks; in fact, they were almost hostile in some of the things they said. Before he got very far into his talk, some of them said, "well, what about the fact that when we call up we can't get anyone here fast enough to do any good? And we can't run away and call for help, we

can't get around that easily." The supervisor spent a great deal of time telling us we had a severe crime problem in town, so that we should realize this. And I couldn't argue with him on that, but he infuriated all of us. . . . But who do these older people turn to when seemingly the police don't react fast enough or don't react with the proper response according to the way these people feel? A major problem with all of this is that a large number of people who should be doing the talking are never heard from. It's the old iceberg business, and I don't know how you get at those people.

Since utilization of many of these alternative agencies or persons in the unofficial system rarely brings the desired relief, the elderly are often left to rely on their own resources. Here they have the option either of taking direct action themselves by confronting the offending party, or of adopting a secondary coping strategy. In many instances, however, direct confrontation is either impossible or strongly inadvisable because the elderly individual either fears being attacked at the moment the act occurs, or fears the possibility of retribution or vengeance at a later time. At lectures to community groups in the area, police advocate a passive role for the elderly when there is the slightest indication that they will be attacked or threatened: women are urged to drop their handbags on the sidewalk, men not to resist a demand for money. Further, the older person who reports a youngster to the youngster's parents for breaking a window runs the risk of escalating one grievance into many, of having other windows broken, or being singled out for special attention as the neighborhood "crab."

Avoidance

Perhaps the most pervasive strategy that is adopted by many elderly in this area is that of avoidance. Avoidance here takes many forms and may be used in a variety of situations. Commonly, the elderly try to protect themselves and to avoid contact with the younger offenders by installation of iron gates at the doors or bars on the windows. One informant reports, "I came home at 10 o'clock, which isn't too late. And if it hadn't been for an iron fence which I have around my house—and they hate, oh, they hate that iron fence. It keeps them from coming up onto my porch." Many of those who do not already have such installations report planning them in the near future to prevent hostile encounters. As one informant who had not yet installed a gate at the entrance to her home noted, "The kids come up and smoke, one or two, to sit on my porch. And one night, I came home, and they wouldn't even move over to let me come up my stairs." Another commented,

"Children come up and play on your stairs. We don't have any metal gates up yet."

Gates and bars may serve to protect the elderly population within their homes, but gates and bars are expensive to install. Further, they do not protect the aged once they go beyond their portals, where they are forced into contact with the potentially hostile social environment of the district at large. In this hostile environment outside their homes, many have adopted a variety of personal coping mechanisms. One informant reported that she simply walks on past her doorway if she notices anyone loitering in the immediate area; she has a preselected alternative location to which she goes if she sees suspicious persons or groups near her home. "I pretend like I don't hear them," she noted. "I don't stop at my door. I never do when somebody is behind me. I never take my keys out and open my door when somebody is behind me. I don't trust 100%." Other informants report crossing the street when they see groups of youngsters approaching or loitering on street corners. Almost unanimously, informants agree that it is best to stay off the streets when the children are out of school. They know what hours children and teenagers are going to or coming from their schools and schedule their outings and shopping trips to avoid contact during these times.

Finally, many informants reported carrying various devices on their persons to ward off attacks or threats. Among women, the most popular items seem to be whistles or spray cans or mace or pepperoil; among men, these items ranged from guns or billyclubs to spray cans. One informant reports carrying her keys in such a way that they protrude between her fingers, so that she can "gouge their eyes out" if attacked.

In recent years a number of agencies and programs have been developed in the district designed to offer an array of services—including legal services—for the elderly. The Senior Block Information Service (described in Chapter 10 of this volume) is one such program that attempts to provide information about legal resources. The staff has conscientiously sought out information and located resources in the legal arena, and provided this information to the population it serves. Almost every newsletter contains information on legal services or programs available to the elderly, or on issues and problems in the legal arena. During the course of our study, the staff has increased its activities in this area, and has placed major emphasis on bringing the elderly together with legal service providers. Not only have speakers in the legal sphere been brought in for the program's monthly meetings but also the District Attorney's staff in charge of the Complaint-Mobile unit—a van modeled after the bookmobile that travels to different locations in the city—has appeared at the meeting site. The program, further, has been instrumental in bringing legal service attorneys into the district. There are now three separate sites in the area at which these lawyers appear at regularly scheduled hours to make themselves available free of charge for consultation on problems brought to them by elderly individuals.

IMPLICATIONS

Despite these major efforts at recognizing the legal needs of the elderly populace, legal services have been restricted to those areas that the legal service providers perceive or define as problem areas for the aged, problem areas that do not necessarily coincide with those perceived by the elderly themselves. The areas with which legal service providers are prepared to deal—consumer complaints, problems with governmental agencies, wills, and probate matters—are not necessarily the areas with which the aged are most immediately concerned, or with which they must deal frequently in their everyday lives. These legal service personnel simply neither seem to recognize nor are prepared to deal with the array of neighborhood injustices discussed in this chapter.

Mrs. Wilson was very ingenious in seeking out a number of alternative remedy agents—whether within or outside of the formal legal system—in seeking resolution of her problems with her neighbors. Most older people, we have found, are not nearly as ingenious, however, nor are they nearly as tenacious. Furthermore, to us it is untenable to argue that the ability to obtain a remedy in a grievance situation should depend upon either ingenuity or tenacity alone. Nevertheless, regardless of either of these elements, the picture that emerges at this exploratory stage is that the elderly simply are not going to obtain the help or satisfaction that they desire with these problems. Our findings indicate that success in obtaining satisfaction in these neighborhood injustice situations does not depend on which agency or which person was contacted for advice or help, or on how many remedy agencies were so contacted. Our data indicate, to the contrary, that regardless of how many or which remedy agents are contacted or of how tenacious or inventive the individual is in seeking resolution, in most cases, there will simply be no relief to these neighborhood injustices."

This inability to obtain relief, then, frequently leaves the elderly with a sense of powerlessness in their own neighborhoods, blocks, and homes, and with a strong sense of frustration and fear. They feel powerless in the sense that they are unable to find a responsive remedy agent or to effect a resolution of the persistent, pressing neighborhood injustices. They are frustrated by and fearful of those in their social environmnent who do not share their values—particularly children and teenagers from "problem families" (Teaff, Lawton, Nahemow, & Carlson, 1978). Further, it is ongoing and persistent fear that causes the elderly to barricade themselves in their homes and to avoid contact with all unknown youngsters at whatever cost. While such avoidance may be the cheapest way of escaping potentially hostile confrontations, avoidance of the younger generation is neither a particularly attractive nor an always possible option for the elderly in this social environment.

In his statement to the U.S. Senate Special Committee on Aging (U.S. Senate, 1970) Senator Harrison Williams observed that "there is far too much evidence that large numbers of older Americans suffer needless anxiety, deprivation and injustice simply because they do not know what help is available to them, or because of wrong-headed decisions made arbitrarily by representatives of government" (p. vii). We have argued here, however, that it is not just that the elderly do not know what help is available, nor is it simply a matter of wrong-headed, arbitrary decision making. Rather, the situation of unredressed neighborhood injustices is as much an artifact of the failure of legal service providers to define or recognize many of the elderly's problems as legal problems as it is of knowledge on the part of the elderly or decision making on the part of governmental officials. Despite major efforts at recognizing the legal needs of the elderly in the district under study, legal services have thus far been restricted to those areas that legal service providers perceive or define as problems for the aged, which, as stated previously, are not necessarily congruent with those with which the aged themselves are most immediately concerned, or with which they must deal most frequently in their everyday lives.

This slippage in the system, created by the lack of congruence in problem definition, knowledge, and access, is not without cost, for it seems clear that the extent to which these legal problems are not satisfactorily resolved or go unattended is directly related to the psychological, economic, and social well-being of the people involved in them. Frustration, anxiety, neglect, and abuse of the aged are some of the more obvious direct and indirect psychological costs that those enmeshed in our seemingly unresponsive legal system must bear. Avoidance of potentially hostile situations or persons; doing nothing about a complaint or grievance, or "lumping it," (Felstiner, 1974) because of fear of retribution; having limited, blocked, or no access to agencies, institutions, or personnel who can (or will) help to deal with these disputes all act to create frustration for the elderly and to precipitate crises that go unresolved. On this point, Felstiner has spoken of a "social pathology" created by the lack of legal recourse and resources available to individuals, particularly those involved in disputes with large organizations.

Avoidance of other individuals or of situations in the neighborhood among the elderly, however, as Danzig and Lowy (1975) have pointed out, is rarely a very attractive option, nor is it a very practical solution on a society-wide basis in terms of the costs involved. Such avoidance may have heavy psychological costs, and may be traumatic; severence of ties or self-imposed "house arrest" may have considerable impact on the emotional health of disputants. Further, as Danzig and Lowy have argued, "avoidance may be anguished and unwilling. Rapes for example infrequently generate complaints, but here the avoidance is practiced largely because of fear of retribution or embarrassment" (pp. 678–679). They note further that "People who stay off the streets at night are practicing avoidance, but we doubt anyone would praise a society which was satisfied with this reaction to street crime because it was a cheap way of dealing with a difficult problem." These are particularly salient observations when placed in the context of our study of the legal problems of the aged, and the psychological costs that the elderly as a category or as individuals must pay in seeking to obtain relief from many of the neighborhood injustices discussed above.

Yet it is not only avoidance that is costly here. Even individuals like Mrs. Wilson who do not "lump" their complaints but who, on the contrary, voice their grievances may suffer psychologically in their dealings with the formal arena. The constant need to do battle with individuals or with agencies and organizations in an effort to enforce one's rights, the seemingly endless numbers of delays met on the way to resolution of the problem, the economic costs involved in taking action, and the hesitancy of taking any action at all for fear of retribution all combine to extort a high psychological, social, and economic cost from those who choose to complain in an effort to gain satisfaction rather than to avoid other individuals, or terminate or curtail the relationships that give rise to disputes.

CONCLUSION

While our findings are preliminary and must be complemented by quantitative survey data if their generalizability is to be ensured, we nevertheless feel that we have identified a significant problem area that legal and social service providers have, by and large, ignored. Further research aimed at determining the primacy of particular problem areas, and the uniqueness or nonuniqueness of these problems to the elderly, is clearly needed. Intelligent policy and program planning, and advocacy and educational programs are all dependent on data that indicate the relative significance of particular legal problems to the elderly population. At this point, although awaiting this additional research, we feel that we have learned enough to urge legal and social service providers to reconsider their own conceptions of the domain of the law, and to direct their attention to the area of neighborhood injustices.

Interestingly, it appears not only that service providers are unaware of this vast range of problems but also that the elderly may not be able to frame or articulate their problems in such a way that communication with service providers can be readily accomplished. They, too, may have trouble recognizing that their complaints may in fact be of the kind which are amenable to legal treatment or assistance, or they may be unable—as was Mrs. Wilson—to convey the urgency of their need for relief.

In both of these areas—problem definition and crisis intervention—programs such as the Senior Block Information Service have a potentially major role to play in informing the elderly of their rights and options when confronted with problems, and in referring them to the appropriate resources. Thus involvement and knowledge at all three levels—social service providers, legal service personnel, and the elderly themselves—are essential. Perhaps if both the service providers and more of the elderly themselves began to think it appropriate for such complaints to be made, these neighborhood injustices could be dealt with more successfully.

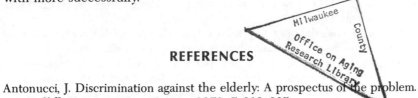

REFERENCES

Antonucci, J. Discrimination against the elderly: A prospectus of the problem. *Suffolk University Law Review*, 1973, 7, 919–935.

Anonymous. Quacks and swindlers bilk aged persons out of millions yearly. *Geriatrics*, 1969, *24*, 56–61.

Bennett, L. Protective services for the aged. *Social Service Review*, 1965, 39, 283–293.

Bernstein, M. Aging and the law. In M. W. Riley, J. W. Riley, Jr., & M. E. Johnson (Eds.), *Aging and society*, Vol. II. New York: Russell Sage Foundation, 1969.

Brostoff, P., Brown, R., & Butler, R. N. "Beating up" on the elderly: Police, social work, crime. *Aging and Human Development*, 1972, *3*, 319–322.

Burr, J. Protective services for older adults: A demonstration project. *Welfare in Review*, 1971, *9*, 1–6.

Clemente, F., & Kleinman, M. B. Fear of crime among the aged. *Gerontologist*, 1976, *16*, 207–210.

Cohen, E. S. Old age and the law. *Women Lawyer's Journal*, 1967, *53*, 96–105.

Collins, W., Flanagan, J., & Donnelly, T. The Senior Citizens Project of California Legal Assistance: An action arm of the National Senior Citizens Law Center. *Clearinghouse Review*, 1972, *6*, 220–221.

Coppelman, P., & Hiestand, F. Legal challenges to relative responsibility in old age security programs: Establishing the right to grow old with dignity. *Clearinghouse Review*, 1972, *6*, 212–220.

Danzig, R., & Lowy, M. Everyday disputes and mediation in the United States: A reply to Professor Felstiner. *Law and Society Review*, 1975, *9*, 675–694.

Denenberg, H. Those health insurance booby traps. *The Progressive*, 1972, *36*, 29–33.

Eichenberg, T. *Housing in the Sunset: A community in transition*. San Francisco: Sunset-Parkside Education and Action Committee, 1974.

Felstiner, W. L. F. Influence of social organization on dispute processing. *Law and Society Review*, 1974, *9*, 63–94.

Fisher, L., & Solomon, J. Guardianship; a protective service program for the aged. *Journal of Social Casework*, 1974, *55*, 618–621.

Forston, R., & Kitchens, J. *Criminal victimization of the aged*, Center for Community Services, School of Community Services, Service Report No. 1. Denton, Tex.: North Texas State University, 1974.

Golick, T., Jennings, E., Kraus, J., & Weiss, J. Interview checklist for elderly clients. *Clearinghouse Review*, 1971, *5*, 303–304.

Gubrium, J. Victimization in old age: Available evidence and three hypotheses. *Crime and Delinquency*, 1974, *20*, 245–250.

Hall, G., & Mathiasen, G. *Guide to development of protective services for older people*. Springfield, Ill.: Charles C Thomas, 1973.

Heyman, D. (Ed.). *Legal problems of the elderly*. Durham, N.C.: Duke University Press, 1974.

Lehmann, V. *Guardianship*. In J. Kaplan & G. Aldridge (Eds.), *Social welfare of the aging*. New York: Columbia University Press, 1962.

Marlin, D., & Brown, R. The elderly poor: An overview of the legal service attorney's responsibility. *Clearinghouse Review*, 1972, *6*, 192–195.

Nathanson, P. Justice for a proud minority. *Trial*, 1974, *10*, 12–13.

Rifai, M. A. Y. *Older Americans' Crime Prevention Research Project: Final report*. Portland, Ore.: Multonomah County Division of Public Safety, Community Affairs/Crime Prevention Unit, 1976.

Regan, J. Protective service for the elderly: Commitment, guardianship and alternatives. *William and Mary Law Review*, 1972, *13*, 569–622.

Silver, L. H. Medical care delivery systems and the poor: New challenges to poverty lawyers. *Wisconsin Law Review*, 1970, 644–681.

Sundeen, R. A., & Mathieu, J. T. The fear of crime and its consequences among elderly in three urban communities. *Gerontologist,* 1976, *16,* 211–219.

Teaff, J. D., Lawton, M. P., Nahemow, L., & Carlson, D. Impact of age integration on the well-being of elderly tenants in public housing. *Journal of Gerontology,* 1978, *33,* 126–133.

Terris, B. *Legal services for the elderly: A technical assistance monograph.* Washington, D.C.: National Council on the Aging, 1972.

U.S. Senate. *Frauds and deceptions affecting the elderly. Investigators' findings and recommendations, 1964.* Report of the Subcommittee on Frauds and Misrepresentations Affecting the Elderly, January 31, 1965.

U.S. Senate Special Committee on Aging. *Legal problems affecting older Americans. Working paper.* 91st Congress, 2nd Session, 1970.

U.S. Senate Special Committee on Aging. *Legal problems affecting older Americans. Hearings, 2 Parts.* 91st Congress, 2nd Session and 92nd Congress, 1st Session, 1971.

U.S. Senate Special Committee on Aging. *Improving legal representation for older Americans. Hearings, parts 3 and 4.* 94th Congress Session, September 28–29, 1976.

Wallin, P. Homeownership problems of the elderly. *Clearinghouse Review,* 1972, *6,* 227–232.

12

The Organization of an In-Home Services Network

LEONARD E. GOTTESMAN
AVALIE SAPERSTEIN

In 1978 amendments to the Older Americans Act placed a new emphasis on in-home services for the elderly by requiring that 50% of all Title III funds be used for in-home, access, and legal services; that the emphasis of such services be on helping the frail elderly; and that area agencies on aging be responsible for developing focal points through which older people can receive services. All of these aspects of this law are in line with increased recent emphasis on home services for older people who might otherwise need institutional care.

About one in four community-resident persons over 65 years old requires some sort of home services according to extensive data from national and cross-national statistics (Gottesman, Moss, & Worts, 1975). Among these the most needful are those aged 75 and over. This group is more impaired and uses more services than any other age group. Four other groups of old people are also high in need for services: people about to enter institutions; those needing protective services; those moving into or living in boarding homes or other sheltered residences; and older people who have few friends or supportive family members. These older people are likely to be physically and/or mentally frail and lack the informal supports to give them the services they need or to help them gain access to services.

For these individuals, entry into a long-term care institution has been the most frequently available alternative. Such a solution has been shown to have many deficiencies. For many, institutional services are not focused on their primary areas of need. Many older people and their families would prefer some other solution. Finally, such treatment makes too little use of available informal services of family and friends.

Responding to this problem, the Congress adopted over the past 15 years Title XX of the Social Security Act, the Community Mental Health Act, Medicare and Medicaid, and the Older Americans Act. Each of these legislative initiatives has provided both increased funds and the structural bases to increase emphasis on noninstitutional services. Service reforms were needed. Existing services were often organized as a group of independent fiefdoms that were difficult to assess, offered limited consumer choice, and created considerable discontent among consumers.

To address these problems legislation has provided incentives for innovative service providers. They may apply for waivers of federal requirements to try new approaches to service coordination and integration and new methods for individual needs assessment prior to and during service delivery. Examples of these approaches include Triage in Connecticut, which uses Medicare waivers and professional assessment to provide an array of needed services. The Massachusetts Home Care Corporation uses multidisclipinary assessment and centralized service billing. The Wisconsin Community Care Organization uses a Medicare waiver to offer integrated services on a capitation basis. Other approaches that emphasize multidisciplinary assessment along with reform in service provision have been undertaken in Rochester, New York, California, and Maryland. Approaches to integrating service providers in a community include those in Pima County, Arizona and Wilkes-Barre, Pennsylvania.

These programs have reinforced the idea that multidisciplinary assessment, service management, and service integration are critically important to the success of a service program. This chapter briefly describes a model neighborhood approach to in-home services developed by the Philadelphia Geriatric Center (PGC), which incorporates all of these features. The neighborhood model is in turn part of a citywide model approach to in-home services. The context for the in-home services program in Philadelphia is the Philadelphia Corporation for Aging (PCA), the local area agency on aging. The PCA operates a central Information and Referral (I & R) service and contracts with a number of neighborhood-based senior centers to provide socialization, congregate meals, and for more frail elderly persons, home-delivered meals and service management. The in-home services for which the PCA pays are contracted for centrally through public bidding and then actuated by service managers in their senior centers on the basis of a standardized individual client assessment and case plan.

THE PHILADELPHIA CORPORATION FOR AGING IN-HOME SERVICE PROGRAM

Prior to the development of a citywide network, an in-home service program was operated by the PGC in a small local area around the center. This program was developed as an Administration on Aging-funded Model Project to demonstrate a means of providing such services from an institutional base, and expanding institutional services incrementally, wherever possible, to serve the needs of residents of the community surrounding the institution. It also served as a prototype area for the citywide system.

Clients

The Logan area served by the PGC In-Home Service Project covers approximately 3 square miles on the border between north-central and northeast Philadelphia. The area is characterized by a high density of older people. About 24% (21,880) of the total population of 90,000 is aged 60 or older. Of these people a high proportion is frail: 22% or 5,970 people are aged 75 or older, and 15% or 4,217 people live alone.

Income statistics indicate that 14% of the older population is at or below federal poverty standards. However, data from a formal needs survey (Gottesman, Moss, & Wortz, 1975) indicate that approximately 40% of the elderly in this area were within $1,000 of poverty level. In reality, people living within $1,000 of the annual poverty level have less spendable income than do Supplemental Security Income (SSI) recipients. These people are not entitled to medical assistance for drugs, nonreimbursable Medicare costs, transportation, or food stamps. Poor old people are also much more likely to live alone, to be over 75 years old, and to be frail.

According to 1970 census data, only 1% of the old people in the service area were of minority status, but this definition of minority excludes many ethnic groups, which are proportionately high in the area. Among these older people, about one third are foreign-born and a substantial percent are not fluent in English. The area also has a rapidly changing racial composition that has recently resulted in the flight of amenities and resources familiar to the elderly population and their replacement by unfamiliar ones or by none at all. As neighbors, friends, family, neighborhood stores, and religious organizations flee, the older people left behind become fearful, often psychologically housebound, and have few neighbors on whom to count for help. In the target area, resources are limited though there are occasional senior citizen weekly meetings in churches and synagogues. Attendance is limited, partially due to the exceptionally poor transportation system in this area. For senior citizens, health services, medical facilities, recreation, and transportation to shopping are scarce. Overall, PCG's In-Home Service Program target area is characterized by a high-density older population of whom a substantial proportion is frail elderly.

Program Staff

To serve these people the program employs six staff. A program director (social worker) plans the overall services, coordinates in-home service activities with the PGC and with the PCA with respect to administrative and fiscal matters, and directs the work of one supervisor. The supervisor (also a social worker) monitors the activities of all workers through frequent discussions about specific clients and about the overall program. Four paraprofessional workers under close supervision do three types of assessments (see below), develop case plans, arrange for services, and serve clients directly where no other formal or informal resource is available or appropriate. A full-time driver delivers meals on wheels, takes clients to medical appointments, to do shopping, and on occasional social outings. All of these staff were given initial intensive training when hired and participate in regular weekly in-service training.

The total service package offered by the program includes information and referral, direct service, service management, and community development.

Program Service Package

Information and Referral (I & R).   This service is directly tied to initial assessment and satisfies the needs of the most capable group of elderly. It is needed because clients are frequently uninformed about available services until they themselves develop a need for service. When in need and under stress, the considerable array of services for the elderly that have developed over recent years is hard to learn about and to assess. There are relatively few services located in the area and clients need help in learning about those available elsewhere in the city.

Because clients on first contact are often under stress and uncertain about the service they want, this contact is particularly important. At that time a decision is made as to whether the information and referral will be all that the client needs or whether more complex direct service or service management will also be needed.

Assessment is central to the in-home service model. Although it occurs as a part of the I & R process it affects all of the in-home service functions. Project workers perform three basic kinds of assessment: initial, simple, and service-management. Initial assessment occurs at intake and obtains basic information for initial problem definition and appropriate client classification. Simple assessment collects enough information about an identified problem so that a simple, direct service may be given. A service management problem is defined by a broad-based multidisciplinary standardized assessment; these problems are complex and are likely to need several kinds of services for their solutions. All clients receive the initial assessment. They then are either given information or a referral to a service or are recommended for the more detailed assessment, either of the simple or the service-management type. The project tailors the type of assessment, level of staff involvement, and type and intensity of services to the client's need. The most capable clients and their families require only to be told where services can be found. For them, only initial assessment is given, followed by the I & R service. They are then able to negotiate for these services themselves.

The intake worker for the in-home service receives all calls and records demographic data, the presenting problem, areas of difficulty, resources, and disposition on an intake form. The major worker tasks in I & R are initial assessment, provision of information or referral, and follow-up.

After assessment, providing the information and the sources for referral congruent with an identified problem are the essential tasks. The I & R worker provides up-to-date accurate information to the client in an understandable way. Where indicated, referral is made to another provider either by giving the client enough information to refer himself or herself or by the worker's making the referral call. Implicit in this task is the necessity of maintaining an up-to-date resource file. All in-home service workers are responsible for reporting all new or changed resource information as they discover it. In this way the resource file is continuously updated.

The third major task of the information and referral service is follow-up. The PGC follows up all referrals of people who may not themselves have that potential. Follow-up can occur by contacting the referred resource or by calling the client.

Direct Service.   Moderately capable clients need only temporary services or perhaps continued help from a single service provider such as meals on wheels or transportation. They were called simple-need clients by the project. For these clients the somewhat more detailed simple assessment is given; services are limited but not always short-term. Worker coordination is also limited in these cases to the development of a contact with the client, a follow-up to make certain that services were started, and a reassessment at the agreed upon time either to terminate or renew the service.

Direct services from the PGC are provided for moderately capable clients and also for less capable clients when no other resources are available outside of the PGC program. These services are analogous to many of the services provided by senior centers. Since no PCA senior center exists in this target area, the PGC's In-Home Service Program provides these necessary services to the older community. These direct services include home-delivered meals, transportation and escort, friendly visiting, telephone reassurance, chore service, counseling, and homemaker.

The philosophy of the project is to call on informal resources first, other citywide services second, and to use project workers' services only where other services are not available or are inappropriate. The direct-service component may thus be viewed as a gap-filling effort. This approach helps keep the client in touch with an informal support network, builds new ties with helpers, and spreads scarce resources over a large number of clients.

The policy of giving time-limited service encourages a return to maximal independence by ensuring that reassessment of need is done frequently and services terminated as soon as they are not needed.

Service Management.   A small group of most vulnerable clients have complex problems requiring long-term services from a number of providers. These vulnerable clients with complex needs require the more detailed service-management assessment, continuing worker involvement in coordinating the group of providers and their package of services, and careful reassessment. The services needed by the most vulnerable are also likely to be in larger quantity and duration than for other clients. Service management is provided for clients whose needs are vague, complex, or multiple, including those for whom protective services, change in living arrangement, or other restrictive treatment is a possibility. This is the population with multiple vulnerabilities who have been designated as having top priority for services (i.e., the old old, the poor, the disabled, and the alone).

Advocacy is often required to insure their access to services and the planful coordination of an entire set of services. For example, if an initial assessment suggests that the client will need meals on wheels for a short time to help aid recovery after returning from the hospital, a simple assessment limited to the personal and environmental factors relevant to this service is done, resulting in a service plan being arranged with the client. By contrast, if the client at initial assessment is found to be homebound, has little family for support, and is having difficulty managing a household, multiple services seem indicated and a service-management assessment would be given. This service-management assessment uses a standardized instrument to summarize the client's assets and problems in six different functional areas: physical health, activities of daily living, social supports, social participation, mental health, and environment. The worker collects information from the client's point of view and then augments it with information from other sources, including the worker's own judgment.

On the basis of this assessment the worker and the client agree on a service plan. This plan not only states goals and the specific services that will be used to help a client reach the goals, but also places the goals within a time limit that never exceeds 6 months and is usually shorter. The plan includes services to be performed by the client, by informal resources such as family and neighbors, and by formal service providers.

The worker then arranges for services from the project staff or from service providers paid for out of PCA's central pool of services or from the PGC. As described for simple-need clients, the PGC is able to provide directly, if necessary, homemaker, home-delivered meals, chore services, counseling, and transportation needs. In addition, the worker can order from PCA homemaker, visiting nurse, and medical transportation. Shortly after a service is ordered, the service manager follows up to be assured that the service has begun as requested. Also, at a time originally designated in the service plan, the worker reassesses the client's situation and functioning to identify changes that have occurred and to decide if a revision or termination of services is called for.

Because the emphasis of service management is on the use of informal resources as the first line of service, relatively little formal service from the PCA is used. In 1977, for example, only 20% of all services used were from the formal pool.

Community Development. The conceptual and operational emphasis of the project on informal resources has motivated a substantial project focus on the development of community resources. When the Logan-area project began operation in 1974, it was confronted with substantial gaps in available resources. Primarily responsible for these gaps was the changing nature of the Logan community. Where once the elderly had depended on family, friends, and neighbors for help, the middle-aged and more privileged older population was in the process of exodus to the suburbs. The social institutions that remained in the community were not prepared to handle the increase of needs among the elderly that had previously been borne by the departed middle-aged population. Although new funding streams were created for aging programs in the 1970s, no new programs or services were being instituted in the Logan community.

A review of other aging programs indicated that agencies typically deployed their energies in two directions: developing funding for their own activities and coordinating the resources of other existing programs. However, the In-Home Service Program recognized the desperately limited resources available within the community as well as the probability that funding for new programs could not keep up with the demand, and would thus be unable to fill the service gaps. Therefore, a different approach was necessary. The program thus designed an additional component, community development, with two major goals: (1) to improve the quality and accessibility of existing services and (2) to stimulate and facilitate the development of new services and access to services.

Community development focuses on working with existing groups, agencies, facilities, businesses, and other organizations. It is not community organizing. Rather, it seeks existing groupings with local roots, current or potential structure, and current or potential leadership.

Four value- and research-supported assumptions guided the community-development component. First, old people are part of the community in which they live, being affected by the community as well as having an effect on it. Second, the needs of an elderly population are best met when an array of service solutions exists. Third, informal resources—family, friends, neighbors, religious groups—are essential for maintaining older people in the community. Fourth, funding lags behind the service needs of the older population.

Community development defines the community as its client. The program works with family, friends, and neighbors; private service agencies and businesses; voluntary associations, civic groups, and religious institutions; and publicly funded services. To all of these it offers community education and help in stimulating new programs.

The community education efforts of the project in its initial needs assessment found a great lack of even elementary knowledge about the needs of the elderly. To overcome this problem the In-Home Service Program met with all existing social service agencies, reached out to the elderly themselves, contacted local churches, local newspapers, and joined local groups. Later strategies involved systematic pamphleting, talking individually with all types of organizations, and making staff available to speak to local groups.

Community education succeeded in sensitizing shopkeepers, stimulating community referrals to the In-Home Service Program, stimulating people to inquire about an elderly neighbor, and creating an impetus for local organizations to modify their current practices or initiate new programs for the elderly. Some groups were strong enough to operationalize their interest in new programs on their own. For others that needed assistance, the In-Home Service Program offered help organized into seven stages.

1.   Using face-to-face meetings, the project helped the group learn more about the issues it was interested in pursuing. The goal was to stimulate the group to take action by modifying existing programs or designing new programs.

2.   The group was helped to analyze its own capacity as reflected by its mandate, funding, size, staffing, relationship to the community, and the political context. Helping to do this assessment typically led the In-Home Service Program to a cooperative working relationship with the organization.

3.   A mutually acceptable decision was negotiated to proceed with a specified project congruent with the resources of the group and the limits of available In-Home Service Program assistance.

4.   During the fourth stage—planning—the roles of the group and the In-Home Service Program staff were clearly detailed, and specific project tasks and timelines were set. Agreement was obtained that the group itself bear major responsibility for the project, with only technical assistance, training, and support being provided by the In-Home Service Program.

5.   In stage five the new program began according to the roles, tasks, and timelines established in the planning stage. The In-Home Service Program stood ready to assist with problems as they arose.

6.   Ongoing project maintenance (step six) was the primary task of the community group. The In-Home Service Program continued its role as troubleshooter.

7.   At the beginning of a community project, both the In-Home Service Program and the community group must agree on an evaluation process (step seven) and on the criteria by which to evaluate the program's effectiveness. Both the community group and the In-Home Service Program assist in gathering client experience data and in its analysis. It is the community group's responsibility to implement the findings of the evaluation.

CONCLUSION

It may appear to be a long way from a wide-ranging service co-ordination and delivery program back to the topic of housing. While the housing-related services component does occur strongly in the form of chore, home-repair, and housing-counseling activities, far more important is the global purpose of the program: the true integration of the physical, human, and service-providing elements of a geographically defined area. The essence of "community" is the mix of informal assistance, use of local strengths, and the judicious infusion of professional expertise when necessary. This approach is directed to the heart of the housing problem, which is rarely a matter of the physical environment alone, but rather of how people use and allocate these physical resources.

The principles described here regarding information and referral, direct services, service management, and community development comprise a network of services focused on assisting people to live in their own homes. The thesis of the In-Home Services Project is that such a network is possible. The results of the project show the thesis to have been supported and the lives of the Logan-area older people to have been enriched.

REFERENCE

Gottesman, L. E., Moss, M. S., & Wortz, F. P. *Resources, needs, and wishes for services in urban middle-class older people.* Paper presented at the Tenth International Congress of Gerontology, Jerusalem, Israel, June 1975.

13
Neighborhood Images and Use: A Case Study

VICTOR REGNIER

The neighborhood within which any housing development is located exerts tremendous influence on the resident's satisfaction with that housing. The larger physical environment provides the context for the retrieval of necessary life-supportive goods and services; therefore, this context must be shaped so as to support the life patterns of a particular population. Dissonance between the supportiveness of the environment and the capabilities of residents normally triggers dissatisfaction. Sometimes the older person will react to the problem by moving, but in most cases the older person continues to maintain his or her present home and tolerate the unpleasantness of the setting.

Urban neighborhoods, particularly those located near the central core, often contain older populations that have chosen to maintain their residence in a familiar neighborhood. Research that has measured the importance of the larger physical environment suggests that as a person ages the neighborhood becomes an increasingly salient concept (Keller, 1968; Pastalan & Carson, 1970) Pastalan's age-loss continuum can be used to explain why older individuals may be more hesitant to leave a familiar environment. Pastalan theorizes that the specific losses of mobility, sensory acuity, and personal relationships through death are related to the age of the individual. As they occur, these specific changes increase uncertainty and decrease one's control over the environment. In the face of increased uncertainty, the older individual may react by seeking to maximize physical and psychological attachment to those items that are stable and familiar. Thus the older dwelling unit in the familiar neighborhood takes on considerable importance.

In their discussion of the older residents of the Strawberry Mansion neighborhood in Philadelphia, Lawton, Kleban, and Carlson (1973) detail the unrelenting terror that older residents tolerated in order to maintain themselves in a familiar lifelong setting. Evidence from the 1973 Annual Housing Survey demonstrates the extremely stable residential patterns of older people. The survey found that 41.2% of all homeowners aged 65 and over had lived in the same home since 1949 or earlier (U.S. Department of Housing and Urban Development, 1979, p. 15). The combination of lowered physical mobility, increased transit dependence, familiarity with the surrounding environment, and a concern for increased control during a period of relative instability together promote lower residential mobility.

The neighborhood also has symbolic qualities. The psychological attachment and identification to the "house" that Cooper (1976) and Werthman (1968) have discussed can also be identified at the larger scale of the neighborhood. Although the neighborhood is more externally controlled than the dwelling unit, the qualities that define "neighborhood" are often considered extremely personal. These standards are based on sociohistoric criteria that define a good neighborhood as one that fits the specific needs and expectations of the neighborhood dweller.

Rowles (1978) suggests that the larger physical environment may encompass several levels of cognition and that emotional and historic ties to a particular area greatly influence the attitudes, preferences, and expectations for that particular locale. A neighborhood park that was the location for Sunday recreational activities 20 years ago may evoke positive fantasies. On the other hand, the present declining nature of the park environment may also reinforce feelings of despair when compared with that same setting 20 years ago. These historic and symbolic characteristics infuse the setting with increased meaning and complicate the link between the older person and the surrounding environment.

Although the neighborhood as a mediator of personal independence and satisfaction is a concept held by policy makers and planners, few studies have examined the relationships between the supportiveness of the setting and the use patterns of the local population. Survey research conducted on a national scale (Harris, 1975) suggests that safety from physical harm is a major factor in both satisfaction and use. The Harris poll found the issue of fear of crime to be the greatest problem reported by the older population. It ranged from 18% in higher income white neighborhoods to 44% in low-income ethnic neighborhoods. Other studies suggest that convenient access to such goods and services as drug stores, small groceries, supermarkets, variety stores, and banks was highly important (Howell, 1976; Lawton, 1977; Newcomer, 1976).

These studies, however, have not measured the complementary and countervailing relationships between the objective physical environment, the perceived environment, and the use of the environment. The remainder of this chapter will present preliminary data on these environmental aspects from an urban low-income neighborhood near the downtown section of Los Angeles. Several different methods were employed to understand more about the use of retail goods and services, parks, public facilities, and social and health services.

Initially, older residents of this area were interviewed to determine their frequency of use of a number of resources. Second, the distance from each subject's residence to each named resource was calculated. Third, the cognitive representation of each subject's neighborhood was determined by two methods. The relationship between the use of the environment, the location of various goods and services, and the cognitive representation of neighborhood are examined in order to (1) determine the dependence for life support on various goods and services, (2) to understand the geographic relationship between the person's residence and frequently visited services, and (3) to measure the utility of cognitive mapping as a procedure for representing salient elements of the environment.

NEIGHBORHOOD DESCRIPTION

The Westlake District is not unlike other older central-city neighborhoods that have attracted high percentages of older people. It is located directly west of the downtown district that will be reported in greater detail in Chapter 19. The aerial photograph in Figure 13.1 illustrates some of the salient environmental characteristics of the area. A large urban park, named MacArthur Park, is located near the center of the neighborhood. The Harbor Freeway defines the east boundary, and the change in the street grid pattern on the west, Hoover Boulevard, defines the western edge. Third Street on the north and Pico Boulevard on the south form the remaining borders. The Wilshire corridor, a highly commercialized strip, cuts through the center of the neighborhood running from the downtown West District to the adjoining Wilshire District. The five east-west streets near the center of the neighborhood are the most heavily trafficked. Alvarado, which runs on the east side next to the park is the only major north-south street. Taller buildings, which often provide visual landmarks, are located in the Wilshire corridor.

The neighborhood is relatively unstable, recently accommodating a large influx of Latino residents. Rental stock is primarily single-room occupancy hotel or studio apartment accommodations. The housing

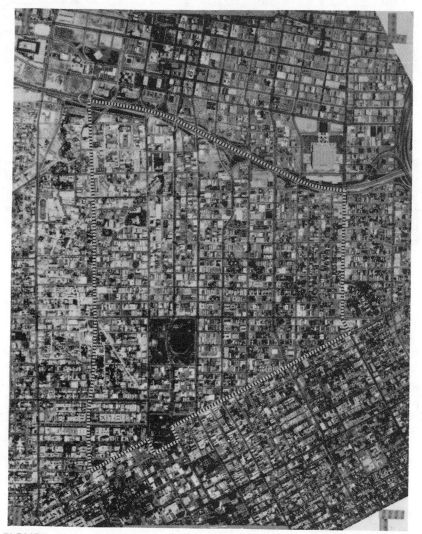

FIGURE 13.1. Westlake Neighborhood. (Photo by Metrex, Pasadena. Reproduced by permission.)

stock is in generally poor condition. Furthermore, per capita crime rates are among the highest in the city.

The neighborhood provides some supports to the older population, which made up 21% of the district's population according to the 1970 census. The area has continued, however, to change so as to accommodate the shopping and other needs of the younger ethnic inmovers and the office needs of commercial business interests. The number of housing units constructed was far below those demolished between 1960 and 1970.

SAMPLE CHARACTERISTICS

The list of eligible respondents for this study was established by a door-to-door screening, which identified all persons aged 60 and over who had lived in the neighborhood for at least 1 year. One hundred respondents were randomly selected from this list of 4,800 eligibles. Figure 13.2 shows the location of all sample respondents. Cluster patterns are generally in proportion to the number of eligibles located in each building.

Respondents have a relatively high functional health level, with only 11.6% reporting difficulty walking one block. The sample is nearly evenly matched in gender. The most predominant ethnic group is white, with a few Chicanos and one Asian making up the remainder of the sample. Most sample respondents live alone, with only 11.9% married and living with their spouse. High familiarity with the neighborhood and the surrounding area is implied, since respondents have lived in the Westlake neighborhood for an average of 10.3 years and the general area for 17.2 years. Finally, the average age is 71.31 years.

Service Use Patterns

Face-to-face interviews queried respondents about the frequency of use, distance to, and specific location of 32 common goods and services. Table 13.1 shows in the first column in rank order the percentage of respondents reporting the use of each service. The first 12 services are utilized by a majority of the sample respondents and thus could be considered the most important as potential neighborhood supports. These top-rated services include five retail stores, five financial and personal services, one eating establishment, and a recreational resource. Although the percentage using the service provides one index

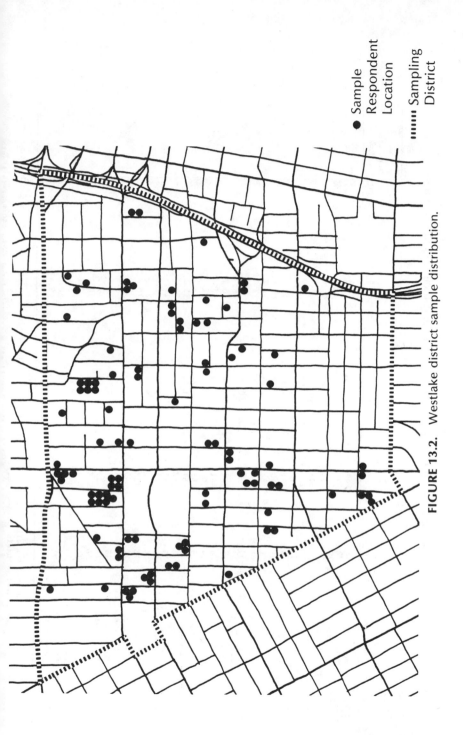

FIGURE 13.2. Westlake district sample distribution.

- Sample Respondent Location
- Sampling District

TABLE 13.1

Amount and Intensity of Use, Distance, and Inclusion in Cognitive Maps of 32 Services

	1 % Who Use	2 No. Trips Per Mo. [a]	3 Mean Trips/Mo. [b]	4 Mean Distance [b] [c]	5 % Of Used Services In Cognitive Maps
Supermarket	88	685	7.78	5.4	43
Bank	82	167	2.04	4.1	56
Pharmacy	79	202	2.55	5.2	60
Physician	79	76	.96	14.9	26
Beauty/barber	75	104	1.39	3.5	66
Variety store	72	193	2.69	4.0	57
Small grocery	72	877	12.17	1.2	76
Department store	69	131	1.90	11.1	5
Restaurant	66	440	6.66	4.9	44
Dry cleaner	61	82	1.34	2.2	69
Eye doctor	61	12	.20	12.0	26
Park	53	449	8.47	4.0	79
Shoe store	47	11	.24	6.3	42
Church	47	181	3.84	10.7	24
Luncheonette	46	441	9.58	3.7	63
Hardware	44	102	2.31	2.7	59
Second hand store	39	69	1.77	4.1	56
Clothing store	37	57	1.53	15.1	25
Library	36	82	2.27	5.7	46
Dentist	33	12	.37	11.3	6
Laundromat	29	77	2.66	1.2	83
Liquor store	26	240	9.22	.9	80
Bakery	25	118	4.72	10.6	64
Book store	22	23	1.05	9.0	32
Filling station	20	71	3.53	4.4	47
Movies	18	35	1.92	8.6	36
Tax service	16	17	1.03	2.5	17
Foot doctor	16	5	.34	6.5	38
Gift shop	15	11	.70	2.7	50
Bar	13	118	9.11	2.4	69
Craft shop	10	5	.47	10.7	20
Food coop	2	5	2.50	3.6	50

[a]This column aggregates all trips made by 100 respondents to the service destinations during a monthly time period.

[b]Means calculated on basis of users only.

[c] . . . for this investigation are calculated to be 750 feet in length.

of neighborhood support, it does not provide a measure of the intensity of use.

The second column of Table 13.1 shows the total number of monthly trips (aggregated over all subjects) made to each of the 32 types of service. This index provides a better measure of the intensity of dependence on each type of service. Eight services appear among the top 12 in both percentage using and intensity of total use: the supermarket, variety store, small grocery, bank, department store, pharmacy, restaurant, and park. Physician, eye doctor, dry cleaner, and beauty/barber services drop out of the second list because, although a majority of the sample uses these facilities, the total number of monthly trips to each of these destinations is much lower. New entries included in the top 12 services by intensity include church, bar, luncheonette, and liquor store. These services are used by a smaller number of respondents but in a relatively intensive manner. In many locations the liquor store, selling goods other than liquor, acts as a substitute for the small grocery, the most heavily visited service. Thus the liquor store probably includes trips for convenience goods and not just alcoholic beverages. For many subjects church activities such as Bible study or daily mass supplement weekly church attendance.

Column 3 of Table 13.1 provides another measure of service dependence, the mean number of trips per month taken to each type of service. These entries represent monthly trip averages for individuals who utilize each service rather than the total number of trips taken. This column includes 9 of the top 12 showing greatest aggregate use in Column 2. However, 3 new services appear: baker, laundromat, and filling station, each representing a destination intensively used by a small number of sample respondents. Because the total number of people who use these services is small, they do not appear among the 12 most used services shown in Column 1 of Table 13.1.

Column 4 shows the mean distance from the user's residence to the service destination, an index of convenience that could have some impact on the average or aggregate frequency of use. By comparison with the trip frequencies shown in Columns 2 and 3, less than half of the closest 12 services were among the most used. Five of the closest services (liquor store, small grocery, luncheonette, bar, and park) are also among the 12 most used services shown in Column 2. The remaining most proximate service entries, which include tax service, dry cleaner, hardware, gift shop, food coop, beauty/barber, and laundromat, are unlikely to stimulate additional trips simply because of their proximity to a person's residence. Of particular interest are those facilities located further from a person's residence that nonetheless generate a high number of trips. The department store and church are good examples of this particular phenomenon. Another service located further than most is the supermarket. This is particularly interesting considering the fact that it is one of the most highly used services, with the second-highest concentration of total monthly trips.

Only 2 services, park and small grocery, appear among the top 12 in Columns 1–4 of Table 13.1. The variety store, restaurant, and supermarket show high use (Columns 1, 2, and 3) but are missing from the most proximate facilities shown in Column 4. These 3 services are important because they are not as conveniently located but generate high demand. The liquor store, bar, and luncheonette appear in Columns 2, 3, and 4, and thus represent proximate services utilized quite extensively by a small number of subjects.

Three services, bank, department store, and pharmacy, are included among the most used only in terms of the percentage who ever use them, and the overall aggregate of use. These services meet the stringent criteria for aggregate use, but are located somewhat further from the respondent's home and thus are not visited as frequently. The beauty/barber shop and dry cleaner are used by a large number of respondents and are located in the proximate neighborhood.

The church appears as a frequently visited service by less than a majority of respondents and tends to be located some distance from the residence.

Identifying the most important supportive services is difficult. However, the best criteria for importance would appear to be those that are used by a large percentage of people and simultaneously generate high overall use. The 8 services that meet these criteria are supermarket, variety store, small grocery, bank, department store, pharmacy, restaurant, and park.

MENTAL MAPS OF THE NEIGHBORHOOD

In addition to gathering information about the use of neighborhood services and facilities the study seeks to understand more about the internalized mental images older people have of the neighborhood. These images are often referred to as cognitive maps, and include salient characteristics of the surrounding environment. Cognitive maps are one way of studying the means by which people learn and cope with the external physical environment. Since this external environment is too vast and complex to comprehend in its totality, a variety of simplifications, schematizations, and even distortions are used in order to reduce the totality to functional scale. Use is partly a function of environmental knowledge. Thus it is important to determine the extent to which what is "claimed" as one's neighborhood is consistent with the use made of that area.

This research utilized two techniques to elicit cognitive maps from respondents. The first required subjects to outline on a cartographically accurate base map of the district (scale: $1'' = 650'$) the area they considered to be their neighborhood. The second provided the subjects with a blank sheet of paper on which they were asked to draw a map of their neighborhood. The hand-drawn map was the first task each respondent was given. Hand-drawn neighborhood maps were consistently smaller than the cartographic outlines of the neighborhood. Both landmarks and streets were used by subjects to define their local familiar surroundings. The maps ranged in complexity from one showing a single street and residence to one with detailed, extensive representations of large portions of the district.

The cartographic map presented to subjects for the neighborhood definition task included an area of approximately 6 square miles within which the sampling district (illustrated by the dotted line in Figure 13.2) was located. The smaller sampling was a district approximately 1.5 square miles in area. This manner of presentation thus provided subjects the opportunity to claim as neighborhood that territory outside of the sampling district. Because subjects' residences were distributed throughout the district each neighborhood configuration was unique. The sizes of maps ranged from 0.15 to 274 square blocks (a block size of $750' \times 750'$ is assumed with regard to square block calculations). The average map size was 0.674 square miles or approximately 33.40 square blocks. The median neighborhood size (21.1 square blocks), however, was much lower because a smaller number of very large neighborhood maps disproportionately increased the mean. Only 12 neighborhood maps were over 65.5 square blocks. Nearly 80% of the neighborhood maps were smaller than 45 square blocks.

Map configurations were classified into six different shapes illustrated in Figure 13.3. Subjects were generally precise about selecting streets as boundaries for neighborhood maps. For example, only 16.1% of respondents selected vague or poorly defined configurations such as the circle or triangle. In fact, the most common configuration type was the irregular shape, which suggests respondents were quite discerning when defining areas as either within or outside their neighborhood. Of interest is the fact that only about one fourth of the sample chose a square or circle shape, theoretically the equidistant configuration assumed to be valid in most neighborhood literature.

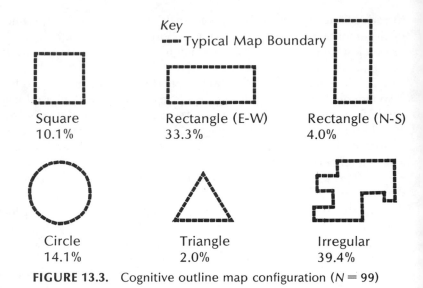

FIGURE 13.3. Cognitive outline map configuration (*N* = 99)

The rectangular shape elongated in the east-west direction was the second most common shape drawn by 30.3% of respondents. This rectangular shape may be more common because of the predominant east-west orientation of major traffic streets. A comparison with the north-south rectangular shape shows that only 4% of subjects selected this shape.

When asked to provide a rationale for selecting the neighborhood boundary, subjects provided two kinds of reasons. One was internally oriented, suggesting the border was selected for reasons relating to the use of or the psychological attachment to the geographic area encompassed by the boundary. The second rationale was externally oriented and generally represented an attempt to exclude areas from the defined neighborhood. Internally oriented reasons were much more common than external delimiters.

About 60% of the sample provided one and 19% provided two internally oriented reasons for boundary placement. The most common reason (provided by nearly 30% of the sample) was that services and facilities used by the respondent were located inside neighborhood boundaries. The second most common reason was simply that the defined area was used by the respondent. Less common were familiarity with the surrounding environment, walking behavior, and responses relating to the location of friends. Non-use was the major externally oriented reason for boundary placement for 28% of the respondents. The remainder considered areas outside their defined neighborhood as dangerous or unfamiliar.

Consensus and Composite Cognitive Map Configurations

Two approaches were utilized to understand the consensus image of neighborhood territory. The first approach utilizes the technique developed by Lynch (1960), which combines elements of the neighborhood defined by subjects in their hand-drawn maps into a composite map. Second, territories defined as neighborhood by all respondents were combined using a synagraphic computer (Regnier, Eribes, & Hanson, 1973). The result is a consensus map that identifies portions of the Westlake District considered by varying percentages of the population to be their neighborhood.

Figure 13.4 illustrates this composite map. The two major elements used by respondents in defining neighborhood characteristics were streets and places. The most popular place was MacArthur Park; nearly 50% of the 95 respondents who completed maps chose to include the park. Four of the most popular elements included on hand-drawn maps wre located around or within a half block of MacArthur Park. These included the Alpha Beta Supermarket, Thrifty Drug Store, and the Elks Building. Nine other popular landmarks were included by at least 10% of the respondents. Five of these nine were retail services. The remaining four elements were the post office, library, hospital, and another park. One interesting feature of these secondary landmarks is their physical location. In contrast to the four most popular places clustered near the park, five of the nine secondary landmarks were located on the border of the neighborhood. The most commonly identified street was Alvarado, near the park. Over 42% of respondents identified this street. Major portions of three heavily trafficked east-west streets, 6th, Wilshire, and 7th Streets, were included in at least 20% of the maps reviewed.

Figure 13.5 illustrates the consensus map generated by a computer synthesis of neighborhood configurations outlined on the cartographic base map. The darker areas denote greater proportions of respondents who included that area in their maps. The highest point of consensus in zone 1 occurred near the intersection of Wilshire and Alvarado. Eighty percent of the respondents included this intersection within their neighborhood. MacArthur Park and the commercial strips along Alvarado and Wilshire adjacent to the park were included in the highest consensus zone (71% to 80% of the respondents).

Zone 2 includes the remainder of the park and expands easterly

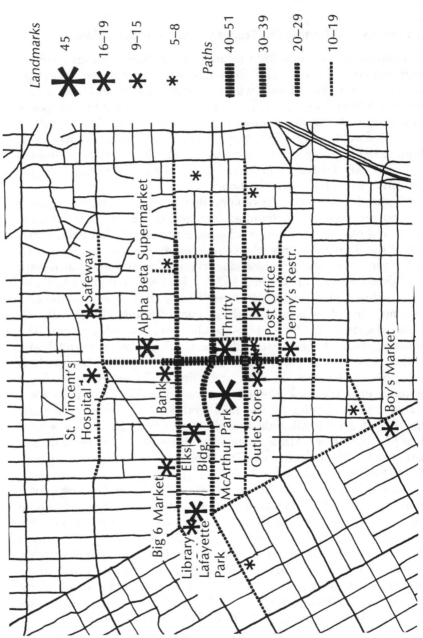

Landmarks

✴ 45
✴ 16–19
✳ 9–15
∗ 5–8

Paths

▮▮▮▮ 40–51
▪▪▪▪ 30–39
▪▪▪ 20–29
···· 10–19

St. Vincent's Hospital
Safeway
Alpha Beta Supermarket
Bank
Big 6 Market
Elks Bldg.
Library
Lafayette Park
McArthur Park
Thrifty
Outlet Store
Post Office
Denny's Restr.
Boy's Market

FIGURE 13.4. Composite of hand-drawn maps.

192

toward a mixed commercial district and southerly from the park into a commercial and residential area. Zone 3 expands in the easterly, southerly, and westerly directions including the commercial areas along several major streets as well as highly dense residential areas. Zone 4 continues expansion in all directions including more residential areas and stretching to the western border of the neighborhood. Zone 5 expands further in a concentric pattern stretching to Temple Street, the northern boundary, and expanding beyond the western boundary into the adjoining Wilshire District. Pico Street maintains a consistent southern boundary.

The two neighborhood image maps share a number of similar attributes. MacArthur Park was included as a central element in both the hand-drawn composite maps and consensus neighborhood map. The strengths of Alvarado and the intervening cross streets of 6th, Wilshire, and Alvarado as a major spine is also reflected in both representations.

One major difference between the two representations is the high number of peripheral elements that appear in the hand-drawn composite map. The consensus neighborhood maps are highly centralized

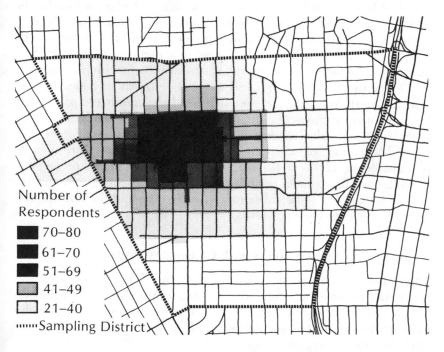

Number of Respondents
■ 70–80
■ 61–70
■ 51–69
□ 41–49
□ 21–40
······Sampling District

FIGURE 13.5. Consensus neighborhood map.

and expand as a series of concentric rings from MacArthur Park. Interestingly, the high-consensus zones 1 through 3 include nearly 60% of the 22 places identified by five or more respondents in the hand-drawn maps.

Comparison of Use Patterns with Cognitive Maps

Individual neighborhood outline maps and the consensus map seem to share a general orientation toward commercial areas that provide supportive goods and services to the older population. In order to measure this relationship, the locations of monthly goods and services trips were compared with both individual neighborhood outline cognitive maps and the consensus cognitive map configuration.

Column 5 of Table 13.1 shows the percentage of sample respondents who included these particular service types within the neighborhood area they outlined on the cartographic map. When compared with the use and proximity information in Columns 1–4, a curious combination of services is seen to be included in individuals' cognitive maps. They include the small grocery, park, and pharmacy, which appear in the list of 8 services common to Columns 1 and 2. In addition, luncheonette, laundromat, liquor store, bar, dry cleaner, beauty/barber, and hardware, which are located within close proximity to most residences are included. The range of inclusion in the cognitive map for these high-ranking services is from 60% for the pharmacy to 82.8% for the laundry. Frequently visited, conveniently located services are most likely to be included in individual cognitive maps. Distant services, such as physician, department store, and church, are rarely included in individual maps. Conversely, the supermarket, which was located an average of more than 0.7 miles from the subject's residence, is included in 42.9% of the maps. The high percentage of services included wthin cognitive map boundaries underscores both the inclusive nature of the neighborhood map outline and the constrained life space of elderly respondents.

Comparison of Use Patterns with Consensus Maps

Table 13.2 compares the areas of the consensus zones with the proportions-of-use units generated in each zone, as well as use outside the sampled district. This analysis provides further evidence as to the convergence between neighborhood use patterns and the consensus configuration of cognitive maps.

TABLE 13.2
Distributions and Comparisons of Area and Use Units

Use Area	% Area of Sampling District	% of Total Use Units	Use Density Index [a]
Consensus Zone 1	2.71	19.6	7.23
Consensus Zone 2	6.29	9.9	1.57
Consensus Zone 3	7.31	5.6	0.77
Consensus Zone 4	13.82	25.2	1.82
Consensus Zone 5	29.24	18.2	0.62
Remainder of sampling district	40.63	6.2	0.15
	100.00		
On map, outside sampling district	-----	13.5	-----
Off map	-----	1.8	-----

[a]The use density index is calculated by dividing the percentage of total use by the percentage of the sampling area within which those trips occurred. A hypothetical even distribution of use units throughout the neighborhood would represent an index value of .847.

Consensus zone 1 (refer to Figure 13.5), which includes the park and some stores near Wilshire and Alvarado, accounts for nearly 20% of the trips respondents make on a monthly basis, but includes less than 3% of the geographic area of the neighborhood.

Consensus zone 2 is twice the size of zone 1 but accounts for only about half the number of trips. Zone 3 expands in a concentric fashion and includes only about half of the number of trips of zone 2 and one fourth the number of trips included within zone 1. Zone 4 nearly doubles the size of zone 3 but shows a high-use density index. This reversal trend can be explained by the fact that four grocery stores and Lafayette park are included in this zone. The total number of trips to these five destinations alone accounts for nearly 1,000 trips. As noted, the major supermarkets were located near the periphery of the neighborhood.

The area defined by zones 1 through 4 accounted for slightly more than 30% of the neighborhood area. Within this area, however, fell more than 60% of the trips the sample made on a monthly basis. The consensus neighborhood map is thus an accurate representation of neighborhood territory that supports the majority of trips taken by respondents.

CONCLUSIONS

If this research is generalizable to other urban areas it would suggest that the local neighborhood is a meaningful and definable concept for the inner-city, transit-dependent older person. The following 8 services are utilized most extensively by a majority of Westlake sample respondents: supermarket, variety store, small grocery, bank, department store, pharmacy, restaurant, and park. Five of these 8 services are located within an average of 5 blocks from the older person's residence. The supermarket, which is the most highly used and second most frequently visited service, however, is located an average of 5.4 blocks from the subject's residence. The department store, among the top 9 most highly utilized services, is an average of 11.1 blocks from the older person's residence.

Certain trips, such as those taken to a physician, are infrequently made to a location a considerable distance from the person's dwelling unit. Furthermore, some destinations such as church services are frequently visited destinations for a small subsample of the population. The locations of these particular destinations may be important in the design of a demand-response transit system or in rating the service accessibility of sites for planned housing projects. The consensus map combining individual neighborhood map outlines provides a unique measure of the common elements considered important. This mapping procedure can be helpful in targeting neighborhood areas for capital improvements, as well as in suggesting locations of senior-specific social and health services.

The close correspondence between cognitive maps and patterns of neighborhood use underscores the utility of mental mapping and the products of these representations. Not only do these maps provide a record of how the environment is mentally conceived and manipulated, but they can have direct application to urban planning interventions. The concept of cognitive mapping has been used by geographers, psychologists, and urban planners. This research has usually been designed to understand better the process of spatial perception and its application for navigational purposes. The preceding research suggests that these procedures can also be used to isolate, examine, reinforce, preserve, or manipulate certain portions of the environment to aid the older person.

REFERENCES

Cooper, C. The house as a symbol of self. In H. M. Proshansky, W. H. Ittelson, & L. G. Rivlin (Eds.), *Environmental psychology* (2nd ed.). New York: Holt, Rinehart & Winston, 1976.

Harris, L., & Associates. *The myth and reality of aging.* Washington, D.C.: National Council on the Aging, 1975.

Howell, S. Site selection and the elderly. In M. P. Lawton, R. J. Newcomer, & T. O. Byerts (Eds.), *Community planning for an aging society.* Stroudsburg, Pa.: Dowden, Hutchinson & Ross, 1976.

Keller, S. *The urban neighborhood: A sociological perspective.* New York: Random House, 1968.

Lawton, M. P. The impact of the environment on aging and behavior. In J. E. Birren & K. W. Schaie (Eds.), *Handbook of the psychology of aging.* New York: Van Nostrand Reinhold, 1977.

Lawton, M. P., Kleban, M. H., & Carlson, D. The inner-city resident: To move or not to move. *Gerontologist.* 1973, *13*, 443–448.

Lynch, K. *The image of the city.* Cambridge, Mass.: MIT Press, 1960.

Newcomer, R. An evaluation of neighborhood service convenience for elderly housing project residents. In P. Suedfeld & J. A. Russell (Eds.), *The behavioral basis of design* (EDRA 7). Stroudsburg, Pa.: Dowden, Hutchinson & Ross, 1976.

Pastalan, L. A., & Carson, D. H. *Spatial behavior of older people.* Ann Arbor, Mich.: University of Michigan Press, 1970.

Regnier, V., Eribes, R., & Hanson, W. Cognitive mapping as a concept for establishing neighborhood service delivery locations for older people: The use of synagraphics as methodological tools. *Proceedings of the 8th Annual ACM Urban Symposium,* New York, 1973.

Rowles, G. D. *Prisoners of space: Exploring the geographical experience of older people.* Boulder, Colo.: Westview Press, 1978.

U.S. Department of Housing and Urban Development. *Annual Housing Survey: 1973 Housing characteristics of older Americans in the United States.* Washington D.C.: Office of Policy Development and Research, 1979.

Werthman, C. *The social meaning of the physical environment.* Unpublished doctoral dissertation, University of California, Berkeley, 1968.

IV
Some Housing and Housing-Service Alternatives

14

The Scope of Residential Repair and Renovation Services and Models of Service Delivery

EDWARD STEINFELD

During the last several years there has been a growing awareness that the housing problems of older people cannot be solved by the construction of new housing units alone. There is an increasing emphasis on helping people to remain in their existing homes and to upgrade their present living conditions. This emphasis is by no means the major focus of federal and state housing programs, which still emphasize new construction. However, the energy crisis has resulted in greatly increased fuel and utility costs, and rapid inflation has had a severe impact on people with fixed incomes. These events have combined to accentuate the problems of the majority of older people who are not served by new construction programs. The emphasis on rehabilitation, renovation, repair, and related services resulted from both an acute need for such services and a recognition that new construction has had, and is likely to continue to have, much less impact on the solution to housing problems for the elderly than is generally believed.

Maintaining satisfactory housing is an important factor in the quality of life for all people. However, older people have more specific housing needs that are related to their socioeconomic status and the processes of aging.

The dwelling is symbolic of the self. Living independently reaffirms to older persons that they are competent and that they do not

Portions of this chapter appeared in Holmes, D. and Holmes, M.B. *Handbook of Human Services*. New York: Human Sciences Press, 1979. Reprinted with permission. Much of the work on this paper was completed under a contract to Community Research Applications, Inc. from the Administration on Aging, U.S. Department of Health, Education and Welfare. Monica B. Holmes was the Project Director and provided editorial assistance.

have to depend on someone else to take care of their personal needs. Like clothing, a dwelling presents an image of the individual to the outside world. This image contributes to the occupant's social identity. A dwelling is personal territory: Everything within it comes under the personal control of the occupant. For many older people this territory may be the only place in which they can have some control over the world and arrange it to suit their individual needs and wants. As a place from which the outside world can be barred, the dwelling can be a haven from the many losses associated with aging. Although a dwelling cannot protect one from loss of spouse, income, employment, or social status, it represents protection from the elements and thus has real meaning as a last line of defense against psychological despair.

A dwelling is familiar ground. Particularly for long-time occupants, which most older people are, the home represents a history of experiences that have contributed to the construction of a personal identity. Moreover, intimate knowledge of familiar surroundings provides a large measure of support in daily activities. For example, it is often reported that new residents in a nursing home may become confused and disoriented. Observers will wonder how the elderly person lived independently for so long. In fact, removal of a person from a familiar setting can bring about the appearance of mental disability, simply because familiar supports and surroundings are absent. Given the deep personal meaning and the physical support provided by the dwelling, it is not surprising that the impact of relocation can be severe.

Income is limited and usually fixed in the later stages of life. For the older homeowner a house is the major capital asset. If a mortgage has been paid, only taxes, utilities, and maintenance costs are required to retain residency. It is usually much more expensive to move into a rental unit or to buy a new house. Furthermore, homeowners often view their houses in terms of legacies. The house has value as both a hedge against the high cost of living and as the most meaningful thing older persons can leave to their children. However, rising costs for utilities, repairs, materials, fuel, and taxes have a great impact on their ability to continue to pay for housing, and thus retain possession of this asset.

Among older people who have physical disabilities or low stamina there is a limitation in their capacity to do major maintenance and ordinary self-help repair work, although they can still take care of personal care needs. In addition, the need for special adaptive features such as grab bars is greater among the aged. Accident prevention, stairway modifications, removal of safety hazards, and fire-safety provisions are also more critical concerns. The aged body generally has a reduced ability to maintain thermal equilibrium. This means that drafty houses and ineffective heating systems can be serious threats to good health. Widowhood, coupled with the onset of chronic physical or sensory impairments, can leave an elderly woman who is living alone not only vulnerable to crime but also without the ability to make minor repairs, do yardwork, remove snow, or do other maintenance tasks.

A relatively high proportion of older people live in inner-city neighborhoods and in depopulated small towns. In both cases, not only is the physical condition of their housing likely to be poor, but also the viability of their neighborhoods is threatened due to lack of public and commercial services, poor maintenance of streets and sidewalks, and generally deteriorated surroundings. Improvement in existing housing, therefore, often must be viewed as part of overall neighborhood and community redevelopment since the livability of a place is not based solely on the condition of the dwelling.

In summary, there is a shift developing in public policy toward a focus on repair and renovation of existing housing. Older people have many specific housing needs that should be addressed through public programs. These include maintenance of a positive self-image and identity, elimination of stress due to involuntary relocation, economic assistance in maintaining possession of homes, support for physical limitations resulting from poor health, and assistance in managing and operating a house. The task of residential repair and renovation services is to address these needs effectively.

The remainder of this chapter identifies and describes a variety of residential repair and renovation services and presents some models of service delivery. The descriptions of services provides an overview of the range of services that can be developed under the rubric of residential repair and renovation. This chapter does not focus on the broader problem of neighborhood and community redevelopment but it must be recognized that improving housing is only one aspect of general improvement of environmental quality.

RESIDENTIAL REPAIR AND RENOVATION SERVICES

Emergency Repairs

Some types of housing defects are so severe that sickness or accidents to the occupants, abandonment of, or major damage to the building may occur unless they are attended to promptly. The scope of emergency repairs must be limited to those things that repair crews can correct, at least temporarily. Twenty-four-hour service is highly desirable. Emergency repair programs should include referral service for people who need other types of assistance. Examples include referrals to the fire department, police, or other emergency services when evacuation and temporary shelter are necessary, as well as referrals to minor repair or major rehabilitation programs for problems not considered to be emergencies. The following problems may require emergency repair services:

- severe roof leaks
- plumbing breakdowns that impede the use of sinks or toilets
- breakdowns in heating and hot water systems and lack of fuel
- utility shut-offs or supply breakdowns
- severe fire hazards such as faulty wiring
- broken windows that present a risk to health or security
- electrical problems that present a hazard or cause a cut-off of electric supply
- damage caused by a break-in or attempted break-in that leaves a dwelling vulnerable to another incident
- snow and ice accumulation indoors where windows or roofing need repair
- serious rodent and vermin infestation
- removal of heavy snow from structures where accumulation is such as to threaten structural damage or prevent egress or entrance

In areas prone to such natural disasters as floods, tornadoes, and hurricanes emergency repair services should be developed to plan for potential disasters and mobilization of aid to elderly people in their wake.

Weatherization

Weatherization includes repairs, modifications, or supplies that protect a dwelling or its occupants from the effects of weather, conserve energy, or provide alternative energy sources to heat or cool a dwelling. Energy conservation and alternative energy sources are usually the primary objectives of weatherization programs because they help reduce utility bills and protect against energy shortages. The provision of reliable fuel supplies is an important weatherization service that can sometimes mean the difference between life and death if there is an energy shortage or utility cut-off.

In terms of energy conservation, the following actions are highly effective measures:

- replacing broken or missing windows
- caulking and weatherstripping windows and doors
- installing storm windows or covering windows with plastic if windows are a high source of infiltration and cannot be caulked
- servicing the heating system
- insulating attics, walls, floors

Since maintaining thermal comfort is so important to older persons and space in their houses is often underutilized, an appropriate approach may be the intense weatherization of only part of a house combined with sealing off the underutilized parts. Such an approach can make a small expenditure go a great distance. Moreover, in regions where summers are hot and humid this approach can allow occupants to leave storm windows in place all year yet still have a cool part of the house in summer.

The maintenance of an adequate fuel supply is an absolute necessity in parts of the country subject to fuel shortages. A weatherization service should include a program that both insures older people protection from shut-offs by utility companies and, if possible, provides emergency fuel supplies. This is possible with fuel oil, bottled gas, coal, and wood, but the maintenance of gas and electricity supplies can only occur through advocacy with utility companies on shut-off policies or through development and support of new legislation. Advocacy with the state public utility regulatory agency is another means of altering shut-off policies.

Weatherization is a high priority for both urban and rural areas and for tenants as well as homeowners. In rural areas weatherization should give specific attention to people living in mobile homes. They may have different needs from those of people living in conventional dwellings. For example, in hurricane zones, tie-downs to prevent homes from overturning in high wind could be provided. Moreover, heat loss and gain in mobile homes is usually very high. Specific ways might be found to reduce heat losses and gains beyond those techniques used in conventional dwellings.

Another aspect of weatherization should be consumer education, including counseling and printed materials for the client that show ways of conserving fuel (e.g., setting thermostats lower, closing off unused rooms, closing drapes at night).

Minor Modifications and Renovations

Many minor modifications and renovations can improve the livability of homes. Most can be made at little cost and may be particularly helpful in allowing chronically impaired older persons to remain in their existing housing. They include security modifications, fire-safety actions, accident prevention measures, and modifications to make a dwelling accessible to and usable by physically disabled people.

Security Modifications.   Having a secure dwelling is a major concern for the older person. The major priorities for any security program should be

- encouraging public surveillance of open space and entrances both from the street and from within the dwelling
- reducing the number of possible entry points
- securing all openings

Some of the most important considerations in security are related to the architectural design of a building and site planning. In multi-unit buildings a significant impact can be achieved through small-scale modifications of entryways and open spaces. Some typical modifications include

- fencing and locking doors to limit access to the site or channel intruders through single, highly visible areas
- decorative elements to define property symbolically and thus keep strangers at a distance
- thinning or removing vegetation that can hide intruders
- adding exterior flood lights or lights along access walks
- eliminating access to fire escapes from the ground
- removing sheds, garbage receptacles, and other items that may be used as a stepladder to reach a window
- equipping locked building entry doors with intercoms located outside the door
- making lobbies visible from outside by lighting and the use of large, transparent, but unbreakable windows in doors
- placing locked mailboxes inside locked entry doors in a highly visible location
- locating lobby waiting and lounge areas adjacent to entry and mailbox areas

- removing exterior hardware on fire exits
- controlling access to the roof when fire escapes have entries there

The dwelling unit itself can be made secure through such hardware, door, and window modifications as

- strengthening or replacing doors, frames, and jambs
- installing escutcheon plates on doors
- protecting exposed hinge pins from removal
- installing secure door and window locks
- substituting break-resistant glass, plastic, or wood panels for glass panels in doors
- installing bars, metal grilles, or window guards on accessible windows (*note*: these should not block emergency egress routes in case in fire)
- installing spinner rings, cylinder guards, or escutcheon plates on protruding lock cylinders
- installing peepholes
- installing mirrors as a means to see around corners in public areas

Fire-Safety Provisions. Fire-safety considerations involve fire prevention, detection and alarm, escape or refuge, confinement, control, and extinguishment. A comprehensive approach to fire safety includes education as well as renovation tasks. Residents can learn how to avoid many fires, for example, by not smoking in bed and by not storing combustible materials. They can also learn how best to escape from their dwellings and how to put out or successfully deal with different types of household fires.

The most important task in fire-safety provisions is inspection of the dwelling for the following hazards:

- combustible materials located close to heat sources, stove burners, or accumulating in confined spaces
- heavy use and improper storage of inflammable fluids
- improperly sized fuses in fuse boxes
- overloaded electrical circuits
- hazardous electrical appliances
- improper maintenance of major appliances (e.g., dryer, stove)
- deteriorated or exposed wiring
- blocked exits

Hazards should be eliminated or repaired before any physical modifications are made. The most important modification is the installation of combined smoke detectors and alarms that can detect and warn about a fire in the shortest possible time. Other physical modifications for improving fire safety include

- installation of a portable fire extinguisher
- installation of a fire-rated door to furnace areas
- installation of ladders at windows to allow easy escape
- refinishing of walls and floors (particularly in furnace rooms of multifamily buildings) to provide lower flame-spread ratings and fire protection

Accident Prevention.   Elderly persons are particularly apt to experience falls, scalds, and burns. As with fire safety, education on accident prevention plays a major role in promoting accident safety. For example, people can be taught how to avoid spattering cooking grease or be encouraged not to climb up on chairs if their balance is poor.

The most common type of home accident involves falls in bathtubs or on stairs. In these two areas minor renovations can play an important role in reducing accidents.

In the bathtub the following measures can help reduce accidents:

- installation of a nonslip surface in the tub
- installation of a secure horizontal grab bar along the wall next to the tub
- installation of a secure horizontal grab bar at one end of the tub
- provision of a seat
- provision of a hand-held shower

Accidents on stairs are caused by inattention to the task of walking and to the stairway itself, inability to see the steps, lack of railings, and tripping or slipping on steps. The following measures can help to reduce accidents on stairways:

- painting the treads so that they can be easily seen and painting a warning stripe on the edge of treads that have risers of irregular height
- repairing loose treads and worn tread edges, removing surface patterns and textures on treads that make the edges difficult to

perceive, and providing a durable slip-resistant surface on each tread

- fastening carpets securely and removing loose or spongy carpeting
- installing secure continuous handrails at both sides and eliminating hazards due to dangerous hardware on handrails
- installing lighting to provide uniform illumination of stairs and handrails, installing permanent night-lights just below the top landing, and installing illuminated three-way switches at the top and bottom landings
- reversing the direction of doors that swing out onto stairways
- rebuilding stairways that are excessively steep or in which the steps are irregular

Other common types of accidents are scalds and burns. There is little that can be done in terms of physical modifications to prevent them other than to cover all exposed hot water or steam pipes a person might touch or grasp, and to provide a safe stove where the placement of controls does not require people to reach over hot burners or pots cooking on the stove.

Accessibility Modifications.   Physically disabled people can live independently if their living environment allows it. There are many kinds of disabilities, and thus the needs of each person for physical modifications to the dwelling are highly specific. Not only must the dwelling be analyzed but the individual's abilities and needs must also be carefully assessed. The major concerns of accessibility modifications are

- gaining entry into the dwelling and all necessary rooms
- using the bathroom
- using the kitchen
- making appliances and mechanical and electrical controls easy to use

The scope of modifications and how they are made are related to the disability of concern. For example, people who use wheelchairs require the most extensive modifications. The blind person has some specific safety concerns but otherwise needs no other special considerations. The partially sighted person has a particular need for the kinds of accident prevention measures discussed in the preceding section. The person with severe hearing loss cannot hear alarms or doorbells. The person with limited mobility and low stamina has many of the same needs as the wheelchair user but not to the same extent. The person with limited use of hands (e.g., severe arthritis) requires modifications to appliances and mechanical and electrical controls. The following changes may be necessary for accessibility, depending on the nature of a person's disability:

- installing a ramp or platform lift to entry level for people who cannot walk stairs
- widening doorways for wheelchairs to pass through
- lowering cabinets, shelves, counters, and sinks; leaving space underneath for pulling in a wheelchair
- installing grab bars at toilets, bathtubs, and showers
- replacing bathtubs with showers
- creating a downstairs bathroom
- creating a bedroom or sleeping space downstairs
- installing a stair lift
- replacing doorknobs with lever handles
- modifying appliance and electrical controls so they can be manipulated without grasping
- installing an easy-to-read number dial on a dial telephone or easy-to-read instructions on major appliances
- improving lighting
- installing visual signals for doorbells, telephones, and fire or smoke alarms

People with disabilities often have special needs for household equipment. They also have a difficult time determining what is available, locating it, and arranging for installation. Residential repair and renovation programs could provide a buying and delivery program for such items, and could give recommendations on reliable equipment, costs, and reputable installers.

Minor Repairs and Improvements (Handyman Services)

There are some small-scale repairs and renovations that usually do not require a licensed contractor to complete. Generally this excludes major structural repairs and rehabilitation, electrical wiring, installation of water, gas, and drain pipes, or major heating repairs. All of the services in the preceding sections could be included in this category except perhaps some emergency repairs or fire-safety measures. A handyman program usually is not limited to specific service tasks such as weatherization or security modifications, but it might include all of those things as the client requires and as the available skills and resources allow. Handyman programs will often perform jobs that specialized services can not do. Handyman programs do not usually provide major rehabilitation work, particularly if tenants must vacate while the work is being done. On the whole, their services substitute for typical, do-it-yourself work of the type that older homeowners can no longer manage. The following are examples of common minor repairs and improvements:

- painting (both exterior and interior), plastering, and plaster repair
- roof and siding repairs
- screen repair and installation
- lamp rewiring, replacing fuses, electrical plugs, and frayed cords
- installation of cabinets and counters
- changing of plumbing fixtures, repair of leaks and stopped-up drains
- laying new floor surfaces
- repair of outhouses
- repairing or replacing doors and windows
- installing new lighting fixtures
- minor repairs or reconstruction of stairs and porches, addition of handrails
- chimney and other masonry repairs
- sidewalk and driveway repairs

In addition to direct services, educational programs can teach older people, their relatives, or neighbors how to make minor repairs and improvements. Another useful service of this type is a lending library of tools. These two services can be particularly useful to tenants. In some cases, young tenants in a building might be trained to make repairs and improvements so that they could help older neighbors as well.

Major Rehabilitation

Major rehabilitation involves extensive repair and reconstruction that usually require skilled tradesmen to complete. In urban areas much of this work comes under the jurisdiction of building codes and has to be done by or under the supervision of licensed workers. In rural areas licensed wokers may not be necessary but the skills required to complete such work would be similar. The following tasks would typically be included in major rehabilitation work:

- major structural repairs such as roof reconstruction, replacement of rotting structural members, reconstruction of fire-damaged areas
- extensive electrical wiring
- installation of major repair of water, gas, and waste plumbing
- major heating repair or replacement
- reconstruction of doors and windows
- re-siding or roofing
- reconstruction of chimneys and other masonry work
- major replastering or installation of dry wall
- replacement of sidewalks and driveways
- installation of indoor plumbing

There are two basic approaches to building rehabilitation: (1) in-occupancy, where occupants remain in the home while the work is done, and (2) nonoccupancy, where buildings are rehabilitated while they are empty. The first approach is the most appropriate for the elderly because it fulfills the overall goal of keeping people in their own homes. The in-occupancy approach is particularly relevant in dense urban areas where a large number of older people live in multifamily rental housing. In such conditions tenants who vacate as a result of rehabilitation work must find a new apartment and are unlikely to realize the benefits of the rehabilitation effort. Nonoccupancy rehabilitation can be effective is it is staged so that several vacant apartments are improved first and existing tenants in the building can move into those apartments; the vacant apartments thus created can then be improved, and so on.

Major rehabilitation programs can focus on organization and administrative tasks rather than on direct construction. For example, a program could identify homeowners or multifamily building owners who need rehabilitation work done and help them to determine the scope of work, obtain financing, coordinate contractors, advise clients during application processing and contracting, and evaluate the work before final sign-off by the client. This type of program could also coordinate major rehabilitation work with other programs available in the community, such as weatherization or modifications and renovation programs.

Urban areas with a large proportion of older homes should be target areas for major rehabilitation services. If neighborhood preservation efforts are underway, the elderly should be targeted as high-priority beneficiaries so that they can participate in the impact of the general uplifting of the neighborhood. Improvement of rental apartment buildings in such neighborhoods can increase rents for tenants. In such cases, it is critical that subsidies such as the Section 8 program of the U.S. Department of Housing and Urban Development or tenant cooperative ownership be initiated in conjunction with major rehabilitation to keep rents within the means of older people. Subsidies, cooperative ownership, and other approaches to keeping rents down can create special problems for older people. Advocacy and counseling may therefore be critical in conjunction with such efforts.

In rural areas, because of the great number of substandard dwellings, the safety and basic adequacy of housing are sometimes relative. Thus the fact that a house cannot be rehabilitated to make it meet a code standard should not be a deterrent to making major safety and sanitation modifications if the repaired dwelling unit is free of significant hazards to health and safety.

Home Maintenance (Chore Services)

Home maintenance or chore services do not include any construction activities. However, these services are housing-related because they contribute to the maintenance of a dwelling's physical condition. They constitute preventative medicine for the dwelling, and can help avoid the need for rehabilitation and renovation in the future. Although a chore-service worker may do housework, this service should not be confused with a homemaker service. Whereas the homemaker is a professionally supervised worker who provides personal care services to the client, the chore worker need not be professionally supervised and does not provide personal care services.

Home-maintenance or chore-service tasks include any indoor or outdoor heavy cleaning or service work. They may also include specialized services, particularly those related to mechanical equipment. The following are some typical home-maintenance or chore-service tasks:

- cleaning floors
- washing windows

- installing storm windows and screens
- cleaning outside gutters and roof drains
- extermination of vermin
- snow shoveling and seasonal yardwork
- removing accumulated litter and debris
- adjustment of pilot lights
- winterization and servicing of heating systems and hot water heaters
- servicing major appliances
- moving heavy furniture
- carrying water, coal, or wood

Many minor repairs may be considered within the scope of a chore service. In fact it may sometimes be difficult to distinguish between the chore service and the handyman service. The major difference is that maintenance requires regular attention; thus clients will tend to be a stable group. On the other hand, minor repairs and improvements are made on an on-demand basis.

Home-maintenance services can include educational programs similar to those discussed under minor renovations. Programs that focus on security, fire safety, and accident prevention can be very effective, particularly if there are no services in the community that provide for physical modifications in these areas.

ALTERNATIVE MODELS OF RESIDENTIAL REPAIR
AND RENOVATION SERVICE DELIVERY

The range of services subsumed under residential repair and renovation is considerable. The various services require the provision of quite different skills and resources, and it is unlikely that any one provider will be able to perform the full range of services. Many communities have active programs already underway in residential repair and renovation and need only to add selected services. Other communities have very little activity in this area and need to develop the full range of repair and renovation services. By focusing on program models, different ways in which the various services can be combined to develop a comprehensive repair and renovation service delivery system can be identified.

Housing-related programs can be operationally characterized along the following dimensions:

Model 1:   Construction model
Model 2:   Advocacy model
Model 3:   Human-service model

In helping to promote and develop residential repair and renovation services, it is important that the service objectives of a particular program be appropriate to the needs of the elderly in the community, that service-need priorities be recognized, and that existing services be coordinated. In some communities a strategy of coordination among several autonomous sponsors may be best. In others, it may be better for an existing provider to develop new expertise and a new emphasis. An understanding of the advantages and disadvantages of the three models of service delivery can be helpful to the planner in analyzing existing community resources and determining the best course of action.

It is important to note that a particular service structure may reflect the personalities and experience of staff more than it does the program sponsor. For convenience, the following discussion refers to specific sponsors as examples of each model. In practice, however, the actual functioning of a program must be studied in depth before any categorization by emphasis can be made.

Model 1: Construction Model

Programs with a construction emphasis place a particular priority on building, repairing, or renovating housing units. They usually focus on a fairly large area, either a state, county, or part of an urban community; however, they may also be restricted to a neighborhood. They may concentrate solely on one service or on many services. Thus programs that incorporate construction expertise usually will have the expertise for doing minor repairs, weatherization, minor modifications and renovations, major rehabilitation, and emergency repairs.

Programs using this model are not concerned with advocacy or human services; basically they are concerned with "bricks and mortar." They are also not necessarily experienced with the full range of repair and renovation services. For example, they may not even know that a chore service exists in the community. Existing housing programs often place heavy emphasis on new construction rather than on repair and renovation services. On the other hand, programs with a construction emphasis are usually familiar with the housing and construction industry and with private contracting, and may need assistance in developing linkages with community outreach mechanisms or needs of older people. Some examples of construction-based activity include

- a community development agency to develop a rehabilitation loan/grant program for specific areas of a city where housing conditions are known to be worse than average
- a rural housing cooperative in an area short of skilled labor working closely with a local Farmers Home Administration Office (FmHA) to provide minor repairs and weatherization to homes of low-income rural people using the FmHA loan and grant programs; the money earned in this work can help finance their own projects
- an agricultural extension service to sponsor a program to do actual construction, including electrical, plumbing, window and door replacement, plastering, and wallboard installation
- public housing authority utilizing funds from a community development block grant to extend its own existing emergency repair services to older people within the community development area

Model 2: Advocacy Model

The focus of programs with an advocacy emphasis is on improving the availability and quality of housing, and on minimizing costs for residents. Usually, programs with an advocacy emphasis serve a small local area or specific group of people (e.g., a tenants' association). Sometimes an advocacy effort is broader in scope and seeks to upgrade an entire neighborhood; this is often called a neighborhood preservation program. Programs with an advocacy emphasis have a multiservice interest because they are concerned with improving housing in general. For example, community action agencies often operate several housing-related programs such as weatherization and handyman. Depending upon their experience, interests, and resources, they may be able to deliver any type of service; in fact some advocacy programs are heavily involved in major construction. Many advocacy programs are also self-help oriented.

Staff in these programs are usually familiar with the planning process, in close contact with residents, and know the condition of housing at the grass-roots level. Being familiar with the target populations, they can identify with specific ethnic and neighborhood interests.

Some residential repair and renovation services are particularly appropriate for delivery through a program using an advocacy model. For example, advocacy-oriented programs can provide the close and continuing client contact necessary for maintenance programs. In addition, those that are organized within small geographic areas are located near clients and, therefore, can provide emergency services quickly. Finally, the grass-roots approach is appropriate for developing self-help competencies and educational efforts in such areas as fire safety, accident prevention, and security. In a neighborhood-oriented program there may be many young people who would be quite happy to provide services to the older residents of the neighborhood, particularly if the neighborhood has a sense of cohesiveness.

There may be some disadvantages to the use of the advocacy model in providing residential repair and renovation services to the elderly. Staff may be inexperienced in administering funds. Since the program may focus on only a small geographic area, an impact cannot be made on a broad, communitywide level. An exception here is the community action agency, which may even serve a multicounty area. Many of these programs will have little construction experience; although they can be effective in this area, they will require technical assistance to compensate for their lack of experience. Although these programs may be quite successful in raising funds for major rehabilitation, they will require technical backup from their own or outside sources. Some examples include

- a neighborhood development association to encourage building owners to rehabilitate run-down apartment buildings using federal funds
- a neighborhood development association to operate an emergency revolving fund to help older people meet utility or loan payments on time
- during the winter, a Community Action Agency to check the availability of heat in homes and apartments of elderly people and to persuade utility companies to restore services if heat is turned off due to nonpayment of bills
- a neighborhood development association to survey the need for weatherization and ensure that it is completed during the warm season before cold weather begins
- a senior center to develop a do-it-yourself club to teach minor home repairs and to work cooperatively on more extensive projects
- a nonprofit voluntary organization through which religious groups, senior clubs and organizations, local industries, and individuals provide volunteer labor, tools, and materials (sometimes called "repairs on wheels," such groups can be particularly effective in rural areas for minor home repairs and chore services)

Model 3: Human-Service Model

Programs emphasizing human services focus on solving problems of individuals through direct service delivery. Usually such programs are limited to one or two services. However, they often operate on a communitywide scale.

Because programs using a human services approach focus on people rather than on housing units, they are often quite aware of the target population's needs and are already in touch with potential clients. Their major disadvantage is that they usually have little experience in construction or knowledge of housing issues. To provide services beyond home maintenance or education related to minor renovations, this type of program requires technical assistance. However, coordination of their efforts with a program using a construction or advocacy model can improve the effectiveness of the total range of services to the community. Some examples are

- a social service agency that provides chore services by hiring retired carpenters with Comprehensive Employment and Training Act (CETA) funds to do minor repairs for clients of its program
- a hospital rehabilitation medicine department that hires college students in architecture, supervised by a faculty member or practicing professional, to design renovations for disabled patients who are being discharged. Title III Older Americans Act funds can be used to pay for a portion of the students' salaries while the college work-study program pays for the rest
- a police department that sponsors programs to inspect homes of older persons and recommends actions to make them secure
- a fire department that inspects homes and ensures the absence of fire hazards
- a senior center where special education programs to teach self-help home-repair skills and safety precautions are developed
- a senior center that uses the services of a group of older persons employed under CETA or Title IX of the Older Americans Act to provide minor repairs (Green Thumb, one of the five national contractors under Title IX, crews have been particularly active in such programs)
- a senior center that encourages the development of a neighbor-to-neighbor volunteer approach for minor repairs and chore services

In conclusion, it is clear that the most effective service to a community will be provided by a comprehensive service delivery system. It is possible that programs with more than one emphasis could be so coordinated as to provide comprehensive repair and renovation services to the elderly of a community. Opportunities for linkages usually occur where there are needs and resources available for

- cash funds and in-kind contributions
- technical assistance
- administrative backup
- equipment and space
- referral and outreach

Each of the three models of service delivery has advantages and disadvantages. Each is more suited to some kinds of services than to others. Planners should consider the relative strengths and weaknesses of each model when evaluating which program among existing service providers would be the best base for a new service.

BIBLIOGRAPHY

American Association of Retired Persons/National Retired Teachers Association. *Your retirement safety guide*. Long Beach, Calif.: AARP/NTRA, 1971.
    This small booklet identifies potential dangers older people face in their physical surroundings. It gives some hints about potential renovation needs in the accident-safety area.
Cavavaty, D. & Haviland, D. S. *Life safety from fire: A guide for housing the elderly*. Washington, D.C.: Federal Housing Administration, U.S. Government Printing Office, 1968.
    This book outlines the problem of fire safety in buildings where elderly people live. It focuses on new construction but includes much useful information on the basic problem of fire safety and fire prevention.
Lawton, M. P. *Planning and managing housing for the elderly*. New York: Wiley-Interscience, 1975.
    A useful general reference book on housing for elderly people. It includes information on basic housing and neighborhood needs as well as descriptive data on housing conditions and programs.
President's Committee on Urban Housing. *A decent home*. Washington, D.C.: U.S. Government Printing Office, 1968.
    This book outlines the broad range of federal commitments to housing and evaluates future trends. A section on federal legislation in the rehabilitation area is included. Programs initiated after 1968 are not included (e.g., Community Development Block Grants).

Reader's Digest. *Complete do-it-yourself manual.* Pleasantville, N.Y.: Reader's Digest Association, 1973.
  A comprehensive book on all phases of home repair, including tool use and maintenance. Very well illustrated.

Steinfeld, H. & Schroeder, S. *Barrier-free design for the elderly and disabled.* Syracuse, N.Y.: Syracuse University Department of Architecture, 1975.
  This set of materials includes two booklets and a slide-tape presentation. It is an introduction to designing buildings to be accessible to disabled people and includes sections on residential applications.

U.S. Community Services Administration. *A community planning guide to weatherization.* Washington, D.C.: Community Services Administration, 1975.
  A guidebook for developing programs for weatherization of low-income dwellings. Includes information on project administration and field work. Designed for use by Community Services Administration programs but has more general applications.

U.S. Department of Housing and Urban Development. *A design guide for home safety.* Washington, D.C.: U.S. Government Printing Office, 1972.
  This booklet illustrates modifications that can be made to homes for greater safety.

U.S. Department of Housing and Urban Development. *A design guide for improving residential security.* Washington, D.C.: U.S. Government Printing Office, 1973.
  Details physical security measures for housing.

U.S. Department of Housing and Urban Development. *In the bank or up the chimney?* Washington, D.C.: U.S. Government Printing Office, 1975.
  Outlines the methods and cost advantages of weatherproofing older homes. Includes various strategies based on climate and cost of fuel.

U.S. National Bureau of Standards. *Home fire safety checklist.* Washington, D.C.: U.S. Government Printing Office, 1974.
  Lists potential fire safety problems.

15
Determinants of
Dwelling Maintenance Activity
of Elderly Households

RAYMOND J. STRUYK
DEBORAH DEVINE

It is now commonplace to assert that elderly homeowners maintain their properties less well on the average than others. In inner-city neighborhoods there is some concern that the elderly homeowner may undermaintain his or her property and hence act as a catalyst to neighborhood decline. This concern is in part responsible for proposals being advanced to assist elderly homeowners through an expansion of the Section 8 Housing Assistance Payments Program, which is presently restricted to renters.

The analysis presented in this chapter deals with the determinants of dwelling maintenance and repair activity of elderly homeowners located in both urban and rural areas. The analysis is especially important in view of various proposals designed to foster better dwelling maintenance by the elderly. The Section 8 approach assumes that the principal determinant of good maintenance is income. No one knows with certainty that this is the critical factor; indeed, nothing is known of the relative importance of income compared to other factors such as the proximity of children who can help make repairs, the role of physical impairments among the elderly, or the structure of the elderly households (e.g., husband-wife household versus female individual). Clearly, formulation of programs to encourage maintenance efficiently requires that knowledge in these areas be developed.

Prior work on dwelling maintenance by homeowners provides precious little assistance. While Sweeney (1974) and Dildine and Massey (1974) have done useful conceptual analyses on the level of

The authors want to thank Deborah Greenstein, Terry Connell, Jim Follain, and Larry Ozanne for helpful comments, and Gwen Stanley and Jim Cogley for expert programming assistance. This work was performed while the senior author was Deputy Assistant Secretary for Research, U.S. Department of Housing and Urban Development.

221

maintenance activity that could most profitably be undertaken, only Mendelsohn (1973) has explored the probability of households making dwelling repairs. Mendelsohn employed the quarterly Census micro data on maintenance, repair, and investment activity by homeowners to estimate reduced-form probability models. The results are highly suggestive, but the information on both the dwelling and the household are quite limited. [There have also been attempts to estimate supply functions for housing services; estimates using macro data can be found in deLeeuw and Ekanem (1971). Micro-based estimates can be found in Ozanne and Struyk (1976).]

In addition, economists have yet to do much analysis of the demand for housing by the elderly. Only recently have analyses using the Annual Housing Survey (AHS) data accurately described the housing situation of the elderly compared to other households (Struyk, 1977a, 1977b).

The data reported here, then, is clearly an initial step in analyzing the housing maintenance and repair activities of the elderly. The first section develops a conceptual model. The second section describes the sample, the data, and the measures employed in the analysis. Analyses of repair activity in both simple and multivariate form are then presented, followed by a discussion and conclusion.

A CONCEPTUAL FRAMEWORK

Seventy percent of the elderly-headed households in the United States are occupied by homeowners. They are, of course, a highly diverse group. By definition the elderly are undergoing a series of changes that have implications for their demand for housing services and their ability to supply them. Such changes include alterations in the composition of the household as children move out or a spouse dies, reduction in income at retirement, and the deterioration of physical and mental capabilities. The elderly as a whole do, then, adjust their housing frequently compared to what might be casually thought. While some elderly make this adjustment by shifting dwellings, more frequently the adjustments are made by altering the current dwelling—by adding handrails and other special fixtures or, if economically necessary, by deferring certain types of maintenance (Newman, 1977; Struyk, 1976).

Ideally, one would like to model the dynamics of the adjustment process. For the present, however, we restrict ourselves to a simple static model of repair activity because the data available for estimation are cross-sectional. A simplified description of the model follows; it is described in more technical terms in the Appendix to this chapter. In the economic model of repair activity the demand for repairs is seen first as a function of two traditional explanatory determinants of repair, household's income and its assets. Assets are important for three reasons: (1) they can be directly used to finance repairs; (2) they influence the household's judgment as to the fraction of income it feels it can devote to housing; and (3) they are indicative of the household's permanent income. In this model, the demand for repair activity is also seen as a function of the household's attitude toward the future, which can have a strong negative influence on the rate of repair as the householder becomes increasingly aged, but which may be offset by a wish to preserve the quality of the housing for bequest purposes. On balance, the discount rate may have little effect on demand. Household composition is also seen to influence the demand for repairs largely through the demand of individual members for a certain quantity of housing services. One can easily imagine one spouse being much more sensitive to dwelling condition than another.

The condition of the dwelling is another obvious determinant of demand. In the extreme, repairs are undertaken for the dwelling to remain habitable. Neighborhood condition is also seen as a determinant of demand. If the neighborhood is declining, for example, maintenance activity would be sharply reduced.

Three price terms—each one representing a different source of supply—are also included in the demand function. One is the price per unit of repairs if the household is making the repair itself; another is the price if a friend or relative is making the repair; and the third is the price of employing someone else or a contractor to make the repairs. Turning first to the household's supplying repairs to itself, the price would include the relevant household members' implicit wage rates, which in turn depend on the degree to which the household members are ill or their activities are impaired, and on the taste and skill of persons for doing these jobs. It would be higher if household members are employed. Household composition influences the price when the household is making the repair itself because two persons may be substantially more efficient than one in performing many tasks. In the case of the price when a relative makes the repair, the wage rate of the relative is assumed to be related to the distance that the relative must travel to the elderly person's home. The price of contracted repairs should remain invariant with the economic demand of the individual household.

THE SAMPLE AND VARIABLE DEFINITIONS

Sample

The data used in this analysis are taken from a sample of 1,575 elderly (over age 62) owner-occupant households surveyed under contract to the U.S. Department of Housing and Urban Development (HUD) in 1975. The sample contains 225 elderly homeowners from each of seven areas, selected for being roughly representative of the location of elderly homeowners nationally. Of the seven areas, five are Standard Metropolitan Statistical Areas (SMSA), each one representing a different SMSA size category: Philadelphia, San Francisco, Dayton, Tulsa, and Pittsfield, Massachusetts. The remaining two areas are a small city (New Ulm, Minnesota) and a rural area (Orangeburg County, North Carolina). Within each area the sample households were selected by a stratified random sample using median homeowner census tract income (or similar data) for stratification. The sample was restricted to dwellings built prior to 1961 in order to include properties more likely to require maintenance and repair activities. This analysis uses only the 1,367 observations for households with elderly aged 65 and over. A more complete description of the sampling procedure is in Jacobs and Rabushka (1976). We have compared several of the broad characteristics of the sample households with those of all elderly homeowners using data from the 1973 and 1974 Annual Housing Survey (AHS). In terms of household composition and income, there is close correspondence between our sample and the national population. On the other hand, the households in the sample have significantly higher ratios of housing expenses to housing income than the national elderly homeowning population.

Variable Definitions

While the survey gathered information on all of the areas critical to understanding the maintenance activity of elderly homeowners, an important question is the accuracy with which the survey data measure the factors hypothesized in the preceding section to be determinants of maintenance activity. Table 15.1 provides a succinct listing of the principal variables actually used in the analysis. The independent or determining variables are divided into eight groups: financial status, household type, family support, dwelling condition, household health, structure type, neighborhood characteristics, and control variables. Many of these specifications are self-explanatory; a few, however, require some explanation.

TABLE 15.1
Variable Definitions

Name and Classification	Description
	A. Independent Variables

Financial Status

TOTINC	Total household income in 1974. Sum of all earnings, income from professional practice, income from farming, dividends, interest, social security, supplementary security, other government sources, pension, rent on property, alimony.
ASSETS	Value of the sum of certificates of deposit, savings accounts, checking accounts, stocks, mutual fund shares, stock through investment clubs, U. S. Savings Bonds, other bonds, property value minus value owed on property, life insurance value.
COSTINC	Ratio of housing costs to average total family income per month. Housing cost defined as sum of monthly property tax, insurance, mortgage payment, electricity, natural gas, fuel oil, coal, other fuels, water, telephone, and other charges.

Household Type

HT1	Household type 1 if respondent is married and living with spouse; zero otherwise.
HT2	Household type 1 if respondent lives alone.
HT3	Household type 1 if respondent lives with others (relative or friend) but not with a spouse.
CH	1 if children of respondent live with respondent.
GCH	1 if grandchildren of respondent live with respondent.

(continued)

225

Table 15.1 (Continued)

CANT	Count of the number of activities respondent found they cannot do (possible 8); includes go up and down stairs, leave home, walk around a room, do own laundry, get in and out of bed, clean own room, shopping alone, changing storm windows.
SFCANT	Takes on value of CANT for San Francisco households only. Defined because one activity--changing storm windows--is not applicable in the Bay area.

Structure Type

ST1	1 if dwelling is a single family detached unit.
ST2	1 if dwelling is a row house.

Neighborhood Characteristics

TRTBLK	Percentage of households in the census tract headed by a black in 1970.
TRTINC	Median family income in the tract in 1970 (in $000).
SATIS	1 if household is generally happy with neighborhood as to location, etc.
NGHQAL	Rating of neighborhood quality by respondent, ranging from 4 (excellent) to 1 (very poor).
RACE	1 if the head of house is white, zero if otherwise.

Control Variables

C4 - C7	Dummy variables for Philadelphia, Pittsburgh, San Francisco, Tulsa (used only in the 5 urban cities sample).
REPAIRS	Total number of repairs made in last two years (maximum of 5).

B. Dependent Variables.

226

Table 15.1

Family Support

VISITMON

Number of family members who visit monthly or more frequently.

TRAVEL2

Number of family members who travel 2 hours or less to reach the respondent.

Dwelling Condition

HQSUM1

Sum of selected interior dwelling defects present in each room divided by the number of rooms (possible 10 defects); includes absence of electrical outlets, defective electrical outlets, absence of light switches, defective light switches, absence of light fixtures, defective light fixtures, room lacks heating outlet, defective wall surface, defective ceiling surface, defective floor surface.

HQSUM2

Sum of selected major interior dwelling defects (possible 6 defects): lack complete bathroom, detached toilet facility; absence of complete kitchen facilities, lacks hot-cold running water, defective toilet facilities, no central heating system.

EHQSUM

Sum of exterior dwelling defects (possible 9 defects) includes defective foundation, paint, exterior wall structure, exterior wall surface, roof surface, roof structure, chimney, entranceway, exterior stairs.

HR

1 if house has been remodeled since 1969.

Household Health

AGE

Age of respondent.

(continued)

227

Table 15.1 (Continued)

Used in Analysis of Presence of Maintenance and Repair Activity	
RPR	1 if any repairs were made over last two years.
REP	Count of the number of repairs (maximum of 5) made over last 2 years divided by five.
Used in Analysis of How Repairs Made, Given Presence of Some Activity	
SELF	1 if respondent or persons living with the respondent did any repairs.
FRIEND	1 if friend or relative not living with respondent did any repairs.
HIRE	1 if any repairs were done for hire, by individual or by contractor.
SLFRTIO	Fraction of all repairs done by self.
FRDRTIO	Fraction of all repairs done by friend.
HIRRTIO	Fraction of all repairs done by individual or contractor.

A set of four variables describes the condition of the dwelling unit; of these, three—HQSUM1, HQSUM2, and HR—describe the interior condition of the unit. One part of the survey involved a detailed room-by-room inventory of the dwelling. HQSUM1, taking advantage of this detail, is defined as the possible presence of each of 10 defects for every room (excluding porches, etc.) and with the sum divided by the number of rooms. Most of these defects are those that could be remedied at modest expense. HQSUM2, on the other hand, totals such deficiencies as the absence of central heating that would be more costly to remedy. The final interior variable, HR, indicates that the unit was at least partially remodeled in the 5 years prior to the survey. Finally, EHQSUM totals 9 exterior deficiencies. All four of the variables weight the included defects equally based on findings of other analyses of the insensitivity of house values to a set of deficiencies weighted in several alternative ways (Mendelsohn & Struyk, 1975). Of the household health variables, CANT is defined as the sum of the number of activities out of 8 that the head-of-house reported needing assistance to do. The activities in this list are similar to those in a scale that has been found to be a reliable indicator of impairment (Rosow & Breslau, 1975).

Two broad types of dependent variables are analyzed: (1) the presence and intensity of any repair activity over the 2 years prior to the interview, and (2) who performed the repair. While the survey explicitly asked that the respondent describe any repair or maintenance task completed and the amount of expenditure, the frequency of activity suggests that households probably limited their response to fairly major tasks (e.g., painting, mending a leaky roof, etc). For example, only 54% reported any repairs having been made and 32% reported only one repair. As documented below, few repairs were made by the respondents. Also somewhat surprising is the frequency with which the elderly paid for repairs to be made. This frequency, of course, might result from the higher income household's ability to afford them, the inability of households to make their own repairs, or some combination of the two.

INITIAL ANALYSIS OF REPAIR ACTIVITY

Before turning to the estimates of the models described in the first section, it may be helpful to spend a few moments looking at the general pattern of repair activity and the simple relationship between repairs and several salient variables.

The first point to note is that the sample differs sharply by location in a number of important respects. The sample areas contain five cities, one rural area (Orangeburg), and one small town (New Ulm). Examination of household and housing characteristics for each of these locations showed that the five cities form a relatively homogeneous group, while New Ulm and Orangeburg are quite distinct. The differences among the three locations are illustrated by the mean values of selected variables provided in Table 15.2. Differences in income, assets, household types, housing quality, and repair activity among the three locations are all substantial. Because of these major differences among the three locations, the remainder of our analysis groups households into these three separate locational groups.

The figures on the amount and type of repair activity shown at the bottom of Table 15.2 indicate that most repairs were done by hired labor (HIRE). The smallest number of repairs were performed by the elderly person himself or herself (SELF). The average cost of repairs

TABLE 15.2
Mean Values of Selected Variables for Three Different
Geographic Areas

	New Ulm	Orangeburg	Five Cities
TOTINC	4,250	2,899	6,633
ASSETS	17,509	4,911	21,418
COSTINC	.34	.44	.32
HT1	.39	.40	.51
HT2	.41	.25	.32
HT3	.20	.35	.17
CH	.12	.22	.15
GCH	.04	.15	.03
VISITMON	1.66	1.42	1.29
TRAVEL2	1.97	1.65	1.47
HQSUM1	.19	1.48	.25
HQSUM2	.35	1.25	.15
EHQSUM	.30	1.54	.42
HR	.17	.15	.16
AGE	74	74	74
CANT	.34	.66	.44
TRTBLK	a	a	6.67
TRTINC	a	a	11,493
SATIS	a	a	.91
NGHQAL	a	a	3.23
RACE	1.0	.58	.96
RPR	.44	.29	.62
REP	.14	.07	.20
SELF[b]	.21	.11	.18
FRIEND[b]	.30	.22	.18
HIRE[b]	.61	.70	.76
COSTSELF[c]	37.5	87.8	135.1
COSTFRIEND[c]	77.3	303.0	279.3
COSTHIRE[c]	622.2	975.0	851.9

[a]Variables only defined for cities.
[b]Frequency of repairs, given some repair activity being done.
[c]Average value of repairs made by this type of supplier.

given in the final three entries seems high. Actually, they are not out of line with the mean expenditures of owner-occupants reported by the U.S. Census Bureau—about $300 in 1970. In addition, Mendelsohn (1973), using these same census data, found that the elderly spend more on the average repair than other households. Still, several arguments might be proffered in support of only the larger expenditures being reported, for example, that major repairs were recalled or thought to be of sufficient importance (Lawton, 1978, has discussed problems of the elderly in responding to questions on current housing conditions). The question itself may not have elicited the correct response, or the cost figures may simply be in error. We have no basis to defend or reject these arguments. Our guess is that the sample is probably biased toward major repair and maintenance activities, as is the census data apparently.

With only about half of the sample households reporting any repair activity over the observation period, one immediately asks whether there is a strong bivariate relationship between the presence of any repair activity and several of the hypothesized determinants. Looking first at income, a positive association of repairs with income is evident; in the urban locations, for example, 53% of those with incomes under $3,000 had performed repairs, as compared to 71% of those whose incomes were $10,000 or more. The ratio of housing expenses to income has little discernible effect on repair activity. This calls into question the hypothesis that high housing-expense burdens by themselves are a good indicator of the household's activity to make repairs.

A somewhat unclear picture emerges when the pattern of repair activity is examined in association with the three measures of dwelling-unit condition. Both New Ulm and Orangeburg generally showed a slight increase in repair activity as the number of defects mounted; this weak pattern held for both interior and exterior problems. On the other hand, no pattern emerged from the data for the five cities.

Finally, for no category of location did the extent of mobility impairment of the elderly household members (variable CANT in Table 15.1) have a strong association with repair activity. For two location types the presence of mobility limitation reduced repair activity slightly; in the third the opposite pattern appeared.

The differences in the extent of repair activity among location types and the weakness of the simple relationship between repair activity and several of prima facie importance suggest that the forces causing repair and maintenance work to be undertaken are quite complex. The multivariate analysis described in the next section attempts to clarify some of the patterns observed thus far.

MULTIVARIATE ANALYSIS

As outlined in the Appendix to this chapter, the estimated models are all reduced-form functions (i.e., a single-equation model in which both demand and supply elements affecting repairs are included). This means that it is frequently not possible to separate the influence of demand and supply factors; it also implies that in some instances countervailing demand and supply influences may cause a particular determinant to be statistically insignificant when it might be significant in a more complete structural model.

The first results to be discussed are the determinants of the probability of the household's undertaking any repair activity over the 2-year observation period. The analysis, shown in Table 15.3, was done separately for the three types of geographic areas. All the models have been estimated using the ordinary least-squares procedure, which is defensible for a dichotomous dependent variable when the mean value of the variable is between .30 and .70 as it is in these cases (Goodman, 1976). Also, the significance criteria used for evaluating the regression coefficients shift between a one-tailed and a two-tailed test depending on the strength of the hypothesis of the net effect of each variable on the probability of repair activity.

TABLE 15.3
Regression Analysis of Probability of Any Repair Activity
(dependent variable is RPR)

Independent Variables	Five Cities		New Ulm		Orangeburg	
	Coeff.	T-stat.	Coeff.	T.- stat.	Coeff.	T-stat.
CONSTANT	.543		.915		.143	
TOTINC	4.5×10^{-6}	2.8	2.2×10^{-5}	2.2	1.9×10^{-5}	2.0
COSTINC	− .010	1.3	.026	.5	.042	1.2
CH	− .063	1.3	− .068	.6	.168	2.0
GCH	.030	.3	.478	.9	.006	.5
VISITMON	.018	1.5	.046	1.6	.043	1.5
HQSUM1	.060	1.5	− .115	.9	.036	.9
HQSUM2	− .007	.2	.062	.9	− .056	1.0
EHQSUM	− .28	1.4	.099	1.6	− .013	.5
C4	.062	1.2				
C5	.063	1.2				
C6	.020	.3				
C7	− .078	1.5				
TRTBLK	− .002	2.0				
TRTINC	.011	2.1				
SATIS	− .083	1.3				
NGHQAL	− .034	.8				
RACE	− .057	.7				
AGE	.0005	.3	− .009	1.5	.0002	.5
R^2	.048		.078		.062	
SE	.480		.489		.453	
F	2.32		1.66		1.26	
df	881		176		171	

In this and later tables each pair of columns gives the results of an estimated regression. The coefficients are interpreted as the effect at the margin that the variables listed in the left-hand column have on the probability of any repairs having been made. So the presence of a child in the home (CH) in the regression for the five cities is estimated to increase the probability of repairs by .06. Finally, standard summary statistics, R^2, SE (standard error of estimate), F, and df (degree of freedom) appear at the bottom of each set of columns.

There are two consistently significant variables: income (TOTINC) and the number of family members visiting at least monthly (VISITMON). Elasticities based on the coefficients indicate that a 20% rise in income would cause a 1% increase in the probability of any repair activity in the five urban areas and about a 4% increase in New Ulm and Orangeburg. A similar percentage increase in visitations by family members would, on the average, have about half the effect of the income increase. In the five cities there are, in addition, two important neighborhood effects. First, the greater percentage of blacks in the area (TRTBLK) the lower the probability of repairs. This result might be due either to the price of materials and contract labor being higher in black enclaves as suggested by some researchers (Schafer, Holshouser, Moore, & Santer, 1975), or to an adverse effect on expectations in transition neighborhoods. Second, higher average income in the tract (TRTINC) has an affirmative influence on the probability of repairs, presumably reflecting general social pressure to maintain one's unit.

As important as these significant coefficients is the inconsistency of the performance of variables indicating the household's ability to make repairs (CANT), the discount rate (AGE), the presence of children in the home (CH), and household type (HT1, HT2) (these last were insignificant when included in the model). Further, the dwelling-quality variables are of inconsistent sign, although sometimes significant. In fact, in only two instances is a dwelling-condition variable both significant and of the expected sign (HQSUM) in the five cities model and EHQSUM in New Ulm. Several explanations for these inconsistencies are suggested. One is that the elderly homeowner may simply be unaware of some dwelling-unit deficiencies, either from ignorance or because they have learned to live with them. This suggestion is borne out by the data in Table 15.4 comparing perceptions and expert evaluations. A second explanation is that a low number of deficiencies signals both good condition and hence little pressure for repairs and a proclivity of the household in the past to make repairs. A final factor at work here is the way the data were assembled: While repairs were ascertained for the 2 years prior to the survey, condition of dwelling

TABLE 15.4
Needed Repairs Perceived by Elderly Respondent and Expert Evaluator
(percent of units needing repairs)

City	Household Perception[a]	Expert Evaluation[b]
Philadelphia	21	54
San Francisco	24	60
Dayton	27	70
Tulsa	25	44
Pittsfield	24	48
New Ulm	27	51
Orangeburg	57	99

[a]Respondent was specifically asked about 28 items that might need repair. These included, for example, the water heater, toilet, wash basin, light switches, electrical outlets, furnace, radiator gutters, walls, ceilings, windows, storm windows.

[b]Includes, in effect, all of items described in footnote a plus a few additional items such as handrails and driveway needing repairs. But the two groups of indicators correspond fairly closely.

was recorded at the time of the survey. Hence a dwelling's good condition on the survey occasion might be attributable to the repairs recorded. It is unlikely that the relationship would be so clean, but this timing problem would surely affect the results to some extent.

Further light is shed on the problem by the analysis of the determinants of any repair activity being undertaken by the respondent (SELF), a friend or nonresident family member (FRIEND), or by a contractor or hired person (HIRE). Estimated regression models employing the data from the five cities are reported in Table 15.5. The neighborhood variables were not included here, since expectations should influence the decision to undertake a repair not the way in which it is done. These models show several highly interesting patterns.

First, an elderly homeowner household was more likely to do the repair itself if it was a husband-wife household; a higher income also increased this probability. The likelihood fell sharply with higher age and mobility limitations.

Second, a family or friend was more likely to make at least one repair if the elderly household had more family visitors in a month. The fact that this likelihood declined with increasing income indicates that the elderly were assisted by family and friends more often when financially constrained to do so (see Shanas, Townsend, Wedderburn, Friis, Milhøy, & Stehouwer, for a general discussion of the household support provided elderly persons by family members). Surprisingly, age and mobility impairments have little effect.

Finally, the probability of the elderly hiring a worker or contractor to make repairs was positively related to income, being a non–husband-wife household, and being older. The significant housing-quality coefficients suggest that hired labor was used more often when units were in good condition, a phenomenon possibly related to past household income.

TABLE 15.5

Regression Analysis of How Repairs Were Made, Given Some
Repair Activity (analysis restricted to five cities)

	SELF		FRIEND		HIRE	
	Coeff.	T.-stat.	Coeff.	T-stat.	Coeff.	T.-stat.
CONSTANT	.713		.140		.319	
TOTINC	$2.7*10^{-6}$	1.4	$-5.8*10^{-6}$	3.1	$6.2*10^{-6}$	3.3
COSTINC	.002	.2	− .004	.3	$2.1*10^{-5}$	a
AGE	− .009	4.5	.0001	.5	.007	3.5
CANT	− .023	1.4	.014	.8		
SFCANT	.033	1.0	.073	2.1		
HT1	.188	4.2			− .096	1.9
HT2	.025	.5			− .033	.6
VISITMON	.001	.1	.040	3.1	− .034	2.2
HQSUM1	.026	.7	.010	.2	− .001	.2
HQSUM2	.009	.2	.028	.8	− .085	2.0
EHQSUM	.022	1.0	.001	.1	− .038	1.5
R^2	.108		.041		.051	
SE	.367		.379		.422	
F	5.85		2.61		3.19	
df	536		538		538	

^{a}less than .05.

The final set of regressions (Table 15.6) explores the determinants of the intensity with which the three methods of repair activity were employed by elderly homeowners. The dependent variable in each case is the number of repairs done by a particular method divided by the total number of repairs undertaken by the household. These models contain the same set of independent variables as those just discussed in relation to Table 15.5, except that the total number of repairs has been added to account for increasing wage rates of the occupant or friends/relatives as the amount of repair activity increases.

The results were generally very similar to those for the probability of using a given method reported in Table 15.5. The number of repairs variable (REPAIRS) did not have the anticipated effect. Looking across the three models, this analysis indicates that over the range (and type) of repairs reported the relevant wage rates were unaffected; indeed, self-made repairs increased as a fraction of all activity as total activity increased.

Another finding of importance is that the dwelling-quality variables were consistently positive in the self equation. This result comes from two countervailing influences. On the one hand, elderly who have

TABLE 15.6
Regression Analysis of Intensity of Repair Activity by
How Repair Was Made (sample restricted to five cities)

Independent Variable	SLFRTIO		FRDRTIO		HIRRTIO	
	Coeff.	T-stat.	Coeff.	T-stat.	Coeff.	T-stat.
CONSTANT	.542		.156		.279	
TOTINC	$2.2*10^{-7}$	.2	$-6.2*10^{-6}$	5.4	$4.8*10^{-6}$	2.1
COSTINC	.002	.2	$-$ .002	.2	.002	1.1
AGE	$-.007$	3.5	$-$ .0003	.1	.006	2.7
CANT	$-.019$	1.4	.016	1.1		
SFCANT	$-.012$	.4	.024	.7		
HT1	.167	4.4			$-.106$	2.0
HT2	.023	.6			$-.043$	.8
VISITMON	$-.002$	.5	.036	3.3	$-.036$	2.4
HQSUM1	.011	.3	$-$ .0005	a	$-.010$	.2
HQSUM2	.027	.9	.042	1.4	$-.063$	1.5
EHQSUM	.036	2.0	.004	.2	$-.039$	1.6
REPAIRS	.022	1.6	$-$ .006	.4	$-.014$	.7
R^2	.104		.043		.051	
SE	.314		.325		.420	
F	5.24		2.49		2.91	
df	542		544		544	

[a]less than .05.

always maintained their units are likely to continue to do so; hence, EHQSUM would have a negative sign. On the other hand, dwellings with numerous defects force the household to make repairs; one expects a positive relation between HQSUM1, HQSUM2, and EHQSUM, on the one hand, and SLFRT10, on the other. The second effect dominates for self-made repairs, but the opposite is true for hired repairs. The two effects apparently cancel each other for repairs made by friends and relatives.

POLICY CONCLUSIONS

What type of policy implications can be drawn from the results presented here? At the outset it must be noted that definitive conclusions simply are not possible because of the limitations of the sample and the ambiguities arising from the reduced-form nature of the estimated models. Even recognizing this restriction, however, several statements are possible that have importance for formulation of policies to assist the elderly homeowner in maintaining his property.

First, the analyses make it abundantly clear that the decision to undertake repair activity is determined by a number of factors. Also, the determinants of this decision appear to vary with local housing conditions and social customs (e.g., extent to which children provide support to their parents). Both facts indicate the need for a high degree of flexibility to be built into any program designed primarily to assist elderly homeowners to maintain their dwellings.

Increased income is strongly associated with the undertaking of repairs/maintenance activity. On the other hand, the elasticity of such activity with respect to income is certainly modest. This low elasticity combined with the sharp difference between the perception by the household of the need for specific repairs and the rating by an expert evaluator suggest the need for earmarking cash grants to be spent on repair activities. Such earmarking could take a variety of forms, one possibility being inspection of the units with continued grants being dependent upon repairs being made similar to the procedure for rental units under the Section 8 program (U.S. Department of Housing and Urban Development, 1977). Alternatively, the full or partial cost of actual repairs could be reimbursed as is being done, for example, under Boston's Housing Improvement Program (City of Boston Office of Housing, 1977). The Section 312 Subsidized Loan Program (of the National Housing Act, as amended) is another vehicle that has the advantage for the elderly of utilizing contractors, but the disadvantage of being administratively complicated. This line of argument also suggests that "circuit-breaker" tax relief for elderly households is a relatively inefficient way to maintain housing quality, although it may provide general income support (ABT Associates, 1975). A similar statement applies to reverse annuity mortgages (Guttentag, 1975). Finally, the income responsiveness of repair activity highlights the desirability of making any assistance income conditional in order to achieve a reasonable degree of target efficiency.

Another set of implications can be derived from the information on how the repairs are actually made. Husband-wife households make more repairs than others, even after controlling for differences in income. This is probably due to the combination of mutual assistance in making the repairs and a reinforcement in the pressure to get them made when a deficiency occurs. In the same vein repairs done by the household fall off sharply as impairments increase. These facts, combined with the general difficulty of hiring people to do small jobs, argue for the provision of chore services, targeted especially to non–husband-wife households and very old or impaired couples. An alternative approach would be for a government-affiliated agency to act in a clearinghouse capacity, arranging for work to be done, providing inspection, appraiser services, and helping to arrange financing (for a description of current activities under Title XX, see Gutowski, 1978). Arguments in favor of providing such institutionalized assistance are given by the aversion of the elderly to impose on friends or relatives for such activity.

Finally, the results suggest that conditions in the neighborhood surrounding the dwelling affect the probability of repairs being undertaken. These conditions have only been captured crudely by the variables included in the present analysis, but the general conclusion seems valid. This finding implies that increasing incomes in declining neighborhoods will produce less dwelling upkeep than in other areas; hence in the declining areas the case for earmarking the assistance rather than providing cash payments is the strongest.

SUMMARY

This study analyzes what causes or prevents elderly owner-occupants from undertaking maintenance activities on their homes. In particular, the work examines the effects that income, household structure, health, assets, the ratio of housing expenses to income, the proximity of grown children living in separate households, and the physical condition of the dwelling and the area in which it is located have on the likelihood of repairs being made and how the repairs are made (i.e., done by the elderly household itself, by a friend or relative outside of the elderly household, or by hired labor or under contract).

The analysis uses data gathered in a special survey of about 1,400 elderly homeowners residing in seven geographic areas—five SMSAs, one small town, and one rural county. Each had to live in a unit at least 15 years old, and, hence one that would be more likely to need some maintenance. Repairs made over the 2 years prior to the 1975 survey date are the subject of the analysis.

The analyses make it abundantly clear that the decision to undertake repair activity is determined by a number of factors. Also, the determinants of this decision appear to vary with local housing conditions and social customs (e.g., extent to which children provide support to their parents). Both facts indicate the need for a high degree of flexibility to be built into any program designed primarily to assist the elderly homeowners in maintaining their dwellings.

Increased income is strongly associated statistically with repairs/ maintenance activity being undertaken. On the other hand, the elasticity of such activity with respect to income is certainly modest. This low elasticity combined with the sharp difference between the perception of the household of the need for specific repairs and the rating by an expert evaluator suggest the need for earmarking cash grants to be spent on repair activities. Such earmarking could take a variety of forms: inspection of the units with continued grants being dependent upon repairs being made, similar to what is presently done in rental units under the Section 8 program (U.S. Department of Housing and Urban Development, 1977); or the full or partial cost of actual repairs could be reimbursed as is currently being done, for example, under Boston's Housing Improvement Program (City of Boston, 1977). The Section 312 (of the National Housing Act, as amended) subsidized loan program is another vehicle, which has the advantage for the elderly of utilizing contractors, but the disadvantage of being administratively complicated. This line of argument also suggests that "circuit breaker" tax relief for elderly households is a relatively inefficient way to maintain housing quality, although it may provide general income support (ABT Associates, 1975). A similar statement applies to reverse annuity mortgages (Guttentag, 1975). Finally, the income responsiveness of repair activity highlights the desirability of making any assistance income conditional, in order to achieve a reasonable degree of target efficiency.

Another set of implications can be derived from the information on how the repairs are actually made. Husband-wife households make more repairs than others, even after controlling for differences in income. This is likely due to the combination of mutual assistance in making the repairs and a reinforcement in the pressure to get them made when a deficiency occurs. In the same vein, repairs done by the household fall off sharply as impairments increase. These facts, combined with the general difficulty of hiring people to do small jobs, argue for the provision of chore services—targeted especially to non-husband/wife households and very old or impaired couples. An alternative approach would be for a government-affiliated agency to act in a clearinghouse capacity, arranging for work to be done, providing inspection, appraiser services, and helping to arrange financing (Gutowski, 1978). This argument is buttressed by the finding of a clear aversion of the elderly to impose on friends or relatives for such activity when their economic circumstances will permit them to do so.

Finally, the results suggest that conditions in the neighborhood surroundig the dwelling affect the probability of repairs being undertaken. These conditions have only been captured crudely by the variables included in the present analysis, but the general conclusion seems valid. One implication of this is that increasing incomes in declining neighborhoods will produce less dwelling upkeep than in other areas; hence, it is particularly in the declining areas that the case for earmarking the assistance is the strongest.

Appendix

THE DEMAND FUNCTION, THE SUPPLY FUNCTION, AND THE COMBINED REDUCED-FORM MODEL

The demand for repairs or repair activities (D) is derived from the demand for housing services and hence the determinants of D closely parallel those for housing services.

$$D = D\ (Y,\ A,\ r,\ HH,\ C,\ N,\ P_1,\ P_2,\ P_3) \tag{1}$$

where Y is the household's current income and A is assets. Assets are especially important for three reasons: (1) they can be used directly to finance repairs, (2) they influence the household's judgment as to the fraction of income it feels it can devote to housing, and (3) they are indicative of the household's permanent income. The household's discount rate, r, can have a strong negative influence on D as the household becomes increasingly aged; on the other hand, this may be offset by a strong bequest factor, so that r on balance may have little effect on demand (Blinder, 1976). Household composition, HH, influences D largely through the demand of individual members for a certain quantity of housing services. One can easily imagine one spouse being much more sensitive to dwelling condition than another. The condition of the dwelling, C, is an obvious determinant; in the extreme, repairs would have to be undertaken for the dwelling to remain inhabitable. N is the condition of the neighborhood; if it is declining, for example, the return to maintenance activity would be sharply reduced.

Three price terms are included in the demand function, one for each of the relevant types of suppliers: P_1 is the price per unit of repairs if the household is making the repair itself; P_2 is the price if a friend or relative is making the repair; and P_3 is the price of employing someone else or a contractor to make the repairs. Each source of supply involves a different production technology and possibly different factor prices. For this reason, repairs can be supplied in the three different ways. The household chooses among them on the basis of their prices.

Turning first to the household supplying repairs to itself, we can write the supply function in the price-determining form as

$$P_1 = P_1(M, L_1, HH, D) \tag{2}$$

where M is the price per unit of materials and L_1 is the relevant household members' wage rates. L_1 in turn depends on the degree to which the household member is ill or his or her activities are impaired (H/I) and on the taste and skill of the person for doing these jobs. Similarly, L_1 will be higher if the household member is employed (CE). Note that the relationship between D and L_1 is likely to be nonlinear after some point (i.e., $\delta^2 L_1/\delta D^2 > 0$, when D is greater than some $D°$) as the effort of doing additional repairs becomes particularly onerous. HH influences P_1 through efficiency: Two persons may be substantially more efficient than one in performing many tasks.

Similarly, the other two supply functions can be written as

$$P_2 = P_2(M, L_2, D) \tag{3}$$

and

$$P_3 = P_3(M, L_3) \tag{4}$$

The wage rate of the relative in Equation 3 is assumed to be related to the distance that the relative must travel to the elderly person's home. It is also assumed that L_2 will rise sharply as D increases beyond a low level. The price of contracted repairs (P_3) should be invariant with the demand of the individual household. With the P_i being unobservable, it is necessary to substitute Equations 2–4 into Equation 1 to obtain a reduced-form model that can be estimated.

Thus far we have tacitly assumed a repair to be a homogeneous good regardless of who supplies it. It is quite conceivable, however, that the repairs are perceived to be differentiated goods depending on who supplies them. One might argue that a job one does oneself is viewed as a superior good, since one "knows" the job was done right. In recognition of the possible differentiation, repairs (and the demand for them) can be distinguished by their source of supply—D_1, D_2, D_3—in much the same way as consumers distinguish among automobiles or cereals. In recent years economists have noted that housing in general is a differentiated good in both demand and supply. The principal distinctions have to do with structural attributes of dwellings and the characteristics of the neighborhoods in which they are located. This is thoroughly exposited in Straszheim (1975).

The greatest experience with the demand for differentiated goods has been in the analysis of international trade of fairly specifically defined but not identical goods. A very thorough discussion and empirical analysis of the differentiated-goods issue is in Kravis and Lipsey (1971).

In other words, if repairs were differentiated goods in demand as well as in supply, the demand function for D (Equation 1) would be replaced in a group of functions, one for each D_i repairs, distinguished by the main source of labor. One can easily write a reduced-form equation for each of the D_i as

$$D_i = D_i(Y, A, r, N, HH, C, M, L_1, L_2, L_3, D_j, K_k) \qquad i \neq j \qquad (5)$$

The levels of D_i are clearly jointly determined, since the P_j and hence the relative attractiveness of the jth activity has been demanded in the relevant time period, except for contractors whose supply schedule to the individual household is flat. In other words, if self-made repairs are the most preferred, the demand for contractor repairs would depend on the relative price of self-repairs. The price would rise sharply as the household makes more repairs itself. Hence assuming the demand for a repair activity (i.e., fixing a broken window), the choice among differentiated goods depends on the household's taste, other demand determinants, and the relative prices of the supply sources, which in turn are driven by the total demand for each repair type to date in the relevant time period.

This line of reasoning suggests that the mix of repair types observed over an extended time period, perhaps 5 years, would be sensitive to the time interval between individual repairs. If repairs were clustered, one would predict a higher fraction of contractor repairs; less bunching would imply a lower implicit wage rate of the householder and/or relative.

REFERENCES

ABT Associates. *Property tax relief programs for the elderly*. Washington, D.C.: U.S. Government Printing Office, 1975.

Blinder, A. Intergenerational transfers and life cycle consumption. *American Economic Review*, 1976, 66, 87–93.

City of Boston Office of Housing. *Housing Improvement Program: Summary.* Boston, Ma.: Author, 1977.

DeLeeuw, F., & Ekanem, N. S. The supply of rental housing. *American Economic Review,* 1971, *61,* 814–826.

Dildine, L. L., & Massey, F. A. Dynamic model of private incentives to housing maintenance. *Southern Economic Journal,* 1974, *40,* 631–639.

Goodman, J. L., Jr. *Is ordinary least squares estimation with a dichotomous dependent variable really that bad?* (Working paper No. 216-23). Washington, D.C.: Urban Institute, 1976.

Gutowski, M. Integrating housing and social services activities for the elderly household. *Occasional Papers in Housing and Urban Development,* 1978, *1,* 110–130.

Guttentag, J. M *Creating new financial instruments for the aged.* New York: New York University Center for Study of Financial Institutions, 1975.

Jacobs, B., & Rabushka, A. *The elderly homeowner: A proposal for further study based on preliminary findings* (Report to U.S. Department of Housing and Urban Development). Washington, D.C.: Transcentury Corporation, 1976.

Kain, J. F., & Quigley, J. M. *Housing markets and racial discrimination.* New York: Columbia University Press, 1975.

Kravis, I. B., & Lipsey, R. E. *Price competitiveness in world trade.* New York: National Bureau of Economic Research, 1971.

Lawton, M. P. The housing problems of community-resident *Occasional Papers in Housing and Community Affairs,* 1978, *1,* 39–74.

Mendelsohn, R. *Housing improvements of single-family owner-occupied units in the United States.* Unpublished senior thesis, Harvard University, 1973.

Mendelsohn, R. Empirical evidence on home improvement *Journal of Urban Economics,* 1977, *4,* 457–468.

Mendelsohn, R., & Struyk, R. *The flow of housing services in a hedonic index* (Working paper). Washington, D.C.: Urban Institute, 1975.

Newman, S. *Housing adjustments of older people* (Part II). Ann Arbor: University of Michigan, Institute for Social Research, 1977.

Ozanne, L., & Struyk, R. *Housing from the existing stock: Comparative economic analyses of owner-occupants and landlords.* Washington, D.C.: Urban Institute, 1976.

Rosow, I., & Breslau, N. A Guttman health scale for the aged. *Journal of Gerontology,* 1966, *21,* 556–559.

Schafer, R., Holshouser, W., Moore, K., & Santer, R. Spatial variations in the operating costs of rental housing (Discussion Paper D 75-4). Cambridge, Mass.: Harvard University, Department of City and Regional Planning, 1975.

Shanas, E., Townsend, P., Wedderburn, D., Friis, H., Milhøy, P., & Stehouwer, J. *Old people in three industrial societies.* New York: Atherton, 1968.

Straszheim, M. *An econometric analysis of the urban housing market.* New York: Columbia University Press, 1975.

Struyk, R. *Housing for the elderly: Research needs for informed public policy* (Working paper No. 229-4). Washington, D.C.: Urban Institute, 1976.

Struyk, R. The housing situation of elderly Americans. *Gerontologist*, 1977, *17*, 130–137. (a)

Struyk, R. The housing expense burden of elderly Americans. *Gerontologist*, 1977, *17*, 447–452. (b)

Sweeney, J. L. Housing unit maintenance and mode of tensure. *Journal of Economic Theory*, 1974, 111–138.

U.S. Department of Housing and Urban Development. *Lower-income housing assistance program (Section 8): Interim findings of evaluation research.* Washington, D.C.: Office of Policy Development and Research, U.S. Department of Housing and Urban Development, 1977.

16
Some Recent Innovations in Community Living Arrangements for Older People

ELAINE M. BRODY
BERNARD LIEBOWITZ

It is now conventional wisdom in gerontology that the heterogeneity of the population of older people should be matched by a wide variety of living arrangements to meet their diverse needs. A theoretical continuum ranges from institutional care to totally independent living in one's own home, with many intermediate points. It includes such specialized housing to which older people move as apartment buildings, retirement communities, boarding facilities, and others. It also includes the older person's own home if that living situation is changed by the provision of supportive services brought to the home (meals on wheels, home care, home nursing, homemaker, and the like), by services that bring the older person to the site of part-time care (such as day care), or by linkage services designed to connect the older person to needed services and facilities (such as transportation).

Some innovative living arrangements for older people have been developing in recent years for which there are no generally accepted names. Among the various titles used to describe them are group homes or residences, cooperatives, and communes. Their most visible characteristics are that they are small, usually serving no more than 20 people under one roof, often use ordinary housing which may be renovated for that purpose, and provide one or more supportive services. They are viewed as noninstitutional and as promoting independence and continued community living.

A striking fact about these innovative arrangements is that the amount of interest in them evidenced by professionals, government, the general public, and the media is not proportionate to the number of older people involved. Since data about them are sparse, no accurate estimate of the population served is possible. It is safe to say, however, that the likelihood is that only a tiny fraction of the elderly population is involved. One can only conjecture about the source of the tremendous appeal of such arrangements. It may lie in their small scale, their resemblance to "normal" living, the fact that they permit continuity of lifestyle, and in their contrast to large, age-segregated apartment buildings and negatively regarded institutions.

In view of the diversity of needs among older people, the criterion of the effectiveness of a service, program, or facility does not lie in its universal applicability. Therefore, the fact that these new living arrangements have struck such a responsive chord warrants further exploration despite the small number of people they serve at present.

In 1971 the Philadelphia Geriatric Center (PGC) developed a project called Community Housing for the Elderly (CH) (formerly called Intermediate Housing), which has been evaluated in the framework of a 6-year research study. In the course of those years, many organizations interested in sponsoring similar arrangements requested information about or visited the housing. An attempt to monitor their progress has met with only partial success. Though we have information about 19 of them (of which 11 are actually in operation), we have no way of knowing how many others exist or what form they have taken. To our knowledge, CH is the only project that has been formally evaluated.

This chapter describes the CH program and research and reviews the other projects about which we have some knowledge. The information is discussed in terms of the potential of such housing and the implications for social policy.

THE COMMUNITY HOUSING PROJECT

Community Housing for the Elderly consists of nine renovated one-family semidetached homes located in a residential neighborhood on two streets bordering the PGC campus. The PGC also includes two high-rise apartment buildings with services for about 500 older people, 460 long-term care beds, a 56-bed hospital fully accredited by the Joint Commission on Hospital Accreditation, and a variety of services designed to serve older people living in the community.

Each of the CH houses contains three private efficiency apartments (bed/sitting room, bath, and kitchen) and a shared living room. The purchase and conversion of the houses were accomplished with the aid of interest abatement under the Section 236 Rehabilitation Program of the Federal Housing Administration (FHA). The rent-supplementation funding made it possible to rent 40% of the apartments at reduced rates to tenants who met the financial criteria (the same as for public housing).

The current version of CH was preceded by the testing of two other models (Bronson, 1972). The creation of the first model in 1965 was stimulated by the many older people known to us who urgently needed new living arrangements but for whom institutions or high-rise apartment buildings were not always suitable, available, or economically feasible. Many wished to maintain as much independence and privacy as possible, but needed some service in order to do so. The first house was not modified architecturally and therefore involved sharing kitchen and baths as well as the living room. In the second, occupied in 1967, each tenant had a private kitchen but the living room was shared. Experience with both models indicated the need for more separate quarters to minimize interpersonal problems and to provide the privacy desired.

In the houses now operating special attention was paid to insuring maximum safety and comfort to the occupants through the elimination of architectural barriers (Brody, Kleban, & Liebowitz, 1973). Included in the basic rental ($98 and $95 for first- and second-floor apartments, respectively) are janitorial and building maintenance services, cleaning of the common areas, and a hotline phone connected to the PGC switchboard for medical or other emergencies. Social services are provided during the application and moving phases, at crisis points, and when tenants need to move elsewhere. The center's group recreational, religious, and social activities are open to tenants. Home-delivered frozen main meals and light housekeeping services are optional extras that can be purchased from the PGC at nominal, nonprofit prices. Medical care is not provided; the tenants retain their own personal physicians.

The Community Housing Research

The short-range and longer-range impact of the housing was evaluated by two research studies (see Brody, Kleban, & Liebowitz, 1975 for a detailed description of the research design). In brief, the experimental group of CH tenants and two control groups were comprised of the 87 older people who applied for tenancy in CH and who met the eligibility criteria. Criteria were age (62 and over), income as specified by the U.S. Department of Housing and Urban Development (HUD), and health such that the individual was capable of functioning with the degree of independence demanded by the physical, social, and service environment of CH (e.g., able to climb stairs, able to manage minimal house-keeping and cooking, and freedom from the needs for supervision or assistance in personal care).

Those in the experimental group of 24 CH tenants were selected randomly in order to eliminate possible biases, though decisions on acceptance rested with the older people themselves. Assignment could not be made to the two control conditions since the individual's own decision to move or not move determined that person's group assignment. The experimental group was comprised of those who accepted the offer of a CH apartment and moved in. One control group—the control movers—elected to move to other types of housing. The second control group—the nonmovers—remained in their original housing. To summarize the moving patterns, the experimentals all moved to CH; the control movers moved to a variety of places such as different apartments, rented rooms, and nursing homes; and the nonmovers remained in their original living arrangements for at least 6 months.

All of the older people received evaluations on instruments and questionnaires administered at baseline (time of application), at 6-month follow-up, and at annual intervals thereafter for an additional 2 years. They were, therefore, followed for a total of $3\frac{1}{2}$ years from the time of application. There were 144 variables that covered demographics; contacts with family and friends; recent interpersonal losses; types of living arrangements and satisfactions and dissatisfactions with those arrangements; social participation; physical, cognitive, social, and behavioral functioning; self-reported health; morale; and self-concept.

The three groups were similar in demographic characteristics with no significant differences in age (mean about 74, range 63–94) or family status (80% widowed, the remainder single, divorced, or separated; mean number of children, 1.45). They also had similar histories of extreme stability in previous living arrangements.

At baseline the three groups also were similar in functional capacities, though there were hints that the control movers were experiencing more health problems. By 6-month follow-up, health problems continued to differentiate control movers and those difficulties had begun to be evidenced by declines in functional capacities as well. The nonmovers were similar to the experimentals at baseline, but by 6-month follow-up five of them had died and the survivors showed differences in the direction of somewhat poorer health.

At baseline the three groups were equivalent in types of living arrangement. As indicated in Table 16.1, most lived alone in apartments or houses and the rest were scattered in rooming houses, hotels, single rooms, specialized housing for older people, or with family. None was in

TABLE 16.1
Living Arrangements at Baseline and at 6-Month, 2-Year, and 3-Year Post-Move Follow-Up

| | All Groups Combined N = 87 | | | | | | | |
| | Baseline | | 6 Mo. Post–Move | | 2 Year Post–Move | | 3 Year Post–Move | |
	N	%	N	%	N	%	N	%
Alone in house	13	15.	6	6.9	2	2.3	1	1.1
Alone in apartment	49	56.4	29	33.3	12	13.8	10	12.5
Rooming house/hotel/ single room	9	10.3	4	4.6	2	2.3	2	2.3
Specialized housing for older people without services	6	6.9	10	11.5	17	20.	13	15.
Intermediate housing	–	–	24	27.5	24	27.	23	26.4
Specialized housing for older people with services	1	1.1	2	2.3	6	6.9	7	8.
Boarding home	–	–	–	–	–	–	–	–
Sharing house or apt. with family	9	10.3	2	2.3	2	2.3	1	1.1
Nursing home or home for aged	–	–	5	5.7	5	5.7	7	9.2
Refusal	–	–	–	–	5	5.7	5	5.7
Deceased	–	–	5	5.7	12	13.8	18	20.
Total	87	100%	87	100%	87	100%	87	100%

Note: There are 5 survivors in the non-mover group who have not moved: 2 continue to live alone in apartments and one each remains alone in a house, at a high-rise for older people, and at a retirement hotel.

institutions or boarding homes though about one fourth of them had applied for nursing-home care. At 6-month follow-up, by definition all experimentals had moved to CH and all the nonmovers had not moved. The fact that five of the control movers had moved to nursing homes is consistent with their poorer health at baseline and their poorer performance on functional measures at follow-up.

There were no differences among the three groups in the nature or number of reasons they offered for wishing to move. The most compelling reasons can be summarized as deteriorated properties in neighborhoods with high crime rates from which families and friends had moved, leaving those who remained lonely, isolated, and fearful. The groups were similar also in the reasons they presented against moving. Though reasons expressed as either in favor of or against moving were not predictive of moving/not moving, a strong predictor proved to be the social workers' baseline judgments of factors operating against moving for each subject. The rating that the older person was reluctant to leave familiar surroundings or would find the prospect of moving too hard psychologically was extremely significant. More than 70% of the nonmovers but only 9% of the control movers and 25% of the experimentals was judged to have such resistance.

The older people's initial reactions to the CH physical environment, though not predictive of whether or not they decided to become tenants, are of interest to potential sponsors. Some objections included the stall showers not compensating for the lack of a tub, too many stairs, and the small size of the apartments. Equal numbers viewed the shared living room unfavorably or favorably. None regarded CH's age segregation as a negative attribute.

The initial data analysis used six variables as criteria for evaluating housing satisfaction at 6-month post-move follow-up: satisfaction with overall living arrangements, satisfaction with apartments, satisfaction with neighborhoods, the wish to move, enjoyment of life, and number of good friends. At baseline there were no significant differences among the three groups on those variables. All were generally dissatisfied.

Six months after moving, the CH tenants clearly fared better than either of the other two groups. They had improved in their overall satisfaction with living arrangements and satisfaction with apartments, their wish to move had dissipated to a much greater extent, and they had increased in enjoyment of life and social contacts. Problems evidenced at baseline in dissatisfaction with neighborhood were solved by both the CH and the control movers but remained for the nonmovers.

Other significant findings from the 6-month follow-up study were:

As a result of not moving, the nonmovers fared very poorly. Their morale had declined, their housing had deteriorated further, and most still wanted to move. In contrast, living arrangement problems had been resolved by the CH tenants. More than the control movers, and much more than the control nonmovers, the CH tenants liked their current living arrangements, had attained freedom from fear and crime, had more close friends, and perceived themselves as being in better health (Kleban & Turner-Massey, 1978).

The data confirmed the idea that favorable neighborhood and residential factors are associated with positive effects on well-being of the elderly, though the impact did not occur in all sectors of functioning (Lawton, Brody, & Turner-Massey, 1978).

The greater satisfaction of the CH tenants with their living arrangements was associated with greater satisfaction with their apartments, neighborhoods, and proximity to facilities. As a group, they were happier, felt safer, enjoyed life more, and had an improved sense of privacy. They had also improved in eating, sleeping, neighborhood motility, social adjustment and functioning, and involvement in enjoyable activities. However, no group is ever entirely homogeneous; there was a subgroup of control movers and a small number of control nonmovers who also fared well in those respects (Kleban, Brody, & Turner-Massey, 1977).

Self-perceived health and functional capabilities were important determinants of where the subjects sought to move. For example, those control movers who moved to nursing homes had more health problems, more hospitalizations, and more functional difficulties. Even within the group of CH tenants, those who selected second-floor apartments that required stair-climbing were healthier and more active (Kleban, Brody, & Turner-Massey, 1977).

Data from the longitudinal follow-up evaluations are still being analyzed. Early findings from analysis of the same satisfaction variables indicate that by the time of the 2-year follow-up, the CH tenants and the control movers were similar in satisfaction with their overall living arrangements, though the CH group maintained greater satisfaction with their apartments. However, it should be recalled that 6 months after moving, the CH tenants had greatly surpassed other movers in overall living arrangement satisfaction. That early sharp boost was attributed to the specifics of the CH environment, including counseling services that focused on conflicts about moving, help with moving plans, and adjustment problems in adapting to their new residences (Brody, Kleban, & Turner-Massey, 1977). The nonmovers fared poorly at both evaluations.

During the longitudinal study all of the older people studied did not, of course, remain in the same location they occupied at 6-month follow-up. Some subsequently moved and some did not; some survived and some died. At the final evaluation 3 years later, 17 of the original 24 CH tenants were still in CH.

Use of Services and Space by CH Tenants

Data on the utilization of services by CH tenants indicate that initially about half of them purchased the PGC housekeeping and linen service and about one third purchased the frozen dinners as steady services, a proportion that remained essentially the same thereafter. Other tenants purchased the meals during periods of convalescence.

A 24-week log of the tenants' contacts with staff following occupancy showed that the highest concentration of service requests occurred during the first week. Contacts then declined sharply during the ensuing 3 weeks and maintained a plateau until another decline occurred in the final 4 weeks of the study. Building maintenance requests, social visits to the project office, and social service requests, in that order, accounted for most contacts. Some building maintenance problems were specific to the newly renovated houses (e.g., windows painted shut), but others related to garden-variety moving problems in general (e.g., installation of fans, air conditioners, and other appliances; movement of furniture; adaptation to new appliances and conveniences). Social services included emotional support, mediation of tenant interpersonal problems, and referral to community resources. Requests for these services were most frequent during the first 4 weeks, then dropped by half, and remained at the same level thereafter.

A study of the communal living room in the CH houses (Ishizaki, Solms, & Turner, 1975) indicated that three fourths of the tenants used it for visiting with other tenants, friends, and family and for solitary activities such as reading, watching TV, and sitting. The remaining 25% did not use that room at all. Cleaning of the living room was done primarily by first-floor tenants whose apartments were adjacent to it, and primarily by those who had contributed furniture to it. There was a tendency for first-floor tenants to dominate the living room. Such territoriality did not extend to the porches, which apparently were viewed as belonging to all the tenants and were used by them equally. This experience suggests that social interaction would be encouraged if each tenant could contribute some possessions to any shared space to convey the sense that it belongs to them equally.

Personality compatibility appeared to be important in fostering or hampering socialization. Some of the tenants who tended not to use the communal living space were continuing a lifelong pattern; they were loners who had never shared social space in previous living arrangements. For others, socioeconomic and perceived social class differences were important; some were unwilling to share with those who were not their "equals." As might be expected, individuals with paranoid tendencies reacted poorly to the shared space; the close contact precipitated disruptive behavior and conflict with others in the house. These observations imply that tenants should be screened for matching of personality and social background when an area is to be shared.

The proximity of CH to the PGC sponsoring agency proved to be a decided asset. The project office acted as a focal point for purposes as diverse as socialization, requests for help, an information center (Where are stores? Where does one vote?), and referral to other agencies for needed services. Twenty-four-hour maintenance service, the protection of the well-lit campus, the numerous social, religious, and recreational events, and the opportunities for socialization undoubtedly add to the tenants' security and well-being. The social work counseling was a major factor in facilitating the move to CH and subsequently in easing transitions in the few instances in which CH tenants needed to go to nursing homes.

IMPLICATIONS OF COMMUNITY HOUSING FOR PLANNING AND POLICY

Community Housing, in existence in its present form since 1971, has proved to be a viable innovation in living arrangements for older people. It has demonstrated the potential of institutions for developing noninstitutional service-supported housing. The capability of the sponsoring agency facilitated the developmental process and the provision of services. The protective proximity of the center and the services offered were influential in fostering the tenants' satisfaction and rapid adaptation to their new settings.

In our opinion, CH has considerable potential for being replicated under a variety of auspices. The two critical components have been identified as the procurement and renovation of the houses and the rent supplements needed to serve a low-income group (Liebowitz, 1978). Initial experience gained by guiding the project through the complexities of FHA regulations led to recommendations that (1) FHA policies and procedures be streamlined for small projects, (2) an FHA expediter be created to give technical assistance to agencies in the mechanics of applications and development, and (3) selective criteria be established for the evaluation, insurance, and administration of small projects (Liebowitz, 1978).

Lawton's (1969) finding that the nature of the services offered in a housing arrangement attracts people who need those particular services was reaffirmed by this study. Thus the CH tenants are somewhat older and in slightly poorer health than the general older population. One quarter of them had applied for institutional care before CH became available. The physical structure of the houses also was a factor in the determination of the tenant population. People who did not wish to climb stairs did not move to CH. The small size of the apartments was a deterrent to the couples who looked at them. It should also be noted that the arrangement affords less privacy than the typical apartment building and less opportunity for socialization within the walls of the house itself.

Another determinant of the population attracted is the nature of the auspice, since the historical goals of any auspice elicit specific expectations in the community. Thus the proximity to the PGC exerted a strong pull for this particular population; the behavior and expectations of the tenants made explicit their assumption of the PGC's continuing social agency function.

Experience with the project leads to a strong recommendation with respect to the service patterns of housing for older people. Inventories of services that should be available often include recreational activities, on-site medical services, on-site meal services, household maintenance, easily accessible shopping, transportation, and information/referral services. To that list should be added outreach and social work counseling during the decision-making, moving-in, and postmove phases of relocation, and help with such potentially overwhelming tasks as locating a new residence, packing and moving, and disposing of possessions (a painful process for many older people).

Certainly, not all movers require intensive counseling. However, most older people (or people of any age) might not be aware of or articulate such a need. Expressed wishes for services are usually keyed to concrete instrumental forms of assistance. Ambivalence, psychological conflict, resistance, and other such concepts are not part of their everyday language. Older people are, therefore, unlikely to identify such problems and take action to resolve them by approaching freestanding counseling agencies in the community. Our observations suggest that older people who are particularly in need of relocation counseling are those whose living situations are clearly undesirable, those who have no supportive family, those who evidence reluctance or resistance to moving despite an expressed wish and need to do so, and those who show strong ambivalence, indecision, anxiety, overdependency, or other problems that prevent them from availing themselves of an acceptable option to move.

The need for such help is supported by the project data, in particular the fact that the experimental movers adapted to their environments much more quickly than the control movers. That initial extra boost is attributed at least in part to the concentrated social work services they received in the decision-making and transitional processes. The service log described above indicates the high utilization of services during the first few weeks after moving in.

Obviously, no one was forced to move, though many CH tenants were given strong support to do so by the project staff when they were fearful, indecisive, too rooted to their old homes and neighborhoods, felt helpless, or otherwise might have stayed in place. Several other studies of urban areas have also noted the resistance to moving even when the older people had been constantly mugged, beaten, burglarized and otherwise terrorized. For example, one such project found that 81% of the elderly Jewish population that resided in a high crime area of Philadelphia were very dissatisfied and indicated that they would like to move (Lawton & Kleban, 1971), yet 2 years later only 20% had moved, though they had had the opportunity to do so (Lawton, Kleban, & Carlson, 1973).

The right of older people to self-determination should not be translated as a hands-off, take-it-or-leave-it policy. The nonmover control group in our study fared very poorly, indeed, in contrast to the two groups of movers at the 6-month follow-up. Though their well-being had deteriorated and 84% still wished to move, they continued to live under conditions of severe environmental stress. Those who subsequently moved did improve, as did the earlier movers. As matters stand, when applications for housing are handled as a straight rental arrangement (as is generally the case), tenant populations of housing for the elderly may fail to include some of the older people who need a change of residence most but who are unable to mobilize themselves to affect the change.

OTHER SMALL-SCALE PROJECTS

A number of other small-scale projects have been reviewed by Liebowitz (1978). Subsequent updating in 1978 has located other projects either completed or in the planning stage. Other organizations that had indicated an interest in sponsoring projects similar to CH had been unable to proceed and identified barriers they had encountered.

A brief review of these projects reveals that:

CH and the other projects all use houses or apartments originally intended as ordinary housing, rather than as buildings to serve as specialized living arrangements for older people.

An essential way in which the other projects differ from CH is that they all provide at least several services as a matter of routine to all their residents (e.g., housekeeping, food preparation, personal care, counseling, and some form of linkage service such as transportation, communication, or referral). In contrast, the optional services available at CH are provided in response to each individual's own request and perception of need.

In the other arrangements a staff person either lives in or is present at least several house daily.

CH is not really a group living arrangement as are the others. In group living situations, services usually are geared to the level of those who need the most service. The CH pattern permits varying degrees or level of services to its tenants.

The physical living arrangement itself at CH differs from the others in that essential components (bath, kitchen, bedroom) are not shared.

The differences between CH and the other arrangements are reflected in their costs, with the CH charge being the only one that approximates rental cost alone.

It is apparent that CH is closest to ordinary housing and normal living. Some of the others have elements of the halfway house, the boarding home, and the personal care home. Many of them provide services similar to those given in an institution; their residents probably are more impaired than the CH tenants. In some cases, they are in fact "mini–nursing homes" in a form that may be more acceptable. None can be accurately characterized as a commune, a concept that has extremely limited potential for current generations of older people.

The three projects in the planning phase at the time of the survey were all under church auspices. One has chosen a site and is currently raising funds. It plans to house 35 older people in a renovated convent with private bedrooms and shared kitchen and baths. Occupants will have to be capable of self-care, but there will be a part-time administrator, a resident manager, a case worker, and a homemaker to prepare meals. The second project has obtained consultation from gerontologists and architects and is still looking for funding, but reports that momentum has picked up. The third project does not involve developing a specific housing site. Rather, it aims to identify and bring together small groups of two to four people who would share existing housing with each other. About a dozen potential groups of such people have been located and they are now in the process of discussing the possibility of living together.

In one case, barriers were encountered while planning inter-generational housing on a college campus. The plan fell through when increased student enrollment made the space unavailable. Two sponsors could not obtain funds, one simply could not mount any support or resources, and two others were handicapped by zoning ordinances that prevented group housing. It is worth mentioning that a few of the projects now actually operating had successfully challenged adverse zoning decision in the court.

In summary, it is apparent that whether CH or any of the other types of small-scale living arrangement is entirely new, is a re-invention, or is a variation on a somewhat familiar theme, they exist and seem to be meeting the needs of some older people. The fact that so few have come into being despite their demonstrated appeal probably relates to the fact that they are not easy to develop, requiring ingenuity and persistence to surmount assorted obstacles along the way to completion. It may be that, given the strenuous efforts needed, sponsoring agencies have preferred to invest their energies and resources in larger Section 202 projects.

It is important to monitor the progress of these small, innovative living arrangements and eventually to clarify nomenclature, definitions, target populations, effects, costs, and standards. In many areas, the usual local housing and zoning codes should accommodate arrangements such as CH that do not involve provision of regular daily services. In any event, at this point it is important not to stifle creative efforts by unrealistic regulations that would press them into a common mold, if not force them out of existence altogether.

REFERENCES

Brody, E. M., Kleban, M. H., & Liebowitz, B. Living arrangements for older people. *American Institute of Architects Journal,* 1973, 59, 35–40.

Brody, E. M., Kleban, M. H., & Liebowitz, B. Intermediate housing for the elderly: Satisfaction of those who moved in and those who did not. *Gerontologist,* 1975, 15, 350–356.

Brody, E. M., Kleban, M. H., & Turner-Massey, P. *Longitudinal evaluation of intermediate housing for the elderly.* Paper presented at annual meeting of the Gerontological Society, San Francisco, November 1977.

Bronson, E. P. An experiment in intermediate housing facilities for the elderly. *Gerontologist*, 1972, *12*, 22–26.

Ishizaki, D., Solms, R., & Turner, P. *Intermediate housing for the elderly: Utilization of the communal living space.* Paper presented at annual meeting of the Gerontological Society, Louisville, Ky., October 1975.

Kleban, M. H., Brody, E. M., & Turner-Massey, P. *The Community Housing Project: Factors contributing to housing satisfaction of older people.* Philadelphia: Philadelphia Geriatric Center, 1977.

Kleban, M. H., & Turner-Massey, P. Short-range effects of Community Housing. *Gerontologist*, 1978, *18*, 129–132.

Lawton, M. P. Supportive services in the context of the housing environment. *Gerontologist*, 1969, *9*, 15–19.

Lawton, M. P. Institutions and alternatives to institutions. *Health and Social Work*, 1978, *3*, 108–134.

Lawton, M. P., Brody, E. M., & Turner-Massey, P. The relationships of environmental factors to changes in wellbeing. *Gerontologist*, 1978, *18*, 133–137.

Lawton, M. P., & Kleban, M. H. The aged resident of the inner city. *Gerontologist*, 1971, *11*, 277–283.

Lawton, M. P., Kleban, M. H., & Carlson, D. A. The inner city resident: To move or not to move. *Gerontologist*, 1973, *13*, 443–448.

Liebowitz, B. Implications of Community Housing for planning and policy. *Gerontologist*, 1978, *18*, 138–143.

17

An Alternative for Elderly Housing: Home Conversion

VIVIAN F. CARLIN
RICHARD FOX

The New Jersey Division on Aging has developed an innovative approach to help low-income elderly homeowners remain in their own homes by providing non-interest bearing loans to convert their dwellings so as to include an income-producing apartment. This approach also increased the supply of suitable apartments for low-income elderly renters at a cost far below that of a new unit in a multi-unit project. As far as is known, this is the first such pilot project in the country. What follows is a description of the program, a discussion of its development, and an evaluation with recommendations for the future.

DESCRIPTION OF THE PROJECT

Support for this project was provided by a $60,000 grant funded under the Older Americans Act Model Projects to the Plainfield Housing Authority. This grant was to be used to remodel five homes so as to produce a rental apartment within the original home. The repayment of the loans would establish a revolving fund for additional conversions. The projected cost of $12,000 per conversion included $955 for administrative assistance, $1,112 for architectural assistance, $9,393 for actual cost of the conversion and $540 for contingency. A more detailed cost breakdown is shown in Table 17.1.

Elderly low-income homeowners in the recent inflationary period have been economically burdened by fixed incomes and rapidly rising property taxes. Some have been forced to sell their homes because of an inability to pay these taxes. Because there are few or no suitable housing choices for low-income elderly, they have at times had to move out of the community, away from family, friends, and familiar surroundings. The state of New Jersey has recognized that low-income

TABLE 17.1
Twelve-Month Demonstration Budget for Five Home Conversion Units,
September 1, 1974–September 1, 1979

Administrative Cost	Per Unit	Program
Zoning variance – preparation, survey, application fee	75	375
Audit	100	500
Clerical	700	3,500
Legal	40	200
Advertisements for bidding	40	200
Administrative sub-total	955	4,775
Architectural Cost		
Architectural, printing, inspection	1,112	5,560
Architectural sub-total	1,112	5,560
Conversion Cost		
Conversion contract cost	9,393	46,965
Contingency	540	2,700
TOTAL	12,000	60,000

elderly homeowners need some form of property tax relief and as a result has instituted a $160 property tax reduction for homeowners over the age of 65 with incomes under $5,000 (excluding Social Security). In most cases, this deduction provides only minimal assistance; many in this income group are able to pay their property taxes only by limiting other necessities such as food and medical care.

The conversion project is designed to defray housing expenses for an elderly homeowner by adding an income-producing apartment upstairs. An eligible homeowner is defined as a person 65 years of age or over (amended to 55 years as the project progressed) who either has a maximum income of $5,000 or is eligible for the State Property Tax deduction. In addition, the homeowner must be in reasonably good health, both mentally and physically, and able to serve as landlord. The two-story house must be in satisfactory repair and suitable for a second-floor apartment. The neighborhood should be fairly stable. It would be preferable for the home to be located in an area that is already zoned for two-family units. However, it was thought that if any zoning variance should be required, it would have a high probability of being granted because of the unusual hardship of senior citizens, prior nonconforming use in various zones, and the moderate nature of the required variance.

The benefits to the homeowner include not only the added income from the rental of the upstairs apartment but also the creation of a safer one-floor living unit for the owner, with the comfort and security of having another person or couple living in the same house. By easing the burden of property maintenance for the homeowner, the project can also contribute to preservation of the neighborhood.

A Suggested Manner of Approach

Although the new apartment could be rented on the open market, it is desirable to have elderly tenants who are eligible for Section 8 rent subsidies. Thus each conversion could be said to create housing for two low-income elderly families.

It is preferable for a housing agency or authority to administer both aspects of the project, that is, the conversion of the homes and the leasing of the apartments. Once an agreement has been entered into with the homeowner, an architect should be employed. Upon finalization of plans, the process of bidding begins: advertisement, receiving the bids, awarding of contracts, and then overseeing construction. The housing authority then leases the units from the homeowner using the Section 8 program and subleases to eligible elderly tenants. The property is jointly managed by the homeowner and housing authority. The housing authority collects rent and pays the homeowner directly. The subleasee's ability to pay rent is determined by a formula, basically 25% of net income. The subleasee's housing is guaranteed for the term of the lease. The lease continues for 15 years, renewable at 5-year intervals. Should the homeowner die or sell the house in the interim the estate or the new owner is obligated to honor the duration of the lease.

PROJECT DEVELOPMENT

The history of project development is one of slow progress due to various delays. The project was first conceived in the fall of 1973. The initial steps involved working with the New Jersey Housing Finance Agency to determine the economic feasibility of such a plan. When it was determined it could work, a grantee for the demonstration was sought. The Plainfield Housing Authority was approached for the following reasons: (1) Plainfield is an urban area, but not as large a city as Newark; (2) there is a significant minority population in the area; (3) the housing authority had existing rent subsidy funds, a good history of pubic housing for the elderly, and a long waiting list of eligible elderly applicants; and (4) the staff of the Plainfield Housing Authority was highly professional, experienced, and capable of meeting the challenge of implementing such an experimental program.

Early in 1974 an attempt was made to obtain funding for the demonstration project. This first attempt failed because of an inability to obtain funds from the housing demonstration program within the Department of Community Affairs. Fortunately, federal Older Americans Act Model Project money administered by the New Jersey Division on Aging, Department of Community Affairs could be used. However, due to bureaucratic procedures it took an inordinately long time to process the contract. Although the Plainfield Housing Authority's proposal was received in July 1974, it was not until August 1975 that the funds were actually allocated. Prior to the start of the program both the Tax Assessor and the Planning Director of Plainfield were consulted to elicit support. Both were enthusiastic. The Planning Director recommended that the program not be implemented in commercial or industrial zones. The Tax Assessor was consulted regarding possible tax increases resulting from the alterations; the alterations added a $1,500 assessment, resulting in a tax increase of $60–$90 per year.

Because of the experimental nature of this program, the Plainfield Housing Authority proceeded to do a thorough analysis of where elderly homeowners who qualified for the property tax deduction were located and then plotted the locations on the zoning map. This took many months and caused quite a delay. Once the zones in which the houses were located were identified (i.e., either one-family zones or zones that permitted two-, three-, four-, or multifamily housing), the people whose homes were in the multifamily housing zones were contacted.

A variety of methods was used to make people aware of this program. Flyers were left at various agencies that served the elderly, spot announcements were made on the radio, articles were submitted to the two local newspapers, speeches were presented to civic organizations, and finally, a door-to-door campaign was conducted in the areas where two-family houses were permitted. This last technique was found to be most effective. It took from August 1975 to August 1976 both to identify the desired five elderly homeowners and to develop the architectural plans and cost analysis.

By September 1976 the five people had signed letters of intent, thereby allowing the bids to be advertised. The bidding process took longer than expected because the first method, consisting of soliciting bids for all five renovations as a total package, proved to be non-productive. This process attracted only large contractors, whose bids were excessive. The second method, in which bids were advertised so that a contractor could bid on a single conversion or any combination of the five, was more successful and, therefore, recommended. Also, the performance bond was eliminated because this mitigated against small and minority contractors. In place of the performance bond, the bidding package was constructed in such a way that the contractor would not get paid until each part of the work had been completed; thus the Housing Authority would always be behind in payments. In addition, 10% was retained until completion of all work to safeguard the Housing Authority and the homeowners during the construction phase. As a result, four of the five houses came in under the maximum allowed for renovation costs, an average of about $10,000 per house. These results were highly satisfactory considering that the estimated costs were $8,000–$10,000 per house when the project began. Four years later and in a period of high inflation the actual costs were about $10,000.

The cost for one of the conversions was too high because the particular homeowner wanted a new roof, a new hot water heater, and drain repairs. Such major repair work was beyond the scope of this project, as it was expected that the bulk of the conversion costs would be for renovations. However, in the interest of maintaining the housing, some money was spent for minor repairs.

Subsequently, four people were left in the program. Unfortunately, one of these homeowners died suddenly during the bidding phase. A third person had to withdraw when her daughter and granddaughter moved into the house. The remaining two conversions have been successfully completed. There are two very happy tenants, one a single man and the other a single woman. Although not by design, both homeowner and renters are black. In 1978 two to three additional homeowners were being sought for additional conversion.

Findings

The projected operating budget for the conversion project was based on an average rent of $262, as provided by the Section 8 program. Anticipated increases in utilities (heat, electricity, water) came to approximately $42 per month. The increases in taxes was based on an additional $1,500 assessed valuation and came to $5.83 per month. Additional homeowner's insurance was projected at $8.33 monthly. The amortization of the principal of $9,393 over a 10-year period came to $78.27 monthly. These increased expenditures resulted in a total of $134.43 per month, leaving the homeowner a net income of almost $128 per month, or $1,536 yearly.

The project has been an overall success and worth replicating; however, legitimate questions remain. The first problem encountered was the tremendous resistance to participate on the part of the older homeowner. The major reason for nonparticipation was that anticipated profit was not high enough. Originally it was expected that there would be a net profit of $500–$600 per year to help defray property taxes. It was thought that this would provide sufficient inducement. The actual new profit was higher, between $1,200 and $1,400 per year, a fact that should provide a significantly greater inducement to future potential participants.

A second reason for resistance to participating was the economic level of the community. The population had a high proportion of persons who had been mainly hourly wage earners. They had no experience with investing money and did not understand the principle of equity investment to produce a rental income. A third reason for resistance was a concern about privacy; people just did not want to have somebody else living in their house, even in a separate apartment upstairs.

A fourth reason was a concern about the level of household disruption during the conversion process. People wanted to be in the program but they did not want a contractor dirtying their houses. A fifth reason, probably one of the most important, was the fear associated with an uncertain social and economic outcome. Since this was an experimental program, there was necessarily skepticism and fear of the end result.

The last and totally unexpected reason was that many adult children vetoed the project. Possibly the children's disapproval was due to fear of what would happen to their inheritance. In most cases, the home was the only inheritance and it was felt that the conversion might jeopardize its value or salability.

It is hoped that because of the two existing successful conversions and the enthusiasm of those homeowners and renters who have benefited there will not be so much resistance among future users. Potentially, the participants could share positive feelings about the program.

A final point to be considered is that through this program it is shown that a rental unit can be produced for an average of $10,000–$11,000, as contrasted with the $35,000–$40,000 it would cost for a comparable unit in a newly constructed building.

RECOMMENDATIONS AND EVALUATION

The first recommendation is that only a municipality where Section 8 subsidies exist be selected. Second, the grantee should be a housing authority or other local housing agency with expertise in designing and managing housing for the elderly. The program might be improved through cooperation with another agency used to find and select homeowners. This agency should have had previous experience in working directly with homeowners in programs such as weatherization, Mr. Fixit, or home repair.

Third, in publicizing the home conversion program, greater use should be made of both the radio and individual contact with homeowners. A fourth recommendation is that there should be at least a part-time salary for a program administrator so that the housing authority does not have to further burden a staff working to capacity. It is felt that had there been an allocation for a project coordinator the project would have moved along at a considerably faster rate. In spite of this, the staff did a remarkable job.

Fifth, a bidding procedure that encourages small and minority contractors should be utilized, and should permit options for the number of conversions that can be undertaken. Finally, the revolving fund concept and other possible ways of funding this program should be reviewed and explored. In place of a revolving fund, another suggestion has been to subsidize just the interest and to use conventional lending institutions as the major funding agency. Thus the housing agency would loan $3,000–$4,000 per conversion and many more homes could be converted for the same amount of money. Also, lending institutions might be stimulated to develop other kinds of home loan programs. Another idea is to investigate the use of Section 8 rehabilitation funds; this would allow higher rents and enable the homeowner to clear $2,400 instead of the present $1,200.

This project is exciting, but it needs more replication before the U.S. Department of Housing and Urban Development can be expected to develop a viable federal program for it. However, it has been demonstrated that home conversions can produce a number of results:

1. The program permits older people to remain in their own homes, if they wish.
2. It provides additional money so that a smaller percentage of their limited incomes goes for their housing need.
3. It provides the support of another person or couple living in the same house thus decreasing isolation.
4. It gives the homeowner the support of a housing authority in handling the landlord duties.
5. It adds additional housing units for those elderly confronted with enormously long waiting lists in subsidized housing at a much lower cost.
6. It helps preserve existing housing stock.

As a result of this demonstration, the Minnesota Housing Finance Agency has proposed a home conversion program. It is not known at this time if it has similar eligibility criteria, but it has restricted eligibility to communities of 2,000 people or less. As proposed, homeowners would be given an outright grant for 50% of the anticipated cost up to $5,000. Homeowners would be expected to obtain the additional money themselves, either through subsidized sources or through repair lending institutions.

The home conversion program can have significant impact on older people's lives. Choices of where to live for the elderly must be increased, particularly for low-income persons who presently have few, if any, housing alternatives. The extension of this and similar programs can be the stimulus that will directly impact the presently unfavorable housing for older people.

18
Single-Room Occupancy Hotels: Their Viability as Housing Options for Older Citizens

BARBARA J. FELTON
STANLEY LEHMANN
ARLENE ADLER

Single-room occupancy (SRO) hotels encompass a variety of housing facilities—hotels, rooming houses, and converted apartment buildings—and contain furnished rooms, usually without kitchens, frequently without bathrooms, and most often in old and deteriorated physical facilities located in or near commercial areas of cities. These hotels are usually inhabited by single adults who, by virtue of their status as ex-mental patients, their skid row lifestyle, or their relative social isolation, are considered "socially marginal."

Physically and socially, SRO hotels range from adequate to disreputable. While many are adequately furnished, well managed, and serve as transient as well as residential facilities, others are seriously deteriorated, neglected, and devoted to collecting welfare subsidies for their absentee landlords with as little investment as possible. It is common for the more dilapidated of these hotels to be located in transitional or commercial areas where there are few other local residents to complain about the erratic or antisocial behavior of the tenants. A handful of these hotels have some social service staff but usually they are part-time and can do little but offer immediate crisis intervention.

Older people constitute a substantial proportion of the SRO hotel population. Many elderly residents of these hotels are ex-mental patients. Deinstitutionalization policies of many psychiatric institutions have favored the relocation of chronic patients, and SRO hotels have become quasi-official community placement sites. Some elderly SRO tenants, however, are longer term residents whose social and economic marginality or lifestyle preferences led them to hotel occupancy long before the advent of their old age. Among this group of elderly tenants are the skid row men for whom hotels have long provided lodging compatible with their transient style of living. Other hotel occupants are marginally middle-class older people whose retirement brought financial exigencies prompting relocation from what had previously been a comfortable and convenient dwelling. Still others have adequate financial resources but prefer the proximity of amenities and access to public transportation that urban living provides; their preference for such amenities outweighs the disadvantages posed by a deteriorating or increasingly commercialized neighborhood.

Although national statistics describing the prevalence of SRO hotels and the size of the total SRO tenant population are unavailable, results of a national survey of housing for older Americans (Goode, Hoover, & Lawton, 1979) indicate that 80,000 "transient" and "permanent" hotel units are occupied by citizens 65 years old and older. Information about the diversity of cities containing SRO hotels (and estimates of the number of units in several cities) suggests that they are not exclusively a large-city phenomenon. The U.S. Senate Special Committee on Aging report on single-room occupancy (1978) cites the existence of SRO hotels in communities as diverse as

> Charleston and Huntington, W. Va.; Big Stone Gap, Va.; Louisville and Lebanon, Ky.; Utica, Syracuse and New York City, N.Y.; Des Moines, Cedar Falls, and Sioux City, Iowa; Portland, Oreg.; St. Louis, Mo.; San Diego, Santa Barbara, San Francisco, and Los Angeles, Cal.; Denver, Colo.; Seattle, Wash.; Detroit, Mich.; Minneapolis, Minn.; Chicago, Ill.; and Richmond, Va. (p. 2)

Despite their large numbers in many American cities, SRO hotels have been slow in attaining the recognition of social planners, scientists, and the public. In the U.S. Senate report on SRO hotels Ehrlich (1976-1977) has described the elderly tenants of SROs as "the invisible of invisible people" (p. 10). Inattention to SRO hotels seems to be due, in part, to their location between the private and public sectors. Most SROs are privately owned but are populated to a large extent through referrals from public social service agencies and mental hospitals. Because they are commercial establishments, they receive no government subsidies and are not licensed; they are regulated only by local building codes that, in a large number of cases, are not enforced.

The recent upsurge in attention given to SRO hotels reflects increasing levels of conflict among SRO owners, residents, professional workers, and local community groups as well as increasing pressure for low-income housing options for elderly urbanites and for habitable community residences for released mental patients. Recognition of the problems surrounding SRO hotels, their tenants, and their neighbors has been reflected in two national conferences on SROs (Ehrlich, 1976-1977), in policy deliberations at the local level, in several monographs, and in articles published in popular periodicals, newspapers, and professional journals.

THE NATURE OF THE CONTROVERSY

The major controversy surrounding SRO hotels stems from conflict about their suitability for habitation. First-hand observations of most SRO hotels tend to provoke reactions of shock. A physically deteriorating building, signs of crime, drug addiction, alcoholism, prostitution, and inadequate heating and sanitary facilities are not unlikely to greet the observer. Journalistic accounts of the conditions of hotel life tend to underline the unsavory aspects of life in some SRO hotels and to use such characterizations as grounds for maintaining that such dwellings are unacceptable as homes for the frail and the elderly.

Poor housing conditions, the presence of burglars, prostitutes, and other petty criminals, and the less than normative behavior of some hotel tenants are frequently at the basis of complaints by neighbors living in more conventional residences in the surrounding area. In New York City, where unofficial estimates suggest that as many as 8,000 SROs may be located within the city, neighbors of SROs have been particularly vociferous (Clark, Hager, Washington, Reese, & Simons, 1978; Koenig, 1978). Whether seen as a threat to safety, property values, or the aesthetics of the neighborhood, SROs have been held responsible for numerous neighborhood problems. Media reports have often portrayed SRO hotels as plagues on the city and as threats to the stability of neighborhoods.

Arguments for maintaining SRO hotels are most usually grounded on the contention that SROs are the dwellings of choice for many tenants. Calls for the preservation of the "SRO lifestyle" (e.g., Ehrlich, 1976-1977) point to evidence that SRO tenants are well adjusted in their accommodations, that they maintain themselves adequately without formal intervention, that the value that such tenants place on their independence does not leave them socially isolated to their disadvantage.

Belief in the right of citizens to select their own housing and to live in whatever accommodations best suit their preferred style of life constitutes another counterargument to the contention that SRO hotels are uninhabitable. As the Senate Special Committee on Aging's report on SRO Hotels (1978) points out: "Society frequently makes assumptions as to what is right and necessary for people to live comfortably based on standards which are not those of people who avail themselves of a particular type of housing" (p. 6).

Economic factors do not resolve the controversy but rather reflect similarly opposing pulls. The "gentrification" of many major American cities, highlighted by the influx of well-to-do citizens into the downtown areas has, in many cities, increased the demand for luxury housing. The opportunity to rid cities of SRO hotels by transforming them into high-rent apartments is attractive to real estate developers and SRO neighbors alike.

On the other hand, SROs provide economical housing for those who choose them as dwellings. As semi-official alternatives to institutionalization, SRO hotels are economically advantageous to society since they are run by the private sector and require a minimum of direct public expenditure. Because many of the residents might otherwise be institutionalized, the savings that this conceivably represents is considerable. To the extent that relocation takes a toll on the physical well-being of older people, maintaining SRO hotels represents indirect savings in medical costs as well.

EVIDENCE TOWARD RESOLUTION OF THE CONTROVERSY

Data-based descriptions of SRO hotels and empirical research on the quality of life for older people in such hotels are relatively limited, frequently restricted to one type of hotel, a single city, or an unreplicated intervention program. However, the accumulating body of literature provides a basis for illuminating some of the factors that make SRO hotels more or less suitable as housing options for the elderly.

While only a few empirical investigations—with the exception of a few journalistic accounts—have as their aim a direct assessment of the habitability of SRO hotels, many of them provide data about the SRO lifestyle. They demonstrate that many SRO tenants are surviving with a measure of integrity and satisfaction, that they are not without social supports, and, in the case of a few, are apparently coping successfully in the absence of an extensive support network.

Before presenting a more detailed review of the findings of these studies, a few caveats are in order. An understanding of the quality and dynamics of SRO hotel life requires recognition of the diversity of physical and social arrangements that fall under the rubric of SRO, and of the equally diverse array of people who constitute the SRO population. The nature of life in a given SRO hotel is a function of the city it inhabits, its immediate surroundings, its physical condition and amenities, its management policies and services, the personalities and styles of its desk clerks, its reputation among tenants, and, most importantly perhaps, of the tenants themselves—their histories, the duration of their tenancies, their social patterns, their health conditions, and their preferred mode of living. A small-town SRO with a benign management and a population of tenants who have lived a skid row existence for most of their adult lives cannot be assumed to be similar in social life or in tenant-management relations to a large-city SRO hotel located in a semiresidential area with a newly arrived and apathetic management and a clientele of formerly middle-class older tenants for whom hotel life offers a preferred alternative to suburban exile or congregate living in a home for the aged.

No formal typology of hotels has as yet been developed. SROs are usually colloquially described as existing at some point on a continuum that ranges from disreputable or horrid to acceptable or congenial. Erickson and Eckert's (1977) classification of SRO hotels in San Diego into "skid row," "working class," and "middle class," however, provides a rudimentary beginning. Their classification system, based on the quality of the surrounding neighborhood, the physical condition of the building, the kinds of services provided by management, and the price of accommodations proved to be closely linked with a variety of characteristics of residents, including sex, age, occupational history, previous incarcerations in jails, psychiatric histories, social relations within the hotel, and patterns of social activities with people outside the hotel.

Personal characteristics and social styles of residents are, in part, a consequence of the physical conditions, service provisions, and perceived safety of the hotels that they occupy. Their patterns of social involvement may conceivably affect the continuing care of the physical facility and the kinds of services obtained. The processes of selection and socialization (Sonquist, 1970) presumably reinforce the congruence between characteristics of the hotel and characteristics of tenants. Thus residents' past histories—economic, occupational, and social—as well as their current physical and emotional status and styles of living provide an additional means of distinguishing among types of hotels.

Elderly SRO Tenants

As briefly indicated, the elderly population of SRO hotels includes people with a diverse array of backgrounds. A certain proportion of elderly tenants are relative newcomers to SRO living. Estimates of the proportions of elderly SRO hotel tenants who have spent most of their adult lives in mental hospitals vary from city to city. Shapiro's (1971) study of nine New York City hotels found 10% of tenants to have been hospitalized at some point in a psychiatric facility. Erickson and Eckert's (1977) study, restricted to older people, found that about 22% of the elderly tenants of skid row and working class hotels had some history of mental hospitalization. An investigation by Felton, Lehmann, and Adler (1977) in three New York City hotels found 32.9% of the total hotel sample and 22.2% of the elderly subsample to have had at least one mental hospitalization.

Another group of elderly SRO tenants whose tenancy began late in life are those middle-class elderly who have chosen hotel living as a way of remaining within their neighborhood or city on a reduced income. "Inexpensive hotel rents, coupled with the availability of needed goods and services, make the downtown practical for some portion of the elderly" (Erickson & Eckert, 1977, p. 446). Several surveys of SRO tenants have located rather large proportions of middle-class tenants: Bild & Havighurst (1976), Lally, Black, Thornock, and Hawkins (1977), and Cohen and Sokolovsky (1978b) found relatively large numbers of middle-class elderly among their samples. Cohen and Sokolovsky (1978b) found one third of their midtown Manhattan sample to have had some college—a proportion twice the national average for older people. While response bias may favor the better-educated tenants, it seems that middle-class elderly constitute a substantial proportion of the SRO tenant population.

Another major group of elderly SRO tenants includes those whose lifelong style of living has been one of transience. The life of the skid-rower, whose social dynamics have been the subject of numerous sociological investigations (e.g., Bahr & Caplow, 1973; Wallace, 1965), frequently includes a series of hotel occupancies. Exact figures on the proportions of SRO tenants who fit into this category are difficult to derive, as the label "skid rower" describes a conglomeration of social and economic characteristics. Erickson and Eckert's (1977) random sampling of 12 hotels in San Diego produced 5 (or 42%) skid row hotels. Judging by hotel type, it seems that skid row tenants are among the largest type of SRO hotel tenants.

Relative Well-Being of Elderly SRO Tenants

A fundamental question is to what extent the SRO elderly are the more fragile, less able, or otherwise less well off than their non-SRO counterparts. Evaluating the adequacy of SRO living arrangements, planning accommodations, and facilities that guarantee the health, well-being, and personal dignity of the elderly requires knowledge of the physical and psychological status of this population. Are SRO tenants the incompetent and fragile residue left behind when others of their generation move to middle-income urban housing or flee to the suburbs? Or are the SRO elderly comparable in functioning to the minimally impaired residents of homes for the aged, distinguishable only by their preference for independence from the regimented standards of social interaction imposed by congregate housing? Have they remained in the inner city because of the accessibility of the resources to be found there and a congenial lifestyle? To what extent do environmental factors aggravate or compensate for the natural changes in health status and well-being that accompany the aging process? Answers to these questions can suggest means and resources that can contribute to the welfare of the rapidly growing urban elderly population.

The number of controlled studies that directly compare the health and well-being of elderly SRO tenants with the status of those among a comparable sample is quite small. Consequently, much of what is known about SRO elderly is based on inferences from case records, informal observations of tenants, and extrapolations from studies of inner-city elderly in a variety of housing arrangements. Most reports of the SRO elderly describe them as a socially and economically marginal group, beleaguered by physical and social impairments accumulated over the years, yet moderately well-adapted to their surroundings. Bohannan (U.S. Senate, 1978) has identified them as "physically and psychologically handicapped—not to say maimed" (p. 11). Both Ehrlich and Jorgen in the U.S. Senate Report by the Special Committee on Aging (1978) noted the premature aging of SRO tenants that makes middle-aged residents appear elderly.

Such images of disadvantage and deficit do not necessarily negate the view of many SRO tenants as effective copers. In view of the invisibility of this population to formal care providers and housing officials, its continued survival attests to a resourcefulness of at least modest proportions. Bohannan (U.S. Senate, 1978) describes the SRO elderly as well adapted to their surroundings: Hotel life affords a freedom from demands imposed by "better" housing accommodations. To lifelong loners, the hotel provides shelter without the costs and demands of sociability, social conformity, and adherence to other middle-class norms. Elderly SRO tenants are thus portrayed as a population that exhibits the problems inherent in the aging process and also presents important individual differences in their styles and preferred means of contending with these problems.

Data comparing the health and well-being of elderly SRO tenants to other elderly residents of the inner city suggest that SRO tenants are moderately to severely disadvantaged. Eckert's (1977) study of the health status of San Diego hotel tenants found the health profile of SRO residents to approximate that of patients hospitalized with emotional disturbances rather than that found among "normal" elderly populations. Emotional complaints among SRO tenants were also comparable in frequency to those of the hospitalized sample. Felton et al.'s (1977) finding that elderly SRO tenants had slightly higher levels of life satisfaction than younger tenants reflects, in part, differences in the rates of psychiatric disturbance between the age groups. The prevalence of psychiatric problems among the total SRO population means that this finding cannot be interpreted as evidence that elderly SRO tenants are optimally adjusted; SRO tenants, as a group, however, seem to be disproportionately plagued by psychiatric disturbances.

Bild and Havighurst's (1976) investigation of six "special groups" of elderly Chicagoans found older urbanites' health status, social, economic, and psychological well-being to be closely linked to income. The two hotel samples included in their study differed substantially in socioeconomic status, and thus resembled both the highest and the lowest groups when all six were ranked on well-being across all the areas investigated. Uptown hotel residents, among the poorest of the six groups studied, were lowest on life satisfaction compared to all six groups and, along with the public housing sample, lowest in self-rated health and physical capacity. Hyde Park hotel tenants, relatively high on income, compared favorably with the other life style groups on perceived health despite their relatively low scores on objective physical capacity. Life satisfaction scores for this group of respondents were second-highest among the groups studied.

In the investigation above, SRO tenants were compared with other urban or inner-city elderly residents. Studies comparing the health status and well-being of inner-city elderly with national samples indicate that the inner-city elderly as a whole suffer personal and environmental disadvantages more severe than those encountered by older people living outside the central core of cities. Reports by Tissue (1971), Lawton and Kleban (1971), Lawton, Kleban, and Singer (1971), and Cantor and Mayer (1976) underline the social, economic, and physical handicaps of the inner-city elderly. Bild and Havighurst's (1976) special groups proved to be lower in life satisfaction than adult respondents to a national sample.

The benefits of urban living and the importance of individual choice in the selection of residence must not be discounted (cf. Clark, 1971). One study that compared inner-city elderly living in housing projects to elderly living in suburban age-segregated housing provides evidence that urban residents remain in the inner city out of choice and preferred lifestyle; they want to be near the hub of activity (Felton, Hinrichsin, & Tsemberis, 1979). There is no doubt that SRO tenants share this preference. Much of their disadvantage seems to stem from their relative poverty and greater economic need rather than from intrinsic environmental deficits.

Social Life in SRO Hotels

Many of the conclusions about the validity of SRO housing for older people are based on inferences about tenants' well-being that are, in turn, based on assumptions about the social isolation of tenants or on observations of the kinds of social interactions that prevail among tenants. Arguments for SRO housing for the elderly rest either on arguments that relative social isolation is a preferred and maximally adaptive arrangement for most SRO tenants, or that SRO tenants are not socially isolated but well integrated into a hotel-based support system that nurtures and sustains them. Conversely, arguments against SRO hotels rest on contentions that social isolation is rampant among tenants and either sustains pre-existing forms of pathology characteristic of many SRO dwellers or increases the vulnerability of these elderly to crises that could be offset if a support system existed, or that the forms of social interaction that take place in hotels are pathological and create deviant and maladaptive behaviors. The reader is reminded to consider the range of tenant types previously described while considering the following descriptions of SRO social life derived from empirical observation.

Shapiro's (1966, 1970, 1971) investigation of Manhattan SRO hotels was the first to provide a systematic account of social interactions within SRO hotels. Her findings suggest that hotel tenants are not social isolates but have high levels of social interaction, mostly within the boundaries of their hotels. The isolation or invisibility of hotel tenants, it seems, describes their relationship to the outside world and to social service agencies intended to serve such "needy" populations. In-hotel activity took several forms, frequently appearing as "quasi-familial" arrangements (Shapiro, 1969) in which several men were dominated by a matriarchal figure. "Bottle gangs," similar to those described in previous investigations of skid row life (e.g., Bahr & Caplow, 1973; Wallace, 1965) and used to refute the portrait of the urban transient as a completely disaffiliated entity, were also uncovered by Shapiro in Manhattan hotels.

Shapiro (1971) suggested that many of the typical patterns of social interrelationship supported and sustained disruptive and self-destructive behaviors. She concluded from her analysis of tenant-landlord relationships (1970) that the reciprocal bonds that link hotel managers and tenants formed a social system that "sanctions emotionally erratic behavior by the tenants and elicits similar behavior from the landlords" (p. 68).

The assumption that pathology-inducing bonds form the basis for hotel social life underlines Levy's (1968) proposal for the upgrading of SRO hotels. In response to policy analyses of the blighting effects of SROs on urban neighborhoods, Levy proposed that architectural arrangements providing physically adequate facilities and common spaces for organized activities and on-site provision of medical, psychiatric, and social services would make SRO hotels more fulfilling for their residents and more congenial to their neighbors.

Stephens's (1974, 1975, 1976) in-depth anthropological study of older residents of SRO hotels in a midwestern city, like Shapiro's studies, documented the existence of intricate and at times extensive social networks within the hotels in her sample. She described in-hotel social linkages as instrumental and aimed at mutual help-giving but at the same time designed to discourage intimacy. This view provides a possible resolution of the conflicting views of SRO tenants as nonattached and yet engaged in many social exchanges. Her analysis emphasizes the tenants' deliberate choice of hotels as living accommodations, and suggests that limiting social encounters to instrumental exchanges permits tenants to have both the autonomy that they desire and the potential for the assistance if needed. Tenants in Stephens's view are not neurotically disengaged from society but consciously self-reliant and scornful of institutions and social bonds which, in their view, promote unnecessary and unwanted dependency.

Ehrlich's (1976–1977) plea for the protection of the integrity of the SRO lifestyle echoes the theme of self-reliance presented by Stephens. The diversity of presentations made at the initial and subsequent St. Louis conferences on SRO hotels called for consideration of the special needs of those who may be physically and emotionally at risk by virtue of having chosen—or without choice ended up in—SRO hotels.

More recent studies of SRO hotel social life (Cohen & Sokolovsky, 1978a; Lally et al., 1977; Rooney, 1976) have provided more refined descriptions of the social networks of SRO tenants and expanded the diversity of SRO sites studied. The relationships between SRO tenants and people outside the hotel appear to vary considerably, primarily as a function of socioeconomic status which, in turn, reflects the quality of social life throughout adulthood. Cohen and Sokolovsky (1978a) make an important distinction between the "ethos" of hotel life and the actual social arrangements that exist. They point out that the norms for self-reliance that characterize hotel social life encourge distortion in the reporting of social activities, particularly when dependency is implied in the questioning. These authors' use of a network analysis strategy reveal larger numbers of interactions and more intimate relationships than previous studies have found; overall, however, Cohen and Sokolovsky's (1978b) mid-Manhattan sample of SRO elderly had social lives comparable in complexity and intensity to those of most inner-city elderly.

Variations in the descriptions of SRO hotel social networks undoubtedly reflect differences in the qualities of hotels studied, differences in the mix of tenant types, and differences in the locations of hotels within the cities. Almost without exception, however, the studies report tenants' adherence to a norm of self-reliance and the existence of effective, if not extensive, in-hotel helping networks. The significance of in-hotel social arrangements is underscored by the finding in the study of three SRO hotels in New York City that in-hotel social contacts were conducive to residents' sense of well-being while contacts outside of the hotel were more likely to have a negative effect (Lehmann & Felton, 1978). An image emerges of SRO hotels as successfully functioning living systems in which moderately disabled people with limited tolerance for social and emotional demands can live, and in some cases thrive, in an environment that provides basic amenities and a modicum of security without overtaxing their somewhat limited psychological resources.

Information about hotel social life does not provide a direct assessment of tenants' well-being; social engagement is not synonymous with mental health. Social activity has been shown to correlate with morale and life satisfaction among samples of older people (Edwards & Klemmack, 1974; Palmore & Luikart, 1972), and social isolation has been found to be more common among older people admitted to mental hospitals than among an elderly control group (Lowenthal, 1965). Cohen and Sokolovsky (1978a) have found in dealing with ex-mental patients living in SRO hotels that those with larger in-hotel social networks are less apt to be rehospitalized. On the other hand, Lowenthal and Chiriboga (1973) found some lifelong social isolates to be as well adapted as some of their more socially active age peers and suggest that late-life increases in social involvement may actually constitute a stress on those whose adult lives have been largely solitary. Current research about the social lives of SRO tenants makes a case for natural helping networks that are instrumental and nonintimate. Such networks are an important resource for those whose lifestyles and needs lead them to seek undemanding and permissive living arrangements.

Effects of Hotel Life: Attempts at Change

Characteristics of SRO tenants—their health status, well-being, and preferred social patterns—are conceptually distinguishable from the nature of the social life of the hotel. In attempting to derive policy recommendations about the best possible disposition of SRO hotels, it is particularly important to know the extent to which the characteristics of the hotel and the nature of hotel life have demonstrable effects—either deleterious or beneficial—on the health and well-being of hotel tenants. Knowing the extent to which hotel life can be modified to improve the well-being of tenants is a prerequisite for intelligent planning.

In actual practice, distinguishing between the nature of hotel life and the characteristics of tenants is a difficult task. The nature of hotel life is thoroughly influenced by the characteristics of tenants. Erickson and Eckert (1977) found tenants' histories of work, incarceration, and hospitalization as well as their age and sex to be closely linked to the quality of services provided by the hotel and to the tenants' in-hotel and out-hotel social links. Levy (1968) maintains that the inability of tenants to fulfill "ordinary human obligations" and their apathy and carelessness, together with the landlords' indifference and the economics of SRO hotel proprietorship, contribute to building deterioration, physical destruction, and sanitary neglect, and lead to tenement-style living. Other evidence suggests that characteristics of hotel social life determine tenants' behavioral characteristics.

Taken together, this evidence on the direction of causation suggests that hotels constitute interactive systems in which the independent contribution of hotel characteristics to the explanation of tenants' social behavior cannot be easily assessed. In cross-sectional studies, for example, hotel effects can be expected to have strong correlations with personal characteristics of tenants. Behavior-environment congruence is typical in settings where selection and socialization processes operate (Sonquist, 1970; Wicker, 1974).

Potential tenants undoubtedly select hotels housing tenants similar to themselves or tenants whose styles of social interaction match their own long-term patterns. Congruence between personal characteristics and hotel style can be expected to be greatest where social service agencies participate in the process of finding hotels for potential tenants or in the task of screening clients at intake, as occurs in some in-hotel social service programs. Hotels' reputations can expedite the selection process, and differing costs for accommodations produce a somewhat predictable stratification of tenants by social class. Socialization processes—transmitted via in-hotel norms for behavior—undoubtedly increase the pressure for conformity and account for some overlap between environmental and personal characteristics.

Studies that evaluate deliberate attempts at change provide us with the most reliable information about the modifiability of the well-being of elderly SRO tenants through environmental alteration. The few evaluations of in-hotel service programs aimed at enhancing the quality of hotel life suggest that hotel environments can be successfully modified so as to reduce disruptive behavior and enhance the self-esteem of hotel tenants.

Plutchik, McCarthy, Hall, and Silverberg (1973) and Plutchik, McCarthy, and Hall (1975) describe an in-hotel service delivery program aimed at overcoming elderly tenants' mistrust and avoidance of hospitals and other service agents. Their multidisciplinary team approach was directed at the primarily ex-mental patient elderly population of a Manhattan hotel. Linking a social service department, a community mental health center, and several educational institutions, the service program instituted a Tenants' Council, a Job Corps program, and a floor counseling service. Initial evaluation of the program showed a substantial increase in tenants' contact with professionals and use of services over the beginning years of the program (Plutchik et al., 1973). A subsequent investigation involving a re-interviewing of 100 tenants after 2 years showed that tenants' incomes had increased, their level of self-care had improved, and they spent fewer hours sleeping (Plutchik et al., 1975). Alcoholics in particular increased in socialization, engagement in hobbies, and self-regard. Some increases in negative affect were found among tenants, and woman and alcoholics were found to spend more time in their rooms alone. Although the studies were hampered by methodological shortcomings, the results show some stabilization of the tenant population as well as some preliminary evidence of constructive consequences of an on-site service delivery program.

Katz and Shands's (1976) account of the same interdisciplinary team intervention noted that increased self-esteem among tenants and decreased disruptive behavior resulted in a decrease in community complaints. In addition, Katz and Shands reported the cost of services to 579 tenants to be $2 per tenant per day; adding to this figure the $10 per tenant per day cost of room and board, the total represents a fraction of the cost of mental hospitalization.

Besides demonstrating that hotel environments can be altered to the benefit of their tenants, these evaluations suggest a viable model for intervention. The reliance of SRO hotel tenants on in-hotel supports (Cohen & Sokolovsky, 1978b; Erickson & Eckert, 1977; Shapiro, 1970) and the insularity of hotel populations from service agencies underscore the advisability of planning programs to increase tenants' accessibility to health, financial, and social services. Further support for the advisability of instituting in-hotel support programs has been provided by Segal and Aviram's (1978) study of sheltered community residential facilities in California; their study showed that where opportunities for social integration were available, urban residential facilities were superior to institutional care in almost every case.

Outreach services proferred to several hotels from a single outpost have been instituted in Manhattan and Brooklyn. While systematic data on the effectiveness of this approach are not yet available, the added efficiency of such an intervention model warrants further application and evaluation.

Other models of intervention that have been attempted include social service agency purchase and management of hotels. Introduced into Long Beach, New York, this form of intervention is aimed less at directly changing the individual than at assuring tenants of clean, secure surroundings and of the presence of a hotel management that provides basic services and oversees building maintenance. Stabilization of rents and the use of a humane and consistent basis for admitting or excluding tenants are additional benefits that can accrue from agency ownership of SRO hotels.

SUMMARY OF EVIDENCE

The investigations above lead to a few generalizations concerning the best route to resolving the controversies about how SRO hotels ought to be considered in the array of housing options available to older people. Elderly SRO hotel tenants are a varied group; their social histories and current financial resources result in a range of preferred social styles running from predominantly male skid row isolation to urban middle-class gregariousness. Most SRO tenants, regardless of their city or type of hotel, are integrated to some degree into an in-hotel social network. These networks, although varied in style, all operate to some extent or another to support the person within an informal system. Such a system obviates the need for reliance on formal helping agents and thus affords tenants a sense of self-reliance and independence.

Relocation of tenants is not a recommended solution to the

problem of SRO hotels. The fragile elderly with health problems and tenuous mental functioning are poor candidates for relocation; the costs of change, including the loss of familiar surroundings and the disruption of a viable in-hotel social network, ought not to be borne by the most disadvantaged of our elderly. Nor is relocation an advisable solution for those tenants who have successfully adapted to hotel life and who have managed to maintain acceptable levels of health and well-being. Individuals' rights to choose their living place ought to be respected.

SRO hotels provide environments well suited to many inner-city elderly. The minimal demands for social interaction, conformity, and responsibility for others make them ideal environments for many whose lifelong style has been one of isolation as well as for many whose experiences late in life make them unable or unwilling to take on the responsibilities of congregate living or of independent living at a distance from familiar surroundings and easily reachable services.

There will undoubtedly continue to be a pool of people whose lifestyles make SRO hotels preferred living sites. Although the size of the skid row population has fluctuated over the years (Wallace, 1965), a sizable group of relatively unattached men has persisted for centuries. Among the more middle-class and more socially integrated, there are increasing numbers of single adults for whom hotel living may become attractive in late life. Older people seeking an independent living arrangement, with people nearby "just in case," are likely to increase rather than decrease in number.

Policy and planning for such groups must be founded on the assumption that SRO tenants, like all other citizens, must be afforded housing that meets universal standards of habitability. Assuring tenants of a sound physical structure with working sanitary facilities is the minimum accommodation. Although local building codes in almost every city and town have provisions for the attainment of such standards, their haphazard enforcement makes it necessary for local federal groups to advocate for the enforcement of such codes.

Health and social services must be made accessible to SRO tenants. Different populations may need different services. For some, in-house provision of formal services may be more necessary than for others. Larger hotels may more easily support service staff. Outreach services—sometimes more economical because they can serve several hotels within a small area—may be better suited to small hotels with relatively unimpaired tenant populations.

The value of providing health and social services extends beyond the benefits that accrue directly to the recipients. Some threats to safety are more prevalent in SRO hotels than in other more sheltered living environments for older people, for example, disruptive behavior frequently associated with alcoholism or psychiatric impairment, drug sales, prostitution, gambling, and other illegal activities. While largely victimless crimes, they may encourage burglary, confidence games, and other more potentially harmful occurrences. The provision of direct services may alter the hotel atmosphere. At least one formal intervention program has been successful in calming the surrounding community as well as enhancing the self-esteem and income level of tenants (Plutchik et al., 1975).

Thus, the roles of service agencies must include not only individual service delivery but involvement in hotel selection processes, advocacy for enforcement of building codes, organization of support from the surrounding community, and pressure on other agencies and government offices for the provision of a safe environment and the education of tenants about benefits for which they are eligible.

Assuring that these roles are assumed requires planning at both local and national levels. Legitimization of SRO hotels by federal housing agents and the provision of guidelines and funding would help ensure their habitability. The failure of the federal government to recognize the housing needs of single adults must be reversed in view of the increasing numbers of single people in the population.

Some of the above policy recommendations may prove, in actual practice, to be in conflict. The provision of in-house services is most economically feasible in large hotels with impaired populations; such hotels may be those most likely to antagonize the local community. The goals of the community and the goals of those concerned with the welfare of tenants are not necessarily compatible. The importance of acceptance by the community to the continued well-being of ex-mental patients (Segal & Aviram, 1978) underlines this concern.

Research is needed in many areas to refine our knowledge about what kinds of policies are most likely to succeed. Little is known about the best mix of tenant types; we do not know what proportion of ex-mental patients can be successfully maintained in a large hotel nor the circumstances under which age homogeneity will be beneficial for older tenants. To date no research has evaluated direct attempts to solicit the support of the surrounding communities. Knowledge about the kinds of neighborhoods most likely to facilitate change efforts within hotels is lacking, as is information about the strategies for gaining the support of local residents. At the individual level, we need to know what kinds of services can be provided that do not threaten the natural support systems that operate in hotels. Research on service delivery attempts is needed to determine how and if the acting-out and mentally frail elderly can be integrated into community-based services for "normal" older people.

The policy goals of preserving the integrity of the SRO lifestyle while assuring SRO tenants of the basic amenities necessary for health and happiness are warranted by both our societal values and knowledge of tenants' needs and preferences. Application of the guidelines presented here requires social and financial commitment, creative energy, and intelligent use of existing knowledge. Continuing evaluations of our efforts should indicate directions for our subsequent attempts at assistance.

REFERENCES

Bahr, H. M., & Caplow, T. *Old men drunk and sober*. New York: New York University Press, 1973.

Bild, B. R., & Havighurst, R. J. Senior citizens in great cities: The case of Chicago. *Gerontologist*, 1976, *16*, 4–88.

Cantor, M., & Mayer, M. Health and the inner city elderly. *Gerontologist*, 1976, *16*, 17–24.

Clark, M. Patterns of aging among the elderly poor of the inner city. *Gerontologist*, 1971, *11*, 58–65.

Clark, M., Hager, M., Washington, E. B., Reese, M., & Simons, P. E. The new snake pits. *Newsweek*, 15 May, 1978.

Cohen, C., & Sokolovsky, J. Schizophrenia and social networks: Ex-patients in the inner city. *Schizophrenia Bulletin*, 1978, *4*, 546–560. (a)

Cohen, C., & Sokolovsky, J. *Sociability of S.R.O. aged—a reassessment*. Paper presented at the annual meeting of the Gerontological Society, Dallas, November 1978. (b)

Eckert, J. K. *Health status, adjustment, and social supports of older people living in center city hotels*. Paper presented at the annual meeting of the Gerontological Society, San Francisco, November 1977.

Edwards, J. N., & Klemmack, D. L. Correlates of life satisfaction: A re-examination. *Journal of Gerontology*, 1974, *28*, 497–502.

Ehrlich, P. *St. Louis "invisible" elderly: Needs and characteristics of aged "single room occupancy" downtown hotel residents*. St. Louis: Institute of Applied Gerontology, St. Louis University, 1976–1977.

Erickson, R. J., & Eckert, J. K. The elderly poor in downtown San Diego hotels. *Gerontologist*, 1977, *17*, 440–446.

Felton, B. J., Hinrichsen, G., & Tsemberis, S. *Urban and suburban neighborhoods and the adjustment of older people*. Paper presented at the annual meeting of the American Psychological Association, New York, August 1979.

Felton, B. J., Lehmann, S., & Adler, A. *Social supports and life satisfaction among old and young S.R.O. hotel tenants.* Paper presented at the annual meeting of the Gerontological Society, San Francisco, November 1977.

Goode, C., Hoover, S. L., & Lawton, M. P. *Elderly hotel and rooming-house dwellers: The population and its housing.* Philadelphia: Philadelphia Geriatric Center, 1979. (Mimeographed report)

Katz, S., & Shands, H. Hotel therapy. In J. H. Masserman (Ed.), *Current psychiatric therapies*, Vol. 16. New York: Grune & Stratton, 1976.

Koenig, P. The problem that can't be tranquilized. *The New York Times Magazine*, 21 May, 1978, 14–17, 44–52, 58.

Lally, M., Black, E., Thornock, M., & Hawkins, D. *Older women in S.R.O. hotels: A Seattle profile.* Paper presented at the annual meeting of the Gerontological Society, San Francisco, November 1977.

Lawton, M. P., & Kleban, M. H. The aged resident of the inner city. *Gerontologist*, 1971, *11*, 277–283.

Lawton, M. P., Kleban, M. H., & Singer, M. The aged Jewish person and the slum environment. *Journal of Gerontology*, 1971, *26*, 231–239.

Lehmann, S., & Felton, B. J. *Peer support systems in marginal population.* Paper presented at the annual meeting of the American Psychiatric Association, Atlanta, May 1978.

Levy, H. Needed: A new kind of single room occupancy housing. *Journal of Housing*, 1968, *25*, 572–580.

Lowenthal, M. F. Antecendents of isolation and mental illness in old age. *Archives of General Psychiatry*, 1965, *12*, 245–254.

Lowenthal, M. F., & Chiriboga, D. Social stress and adaptation: Toward a life-course perspective. In C. Eisdorfer & M. P. Lawton (Eds.), *The psychology of adult development and aging.* Washington, D.C.: American Psychological Association, 1973.

Plutchik, R., McCarthy, M., & Hall, B. Changes in elderly welfare hotel residents during a one year period. *Journal of the American Geriatrics Society*, 1975, *23*, 265–270.

Plutchik, R., McCarthy, M., Hall, B., & Silverberg, S. Evaluation of a comprehensive psychiatric and health care program for elderly welfare tenants in a single-room occupancy hotel. *Journal of the American Geriatrics Society*, 1973, *21*, 452–459.

Rooney, J. F. Friendship and disaffiliation among the skid row population. *Journal of Gerontology*, 1976, *31*, 82–88.

Segal, S. P., & Aviram, U. *The mentally ill in community-based sheltered care.* New York: Wiley, 1978.

Shapiro, J. Single-room occupancy: Community of the alone. *Social Work*, 1966, *11*, 24–33.

Shapiro, J. Dominant leaders among slum hotel residents. *American Journal of Orthopsychiatry*, 1969, *39*, 644–650.

Shapiro, J. Reciprocal dependence between single-room occupancy tenants. *Social Work*, 1970, *15*, 66–72.

Shapiro, J. H. *Communities of the alone: Working with single room occupants in the city.* New York: Association Press, 1971.

Sonquist, J. A. *Multivariate model building.* Ann Arbor, Mich: Institute for Social Research, 1970.

Stephens, J. Romance in the SRO: Relationships of elderly men and women in a slum hotel. *Gerontologist,* 1974, *14,* 279–282.

Stephens, J. Society of the alone: Freedom, privacy and utilitarianism as dominant norms in the SRO. *Journal of Gerontology,* 1975, *30,* 230–235.

Stephens, J. *Loners, losers, and lovers: A sociological study of the aged tenants of a slum hotel.* Seattle: University of Washington Press, 1976.

Tissue, T. Old age, poverty and the central city. *Aging and Human Development,* 1971, *2,* 235–248.

U.S. Senate, Special Committee on Aging. *Single room occupancy: A need for national concern.* Washington, D.C.: U.S. Government Printing Office, 1978.

Wallace, S. E. *Skid row as a way of life.* Totowa, N.J.: Bedminster Press, 1965.

Wicker, A. W. Processes which mediate behavior-environment congruence. In R. H. Moos & P. M. Insel (Eds.), *Issues in social ecology.* Palo Alto, Calif.: National Press Books, 1974.

19
Recycling Buildings
for Elderly Housing

VICTOR REGNIER
JAMES BONAR

City development is a cyclical ecological process that involves a constant rebuilding, redevelopment, and changing of land and building uses. In some cities building resources formerly of great value may lie dormant for some time awaiting recycling into a second appropriate use.

The advent of post–World War II decentralized development has had a major effect on the central-city areas of most metropolitan American cities. In some cities older buildings with much usable space have been abandoned or underutilized because their location and physical characteristics are not conducive to current commercial or industrial demands.

Downtown areas support a higher than average population of older people because settlement patterns and the centralization of services have attracted or maintained a large elderly population base. According to the 1970 census, 61.2% of the population aged 65 and over lives in a metropolitan area and over 50% of this metropolitan population lives in central-city neighborhoods (White House Conference on Aging, 1971). Although there is some evidence of future population decline in these extremely urban centers, accompanied by growth in suburban areas (Golant, 1975), one can still assume that substantial future population concentrations, particularly minority populations, will be concentrated in central-city environments.

The need for expanded housing opportunities for the aged is apparent in nearly every large metropolitan area. The many problems of adequate housing have continued to increase as opportunities for resolving this critical issue have declined.

The lofty goals established in the report of the President's Committee on Urban Housing issued in the late 1960s have not been met (U.S. Congress, 1968). Rapidly rising costs have been a major barrier to the increased production of newly constructed low-income housing stock. The hopelessness of total dependence on new construction has led to such alternative solutions as the rehabilitation of older units for elderly occupants or the sharing of housing with nonrelated individuals.

A policy emphasis on the recycling of older housing stock produced active rehabilitation strategies and the extensive use of the Section 8 program in the 1970s. The case study presented in this chapter considers the potential of older buildings for use as planned housing for the elderly.

The downtown Los Angeles business district has undergone radical changes in the past 20 years as efforts toward the reconstruction of a modern downtown have substantially altered the appearance of the central city. This redevelopment activity has had two major impacts on the downtown area: the demolition of a substantial number of low-rent housing units inhabited by an older population and the abandonment of millions of square feet of office space in older 8- to 13-story mid-rise buildings on the east side of the downtown district. The narrowing of rental opportunities is reflected in a decrease of the elderly population in this area from 9,900 in 1960 to 3,800 in 1970. Figure 19.1 locates the abandoned office core in relation to the present new downtown office core.

The Los Angeles Community Design Center, a nonprofit community organization constituted to provide technical assistance to projects involving low-income citizens, was asked by the Program of Retired Citizens to analyze opportunities for the creation of additional housing for low-income older people. A 1972 development plan for downtown had all but ignored this issue while making recommendations that favored financial and commerical interests.

The interest of the Program of Retired Citizens was aroused for several reasons: (1) fear that future planning would preclude the elderly; (2) the size of waiting lists at local low-rent hotels and apartments had increased greatly; and (3) the number of older people seeking housing in the downtown area had also increased.

CHARACTERISTICS OF THE DOWNTOWN DISTRICT

A comprehensive analysis of housing problems and opportunities was conducted utilizing interviews with key community informants, housing managers, service providers, and older people. The following characteristics of the downtown district were identified:

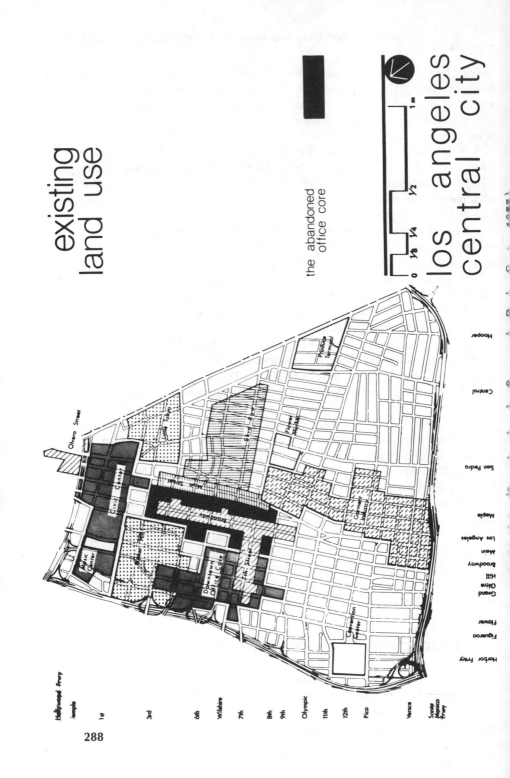

existing
land use

the abandoned
office core

los angeles
central city

288

- Most hotels and apartments had rents that were reasonable for older low-income individuals.

- Close proximity of residential to commercial land use provided a convenient supportive environment for even the most frail.

- Convenient neighborhood medical, social, food, and transportation services were available.

- High residential concentrations of older people provided increased opportunities for social interaction, companionship, and recreation.

- Existing low-rent housing stock was inadequate to meet the demand.

- A vast amount of older office space was vacant throughout the downtown area.

- The structural condition of the majority of available empty buildings was substantially closer to meeting current code requirements than was the existing housing stock.

The current downtown population of older residents is predominantly male, most of them living alone on an income near or below the poverty level. The 1970 census population density of individuals aged 65 and over was 20%, nearly twice the Los Angeles County average.

Although the downtown low-income population decreased over the past two decades, the area remains popular as a low-cost shopping district. Figure 19.2 locates various key services for the elderly. Supportive goods and services are conveniently located within easy walking distance from most areas near the central downtown core. More importantly, most services available east of Hill Street are targeted to moderate-income clientele rather than the upper middle class.

Using standard measures of site acceptability for the elderly (Lawton, 1977; Newcomer, 1976; Noll, 1973), almost all areas are within two blocks of critical goods and services. Public transportation is good and opportunities for recreation are exceedingly rich.

The downtown office core along Spring, Hill, and Broadway had for 50 years maintained its preeminence as the civic and business center of the City of Los Angeles. In the early 1960s major financial services and their supportive enterprises began a move six blocks west to the newly redeveloped section of the downtown. Several obvious reasons underlay the exodus. The older Spring Street buildings were inflexible and meeting tenant office requirements was often a problem.

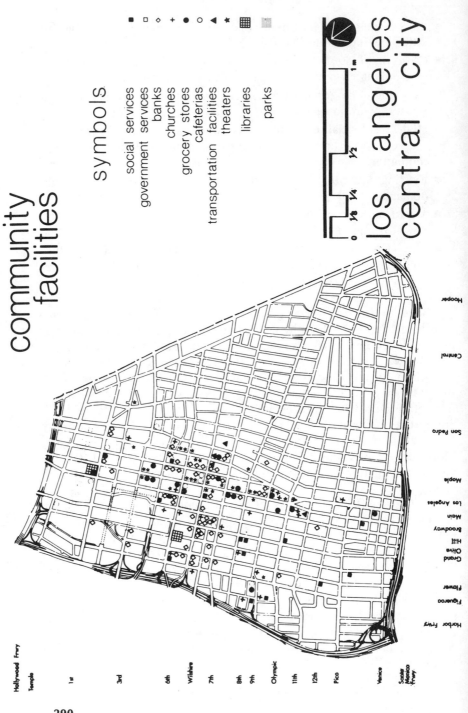

community
facilities

symbols

■ social services
□ government services
◇ banks
+ churches
● grocery stores
○ cafeterias
◀ transportation facilities
★ theaters
▦ libraries
▥ parks

los angeles
central city

Also, the buildings in this area were all constructed at a time when the code limited office buildings to 13 stories. The redevelopment on the western edge of downtown provided the chance for the construction of 40- to 60-story buildings that towered above the low-rise skyline of Los Angeles.

Additionally, the skid row area east of Spring Street has persisted tenaciously and thus has increasingly tarnished the business's image of the String Street district. The shift of the Broadway commercial strip to a Latino/Chicano shopping district also increased the momentum for the westerly relocation of status-conscious financial institutions.

Almost all structures are steel or reinforced concrete buildings that would require few, if any, structural modifications for residential use (see Figure 19.3). Beyond their obvious value for recycling is the heritage reflected in the unusual architecture of these structures. Terra-cotta cornices, cast-stone fascia details, elaborate window moldings, marble staircases, and stained glass skylights are just a few of the delights to be appreciated in the design of these old buildings (Figure 19.4). The threat of loss of these irreplaceable landmarks should be motivation enough to consider alternative adaptive uses.

ALTERNATIVE USES OF OFFICE SPACE

Alternative use of the abandoned office space for garment industry or office space has not materialized because of locational characteristics and the special building needs of various alternative users. The expanding garment district located several blocks south of the old office core is a logical tenant group for this space. However, garment manufacturers located there tend to be low-budget piecework operations that are tightly clustered around the wholesale market building and its services. Major constraints to their utilization of the abandoned building space include insufficient elevators and the need for increased electrical service to power garment-assembly equipment. Unfortunately, this type of operation often also destroys irreplaceable building details because of its need for functional improvements in spatial layout and building services. Furthermore, the garment industry and its low-budget operation more often turn out to be scavengers than renovators. As a result many building owners have resisted garment manufacturing occupancies.

Contemporary office use is limited because of narrow structural bays (12'–20') and the small square footage per floor typical of most

FIGURE 19.3. To the left, a typical reusable office building and its immediate surrounds. (Photo by Cliff Allen, Los Angeles Community Design Center.)

older structures. Newer office buildings utilizing sophisticated air handling and lighting equipment are constructed with a central service core surrounded by higher per-floor office space. Pre-1939 office construction was typically narrow and rectangular, guaranteeing that no space would be less than 25 feet from light and ventilation. The small floor areas in conjunction with the narrow space configurations limit rental clients to those desiring smaller offices, thus eliminating larger organizations that might require their operations on one floor. Finally, low ceiling heights make the addition of air handling equipment and overhead lighting more difficult.

FIGURE 19.4. Some details that are worth preserving. (Photo by Cliff Allen, Los Angeles Community Design Center.)

Industrial use such as warehousing is discouraged by the lack of loading dock facilities and the inability of these structures to accommodate large semitrailer trucks. Additionally, the floor space is not designed for the heavy structural loads associated with warehouse storage.

RECYCLING FOR HOUSING

The use of these abandoned structures for housing, however, is a much more feasible alternative. Most of the criticisms raised for the alternative uses suggested are not relevant for residential use. For example, the structural loads that the floors have been designed to accommodate are adequate for residential use. The narrow bay widths that can pose problems in a large office become natural partitions for separating units. The existing ceiling height of 9' is above the minimum standard height for residential use and the smaller units can be outfitted with mechanical and electrical systems that do not require lowering the ceiling height. The smaller square footage per floor that constitutes a liability in commercial office applications provides a much more intimate scale for the clustering of residential units. Finally, the building configurations limit the width of the building and provide wells for access to natural ventilation and light. These narrow building widths are perfect for residential units that must have access to natural light.

Figure 19.5 outlines the locations of 50 structures deemed financially and structurally feasible for recycling. These structures are clustered around Spring Street and Broadway and meet the requirements for classification as Class A buildings. All of these structures are eight stories or more in height and include underutilized or abandoned space. Most of the structures in this area have rented retail spaces on the first floor with the office space in the floors above abandoned. These buildings' reservoir of 7 million square feet of abandoned space could easily provide for 7,000 elderly housing units.

The Community Design Center staff scrutinized three buildings to develop an architectural program for each structure, calling for a mixture of one-bedroom and studio apartments. Figure 19.6 provides a rendering of one of those structures, the Arcade building. Figure 19.7 represents a remodeling scheme for typical floors of the Arcade structure. Cost estimates developed for the acquisition and remodeling of this building realistically forecast feasible project expenses. The construction cost estimates are comparable to projects located on scattered sites in suburban neighborhoods. Construction costs are substantially lower than new construction in comparably convenient locations near central-city social and health services.

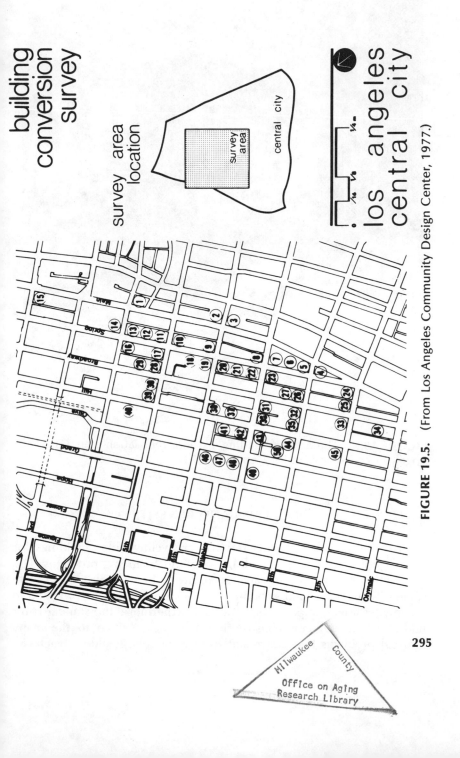

FIGURE 19.5. (From Los Angeles Community Design Center, 1977.)

building
conversion
survey

survey area
location

survey
area

central city

los angeles
central city

FIGURE 19.6. The Arcade building, exterior renovation plan. (From Los Angeles Community Design Center, 1977.)

PROBLEMS AND BENEFITS

Most of the problems associated with recycling older buildings for elderly housing relate to building code and financing problems. The reuse of older buildings in earthquake-prone Los Angeles does create some difficulties. Added structural reinforcement must be provided to comply with contemporary standards. Furthermore, the standards for mid-rise and high-rise construction are not sensitive to the many unusual problems that can result from remodeling older structures.

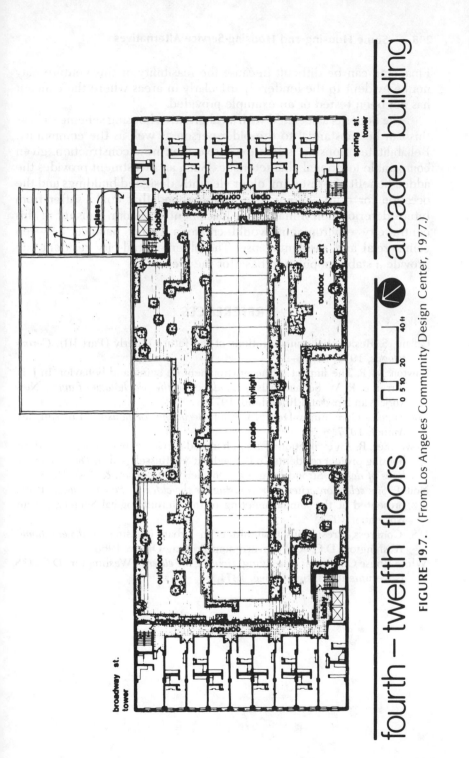

fourth–twelfth floors

FIGURE 19.7. (From Los Angeles Community Design Center, 1977.)

Financing can be difficult because the feasibility of this venture may not be evident to the lenders, particularly in areas where the concept has not been tested or an example provided.

The benefits associated with an alternative housing scheme such as this can be substantial to the older person as well as the community. Rehabilitated housing is less expensive than new construction, given comparable locational characteristics. Such an investment provides the added benefit of preserving older elegantly designed buildings and the occasion for reinvestment in a neighborhood that could suffer from future deterioration. Finally, the placement of senior housing in this central-city environment would create a better balance between commercial and residential use. The older central-city resident can provide a stable population base for the area.

REFERENCES

Golant, S. Residential concentrations of the future elderly (Part III). *Gerontologist*, 1975, *15*, 16–23.

Lawton, M. P. The impact of the environment on aging and behavior. In J. E. Birren & K. W. Schaie (Eds.), *Handbook of the psychology of aging*. New York: Van Nostrand Rheinhold, 1977.

Los Angeles Community Design Center. *Recycling for housing*. Los Angeles: Author, 1977.

Newcomer, R. An evaluation of neighborhood service convenience for elderly housing project residents. In P. Suedfeld & J. Russell (Eds.), *The behavioral basis of design*. Stroudsburg, Pa.: Dowden, Hutchinson & Ross, 1976.

Noll, P. *Site selection criteria for housing for the elderly: Policy change*. Paper presented at the annual meeting of the Gerontological Society, Miami, November 1973.

U.S. Congress, President's Committee on Urban Housing. *A decent home*. Washington, D.C.: U.S. Government Printing Office, 1968.

White House Conference on Aging. *Housing the elderly*. Washington, D.C.: U.S. Government Printing Office, 1971.

20
An Overview of the Elderly Experience in the Experimental Housing Allowance Program

TERRENCE L. CONNELL

In response to Congressional authorization in the Housing Act of 1970, the Experimental Housing Allowance Program (EHAP) was designed to test the concept of housing allowances. Housing allowances are cash payments made directly to low-income households that obtain or are already living in private market dwelling units meeting program housing requirements (such as occupancy and quality standards based on health and safety). Under the housing allowance concept, households have freedom of choice in selecting dwelling units and locations in which to live. Also, the use of existing units in the private market might hold subsidy costs down compared with alternative housing assistance programs. EHAP was designed to determine the effect of a housing allowance program on both participants and nonparticipants. The EHAP analysis was also planned to consider various administrative issues and cost comparisons with alternative assistance programs.

Since enrollment began in EHAP in 1973, over 23,000 households at 12 sites had received housing allowances enabling them to obtain adequate housing by 1978. About 25% of the recipients of allowances have been elderly households. This chapter discusses some of the housing choices of these elderly households participating in EHAP and makes comparisons with nonelderly households.

Issues concerning elderly participation in a housing allowance type of program can be examined utilizing the first 3 years of

The statements and conclusions contained herein are those of the author and do not necessarily reflect the views of the U.S. Government in general or HUD in particular. Neither the United States nor HUD makes any warranty, expressed or implied, or assumes responsibility for the accuracy or completeness of the information contained herein.

experience in EHAP. A number of reports based on the EHAP experience are available and more will be prepared in the future dealing with issues of current interest and broad applicability (ABT Associates, 1977a; 1977b; forthcoming; Office of Policy Development and Research, 1978; Rand Corporation, 1978).

EHAP consists of three experimental components:

1.   The Demand Experiment, which provides information regarding the response of low-income households to various forms of housing allowances, and how those allowances are used. The Demand Experiment was conducted in Allegheny County (Pittsburgh), Pennsylvania and Maricopa County (Phoenix), Arizona. About 1,250 households were offered allowances at each site. A central part of the analysis in the Demand Experiment is a comparison of the housing choices of these households with the choices of approximately 550 additional households per site, which were not offered allowances but were otherwise similar with respect to demographic and initial housing characteristics. Analysis of the data was completed in 1979.

2.   The Supply Experiment, which investigates the effect of a full-scale housing allowance program on the housing market and on prices in particular. In contrast to the Demand Experiment, where a limited number of households was approached on a random basis and offered allowances, the Supply Experiment makes allowances available to all income-eligible households that apply and meet the housing requirements at the two sites. The Supply Experiment is being conducted in Brown County (Green Bay), Wisconsin and St. Joseph County (South Bend), Indiana. The collection of survey data was completed at the end of 1978 and analysis will continue for about 3 more years.

3.   The Administrative Agency Experiment (AAE), which examines the consequences of utilizing different administrative methods in managing an allowance program. The AAE was conducted in eight sites. Analysis by the AAE contractor has been completed.

For a more complete description of EHAP, a discussion of current findings, and a bibliography of available reports, see Office of Policy Development and Research (1978). Unless otherwise noted, the basis for this chapter comes from a report on the elderly in the AAE (ABT Associates, 1977b), a report on participation from the Demand Experiment (ABT Associates, 1980), and an annual report from the Supply Experiment (Rand Corporation, 1978).

Although EHAP was specifically designed to test the housing allowance concept, a massive amount of information has been gathered concerning the operation of assistance programs in general and programs related to housing in particular. Information from EHAP includes how households respond to offers of assistance, how different administrative procedures and techniques affect program outcomes, and, in the case of a housing allowance program, how the housing market responds to the presence of the program. Many of the findings from EHAP may be considered directly applicable to or indicative of what would happen in other assistance programs.

In this chapter comparisons are made between elderly and nonelderly households with· respect to participation in a housing allowance program and the changes in housing costs, quantity, and quality that occur as a result of such assistance. Some explanations are offered for the differences observed. Particular note is made of the similarity of housing choices of the elderly and nonelderly participants when household characteristics are taken into account.

AGE DIFFERENCES IN PARTICIPATION RATES

To date, one of the principal findings from EHAP is that a relatively low level of participation may be expected in certain types of assistance programs. In particular, less than half of all income-eligible households and less than one third of the income-eligible elderly households seem likely to participate in an ongoing open-enrollment (i.e., supply) housing allowance program.

This section examines some of the evidence to support that finding and also looks at how participation varies according to different types of programs, program features, and demographic characteristics, with particular reference to the elderly.

In order to participate in a housing allowance program, households must first apply for enrollment. Households are accepted as enrollees by the agency administering the program only if they meet the eligibility requirements with respect to income, assets, and household composition. (Under the last requirement, certain households such as those made up of nonelderly singles or students may be excluded depending on program rules.) Enrolled households then must meet further housing-related requirements, which assure that assistance is provided only to help households to exist in adequate units. In the case of an allowance type of assistance program, households satisfy the housing requirements if they move to or already live in dwelling units meeting certain program occupancy and quality standards based on health and safety. Units may also be improved to meet the requirements. Enrollees meeting the housing requirements are then eligible to become recipients of assistance payments, enabling them to obtain adequate housing at a reasonable cost.

Experience in EHAP indicates that a number of program and household characteristics affect participation in assistance programs. These factors affect enrollment rates and the probability that enrollees become recipients (by meeting housing requirements) in different ways. Because of this difference, the two stages of participation— becoming enrolled and becoming a recipient—have been examined separately.

Enrollment

In the Supply Experiment, where all income-eligible renter and homeowner households can enroll, enrollment rates are relatively low. After more than 3 years of operations, enrollments seem to have leveled off at about 60% of eligible renters and 30% of eligible homeowners. The rates in the Supply Experiment are more likely to reflect what would happen in a ongoing open-enrollment program than the rates in the Demand Experiment, since that is precisely what the Supply Experiment is. Households enroll in the Supply Experiment after having heard about the program from advertisements, public announcements, referrals, friends, or other sources.

Unless special efforts are made, certain groups of the eligible population will enroll at relatively low rates; others will enroll at much higher rates than average. In the Supply Experiment, the open-enrollment assistance program, large differences in enrollment rates for renters appear between elderly households and those younger households that include children. As shown in Table 20.1, young couples with children enrolled at rates that are about 10 percentage points higher than elderly couples. Even greater differences occur between enrollment rates for households with single heads. Single heads of households with children enrolled at rates that are 23 to 44 percentage points higher than those of single elderly households. Table 20.1 also shows that single heads of households, whether young or elderly, enrolled at greater rates than couples.

Among the elderly, more homeowners than renters enrolled in the Supply Experiment. The opposite was true for nonelderly households. For homeowners, Table 20.1 shows that single-headed households enrolled at greater rates in the Supply Experiment than couples, whether elderly or not. This was the case for renters also. Similarly,

TABLE 20.1
Enrollment Rates by Tenure and Type of Household in the
Supply Experiment

| | Percent Enrolled at End of Year Two[b] | | | | | |
| | Brown County | | | St. Joseph County | | |
Type of Household[a]	Renter	Owner	Total	Renter	Owner	Total
Young couple, young children	40	22	31	33	16	23
Single head with children	69	52	64	81	42	64
Elderly couple	30	22	24	22	16	16
Elderly single person	46	43	44	37	27	29
All other	70	35	51	54	30	38
All types	53	33	42	54	25	34

[a]Selected stages of household life-cycle. Young couples are under 46 years of age; young children include at least one child under six; elderly couples and singles are at least 62 years old; "all other" is comprised of young couples with older children, older couples (46 to 61 years of age) with children of any age, and childless couples under 62.

[b]Number enrolled at the end of Year 2 as a percentage of the number eligible when the program began in each site. Year 2 ended in June 1976 in Brown County with about 3400 enrolled and in December 1976 in St. Joseph County with about 5300 enrolled.

Source: Rand Corporation, 1978.

single-headed homeowner households with children enrolled at greater rates than elderly singles. No difference was observed between young and elderly couples, however.

The rates of Table 20.1 are actually the number enrolled at the end of the second year as a percentage of the eligible population at the start of the program. To the extent that the eligible population has changed, the percentages will differ. After 2 years, the programs appear to be fairly close to a steady state with respect to enrollment. The overall enrollment rates as a percentage of the initial eligible population were only about 2 percentage points higher in Brown County after about 20 more months of operations, and 6 percentage points in St. Joseph County after about 14 more months. For renters only, the increases were 9 and 5 percentage points in the two sites, respectively.

In the Demand Experiment, households were contacted individually and the program was explained. Only those who listened long enough to be given an estimate of the amount of the payment were considered in computing the enrollment rate, which was about 85%. This experimental component of EHAP was designed to allow for comparisons of household responses to a total of 17 different forms of housing allowances. Control households that were not offered allowances are also included in the Demand Experiment. Because of the design of the Demand Experiment, differences in participation rates between groups of households are of more importance than the absolute levels involved.

Acceptance of an offer to enroll in the Demand Experiment shows a slightly different picture among age groups, as contrasted with the Supply Experiment. The age of the head of household made no difference in one of the two sites (Phoenix), but in the other, acceptance rates decreased significantly as age increased.

Analyses were performed in the Demand Experiment to determine which of several household characteristics affected enrollment decisions. In multivariate analyses taking age, sex of head of household, income, household size, welfare status, race/ethnicity, and number of moves over the past 3 years into account simultaneously, the same results occurred with respect to age as given above; that is, acceptance rates decreased with age in one site and made no difference in the other.

Effect of Outreach

The Administrative Agency Experiment (AAE) was designed to assess the impact of various administrative procedures as chosen and implemented by agencies in the eight different sites. Each of the programs developed independently and it was observed that various outreach procedures produced different results. Because enrollment rates depend on demographic characteristics, outreach efforts that focus on different groups will produce different levels of enrollment. The AAE demonstrated, however, that outreach can be targeted to some specific groups such as the elderly only to a limited degree (ABT Associates, 1977a). Generally, the AAE found that the results of targeting were indistinguishable from the effects of increasing the overall level of outreach. That is, more applications were received from both the group at which outreach was aimed and from others.

Becoming a Recipient

Before assistance payments are made to an enrolled household, the program housing requirements must be satisfied. In analyzing the effect of housing requirements on becoming a recipient, evidence from EHAP is presented concerning the relationship between household characteristics and the probability that an enrolled household meets requirements.

Housing requirements were developed independently in the different experimental components of EHAP. In the Supply Experiment, dwelling units that do not meet housing requirements at enrollment can usually be upgraded with relatively inexpensive repairs, such as installation of a handrail. In the Demand Experiment, the housing requirements were more stringent and, compared with the Supply Experiment, households were less likely to meet requirements in the units that they occupied at the time of enrollment. It was also more difficult to upgrade units that did not meet requirements in the Demand Experiment. In part because of these differences, the effect of household characteristics on the rate of becoming a recipient varies among experiments.

In determining the effect of various household characteristics on the probability of enrollees meeting requirements and becoming recipients it is of particular interest to examine participation only for those 65% of enrolled households in the Demand Experiment that did not meet the housing requirements at enrollment. After 1 year, 50%–60% of those who moved met the requirements. Less than 25% of those who stayed in their initial units met requirements after 1 year. Thus mobility of the household can be a key determinant of the ability of enrolled households to become recipients.

Table 20.2 shows that elderly households enrolled in the Supply Experiment at the end of 2 years were more likely to have been recipients than were other types of households. It has also been observed that the elderly who enrolled in the Supply Experiment were about 20 percentage points more likely to live in units already meeting housing requirements than were those under 62 years of age.

In contrast to the Supply Experiment, after 1 year of enrollment in the Demand Experiment, elderly households had met housing requirements and become recipients at lower rates than younger households at both sites. In one of the Demand Sites (Pittsburgh), however, age had no independent effect when the impact of other characteristics on meeting housing requirements was taken into account. That is, given similar income and household size, elderly households met housing requirements in Pittsburgh at about the same rate as the nonelderly. It is relevant to ask if there was an age difference in whether housing requirements were already met at enrollment. In Pittsburgh, where age made no significant difference in the probability of enrollees becoming recipients, there was also no significant differ-

TABLE 20.2

Recipient Rates by Tenure and Type of Household in the
Supply Experiment

Type of Household	Percent Participating at the End of Year Two[a]					
	Brown County			St. Joseph County		
	Renter	Owner	Total	Renter	Owner	Total
Young couple, young children	73	82	77	60	77	67
Single head with children	84	88	85	68	81	73
Elderly couple	82	90	88	79	92	90
Elderly single person	89	91	90	82	90	88
All other	81	83	82	71	82	77
All types	82	87	84	70	86	79

[a] Number of recipients at the end of year two as a percentage
of the number enrolled at least six months before the end of
year two, so as to exclude those still repairing their dwellings
or looking for alternatives.

Source: Supply Experiment, table provided by the Rand Corporation,
March 1978.

ence in the probability that the elderly already met housing requirements at enrollment. In Phoenix, where age did make a difference in
the rate of enrollees becoming recipients, the elderly were less likely to
have met the housing requirements when first enrolled than younger
households.

The experience in the AAE shows an inconsistent pattern with
respect to whether elderly enrolled households are more or less
successful in meeting housing requirements. In three of the AAE sites
the elderly were less successful than the nonelderly. In the other five
sites the elderly were more successful.

There are many experimental and site factors that might explain
these differences. These factors include the different housing requirements, the way in which the program was administered in
different sites (each of the AAE agencies developed its own procedures), and differences in the quality of the housing stock and
availability of adequate dwelling units at the various sites. In general, no
overall statement seems appropriate regarding the relative success
elderly and nonelderly households might have in meeting housing
requirements in an allowance program.

Comparison with Homeowners

At both sites in the Supply Experiment, the elderly enrollees, whether renters or homeowners, were more likely than other types of enrollees to meet the housing requirements. Whether the head of an elderly household was single or not single did not seem to have much of an effect.

Although homeowners enrolled at lower rates than did renters in the Supply Experiment (as shown in Table 20.1), they were more successful in meeting the housing requirements. A comparison of Tables 20.1 and 20.2 shows that this appeared to be true for each of the four household types given.

It is apparent that homeowners behave very differently from renters. Programs serving both populations need to take this into account in their planning and operations, but it seems clear that substantial proportions of both types of household desire to participate in an allowance program when offered the opportunity.

HOUSING OUTCOMES

There are a number of differences between elderly and nonelderly households with respect to the cost, quantity, and quality of housing consumed. In some cases, however, these differences can be attributed to a difference in the household characteristics of the two populations, such as size of household. This section examines these differences and the effect that a housing allowance program has on the consumption of housing.

Rent Burden

Rent burden is defined as the percentage of gross income spent on gross rent (including utilities). At enrollment, rent burdens averaged 52% for the elderly and 44% for the nonelderly in the AAE.

Table 20.3 presents evidence from the AAE that shows that rent burdens were greatly reduced as a result of participating in an allowance program. In fact, rent burden was cut in half for both elderly and nonelderly households. Table 20.3 also illustrates that there was a large difference in rent burden of enrollment between the elderly and nonelderly low-income populations of all household sizes together, but that the difference was much smaller when household size was taken

TABLE 20.3
Mean Rent Burden within Household Size Categories at Enrollment
and First Payment, Elderly and Nonelderly

	Mean Rent Burden			
	At Enrollment		At First Payment	
Household Size	Elderly ($\underline{N}$ = 1159)	Nonelderly ($\underline{N}$ = 4215)	Elderly ($\underline{N}$ = 1158)	Nonelderly ($\underline{N}$ = 4215)
One	.56	.60	.27	.30
Two	.46	.50	.23	.27
Three – Four	.39	.43	.18	.22
Five or More	.33	.35	.10	.15
All Households	.52	.44	.26	.22

Source: Abt Associates, March 1977

into account. Although average rent burdens were 8 percentage points higher for the elderly than for the nonelderly at enrollment, this difference was no greater than 4 percentage points when considered by household size. Table 20.3 also shows that rent burdens seemed to decrease with an increase in household size both at enrollment and after becoming a recipient of assistance payments.

Housing Quality

In the EHAP experience no overall statement can be made regarding whether the elderly or nonelderly lived in better housing at enrollment. In the Supply Experiment the preceding section noted that about 20% more of the elderly met that experiment's housing requirements at enrollment than did the nonelderly. It was also pointed out that the reverse was true in one of the Demand sites, and that there was no difference between elderly and nonelderly in the other site. In the AAE the elderly lived in slightly better housing at enrollment. Depending on the relative importance placed on various housing attributes, Table 20.4 shows that there was little difference between elderly and nonelderly households with respect to housing quality at enrollment for those who moved prior to first payment.

Of greater interest is a comparison between the elderly and

TABLE 20.4
Percentage of Recipient Movers Living in Units with
Common Deficiencies at Enrollment and at First Payment

| | At Enrollment | | At First Payment | |
Substandard Attribute	Elderly (N = 51)	Nonelderly (N = 300)	Elderly (N = 51)	Nonelderly (N = 300)
Unit has leaks	18%	23%	6%	7%
Unit has rats	14	24	8	8
Unvented space heaters, portable electric heaters, or no heat	12	9	2	2
Unit has structural hazards	18	14	4	4
Unit has safety hazards	31	33	17	20
Unit has major plumbing deficiencies	22	19	4	10
Unit is unfit for habitation	16	16	2	7

Source: Abt Associates, March 1977

nonelderly of the change in quality from enrollment to first payment as a recipient. Indeed, one of the principal goals of EHAP is to analyze changes in housing quality as a result of participation in the experiment. The main changes occurred for those who lived in housing that failed the requirements at enrollment but who subsequently moved to housing that qualified. Given the fact that the elderly are not as mobile as the nonelderly, the overall change in housing quality was greater for the nonelderly. Considering only those who moved, however, little difference was seen between the elderly and nonelderly. Table 20.4 illustrates this point concerning movers in the AAE, using incidence of various common deficiencies as a measure of quality. Thus it appears that few differences occurred with respect to changes in housing quality between elderly and nonelderly households if mobility was taken into account.

Occupancy

A look at changes in number of rooms occupied shows that there was improvement in this measure of housing consumption. On the average, elderly participants in the AAE occupied units with substantially fewer persons per room than the nonelderly both at enrollment and at first payment. At enrollment, the average was 0.42 persons per room for the elderly and 0.80 persons per room for the nonelderly. This large difference, however, simply reflects a different mix of household sizes in the two populations as is shown in Table 20.5, where both recipients of assistance payments who stayed in their original dwelling unit and those who moved are examined. Without such disaggregation, an erroneous conclusion might have been reached that the elderly were grossly overconsuming compared with the nonelderly.

Neighborhood Quality

To measure improvements in neighborhood quality, a socioeconomic index (SEI) was utilized in the AAE analysis that took into account the levels of income, education, and white-collar employment in the census tract. (An "average" tract in each program area would have a value of 1.00 on the index.) The average SEI for all elderly enrollees changed from 0.83 at enrollment to 0.87 at first payment. For the nonelderly the SEI changed from 0.80 to 0.87. It appears at first look that the nonelderly benefited more from the program based on change in SEI. In fact, for those who moved outside their census tracts, the elderly had a larger increase in SEI than the nonelderly (changing from 0.80 to 1.01 for the elderly and from 0.75 to 0.91 for the nonelderly). The apparent larger gains for the nonelderly can be attributed to the fact that more of them moved.

SUMMARY

In general, a smaller proportion of eligible elderly than nonelderly households enrolled in EHAP. No such overall statement, however, can be made with respect to the relative success elderly and nonelderly enrolled households had in meeting the program housing requirements. In the two Supply Experiment sites and in five of the eight AAE sites, the elderly became recipients by meeting the housing requirements at a greater rate. In the other three AAE sites and in the two Demand Experiment sites the elderly were less successful than the nonelderly. The reasons for this lack of consistency are not fully known but may depend, in part, on differences between the experiments and sites with respect to stringency of housing requirements, administration of the program, and various site characteristics.

TABLE 20.5
Persons Per Room within Household Size Categories,
Recipients Who Stayed and Recipients Who Moved
at Enrollment and First Payment

| | Recipients Who Stayed | | Recipients Who Moved | | | |
| | | | At Enrollment | | At First Payment | |
Household Size	Elderly (N=911)	Nonelderly (N=2248)	Elderly (N=318)	Nonelderly (N=2279)	Elderly (N=318)	Nonelderly (N=2279)
One	.35	.35	.37	.45	.32	.33
Two	.51	.53	.56	.59	.50	.50
Three-Four	.81	.74	.72	.84	.66	.72
Five or More	--	1.11	--	1.24	--	1.06
Total	.40	.72	.45	.87	.42	.73

Source: Abt Associates, March 1977

Depending on the site involved, from 18% to 70% of the enrolled households that became recipients had met the housing requirements at enrollment. Thus the characteristics of the recipient population are already determined to a large extent by whatever factors are involved in meeting housing requirements at enrollment.

Care must be taken in analyzing and comparing the housing choices of the elderly and nonelderly populations. Differences that appear when data are aggregated frequently become smaller when household characteristics are taken into account. The data in this chapter illustrate that some of the differences observed between the elderly and nonelderly are due simply to the different mix of household characteristics such as a difference in the proportion of various household sizes. The implication is that for certain housing choices there may be no real difference between elderly and nonelderly households, given that they have the same characteristics other than age. For example, since the elderly are less mobile and have smaller sized households on the average, their aggregate behavior will differ from that of the nonelderly where those characteristics have an impact. Conversely, elderly and nonelderly households with similar mobility and size characteristics are likely to make similar choices.

Although the elderly pay greater portions of their incomes for rent than the nonelderly, about half of the difference disappears when the difference in household size is considered. This was true both before and after becoming recipients of assistance in EHAP. Similarly, with respect to number of rooms per household member, it was observed in the AAE that on the average the elderly occupied about twice as much space as the nonelderly. Taking household size into account, however, there was virtually no difference between the elderly and nonelderly with respect to amount of space occupied.

Among households that moved, little difference was observed between the elderly and nonelderly with respect to change in housing quality. Looking at neighborhood quality, the nonelderly seemed to benefit more from the program than the elderly on the average; this proved to be an artifact due to the nonelderly's having moved more frequently. Among only those who moved outside their enrollment census tract, the elderly experienced a greater improvement in neighborhood quality.

Overall it appears that the principal factor causing different housing outcomes for the elderly and nonelderly was mobility. Other than mobility, differences were largely explained by taking into account characteristics such as household size.

Based on the elderly experience in EHAP, housing assistance programs providing cash assistance directly to households can enable many elderly households to meet their housing needs. The early experience in the Section 8 Existing Housing Program, which is similar to EHAP in many respects, confirms this also. As the results reported in this chapter indicate, housing assistance program planners and administrators need to be aware of the special needs of the elderly, but those special needs may be due, in large part, simply to a different mix of household characteristics and/or a lesser ability or desire to move from what may be inappropriate dwelling units.

These results also remind researchers concerned with elderly housing issues that often a simple one-dimensional comparison of elderly and nonelderly households may yield misleading results. Where differences occur between elderly and nonelderly households, it may be explained by taking into account the differing compositions of these two populations. Such explanations need to be pursued in order to avoid inappropriate conclusions and also to enable policy makers, planners, and administrators to better understand the basis for differences in behavior and housing choices.

REFERENCES

ABT Associates. *Outreach: Generating applications in the Administrative Agency Experiment.* Cambridge, Mass.: Author, February 1977. (a)

ABT Associates. *Elderly participants in the Administrative Agency Experiment.* Cambridge, Mass.: Author, March 1977. (b)

ABT Associates. *Report on participation under a housing gap form of housing allowance.* Cambridge, Mass.: Author, 1980.

Office of Policy Development and Research. *A summary report of current findings from the Experimental Housing Allowance Program.* Washington, D.C.: U.S. Department of Housing and Urban Development, 1978.

Rand Corporation. *Fourth annual report of the Housing Assistance Supply Experiment.* Santa Monica, Calif.: Author, 1978.

Index

Index